A WOUNDED THING MUST HIDE

A WOUNDED THING MUST HIDE:
IN SEARCH OF LIBBIE CUSTER

JEREMY POOLMAN

BLOOMSBURY

First published 2002
Copyright © 2002 by Jeremy Poolman

Title page photograph of Libbie Custer, courtesy of the
Little Bighorn Battlefield National Monument

The moral right of the author has been asserted

Bloomsbury Publishing Plc, 38 Soho Square, London W1D 3HB

A CIP catalogue record for this book
is available from the British Library

None of the characters in this book is wholly fictitious,
and any resemblance to actual persons,
living or dead, is only to be expected.

ISBN 0 7475 4949 4

10 9 8 7 6 5 4 3 2 1

Typeset by Hewer Text Ltd, Edinburgh
Printed in the United States of America by
R.R. Donnelley & Sons Company, Harrisonburg, Virginia

For Oskar, Charlie and Sarah

Prologue

Ghosts in the Park

On the afternoon of Sunday April 2nd 1933, two months and three days after a 43-year-old corporal named Adolf Hitler became Chancellor of Germany and democracy's bastard child was born, an elderly lady, an adopted New Yorker, suffered a heart attack and died in her apartment overlooking the East River. She was just four days shy of her ninety-first birthday. Her name was Elizabeth Bacon Custer.

Today, with perhaps the sympathetic synchronicity of history, the apartment in which she lived and in which eventually she died belongs to the widow of another fallen soldier – a now-elderly woman whose father, a Jew, fled Austria with his wife and young daughter in 1938, so escaping the approaching Nazi terror. It was here, in this apartment filled with the sentimental detritus of an exile's dreams of home, that I first really learned of Libbie Custer – and here that, consequently, the first stones of an obsession were laid, the final monument to which is this book. It was here, amongst the crystal-filled cabinets, sipping tea from fine Dresden china and sitting awkwardly on an over-stuffed sofa beneath the stern but benevolent gaze of a long-dead father and mother, that I first learned something of her extraordinary life – that I heard my first stories of her deep and obsessive love for her darling golden boy.

'You've heard of General Custer, I suppose.'

And it was later, standing at the window at which *she* had stood, watching the sun slipping low between the buildings of Manhattan as *she* had watched it, that I knew some day I would follow her, that I would feel in time compelled to chase her shadow around the world on a search the real reason for which I only now, at that search's end, understand.

'Of course,' I said. 'Everyone has, haven't they? Custer's Last Stand —'

And I did. I have. Since that day, I have watched a woman quite her double eating sweet sickly cake in a café in Vienna and I have listened to her image playing Chopin's Raindrop Prelude in the twice-reconstructed house on the north side of the parade ground at a fort way out on the great northern plains of Montana. I have stood where she stood in the Winter Palace at St Petersburg, and placed my feet where hers were placed in the hangman's room in a red-brick English jail. Indeed, I walked so close and for so long in her footsteps — feeling the brush of her skirts and her breath on my face — without ever quite reaching her that I came to believe I never would.

But I have. I did.

'Well, everyone knows *that*. But did you also know he had a wife?'

I have stood in her presence, felt the warmth of her hand, her gaze returning mine.

'Well, did you?'

But all that, then, was still to come. I shook my head. For then — for now — it was time to go, the duty visit to my mother's friend done.

'Here —'

A photograph. Black and white. A woman, maybe sixty, dressed in mourning black, delicate hands caressing the pages of a book, her gaze straight at the camera benevolent but above all strong — so strong.

'She's beautiful, don't you think?'

'She is, yes.'

'Even at eighty-two.'

'She was eighty-two when this was taken?'

'Eighty-two. And you know *where* it was taken? Right here. In this very room. Do you see how the light in the picture falls on that table?'

2

I looked.

'And do you see how it *still* falls?'

The last of the day's light was striping a high-polished surface. 'You mean it's the same table?'

My mother's friend smiled. 'Same table. Same cup. Different tea, though.'

I looked again at the picture.

'Speaking of tea –'

And slowly the hands of the past crept over me – fingertips, the lightest of touches.

'Would you care for a little more?'

There was no mistaking it. The face was a face I'd seen before. It was the picture of youthful old age projected upon the face of the girl with whom I have so long been in love. The girl about whom all my books have been written.

'Hello?'

I blinked; the image faltered.

'Are you all right?'

'I'm all right, yes,' I said. 'All right.'

That evening, over lobster and beef at the Union Square Café, she told me, at my prompting, all she knew about the wife of the general, and then of her own life alone. She told me how, like Libbie before her, she walked the length of Fifth Avenue every day for the exercise and how she hated Trump Tower (and how Libbie for sure would have hated it too), and how they both loved to wander in Central Park Zoo. The zoo, she told me, still contained some descendants of the creatures sent back by General Custer from the frontier.

Later still that evening, sitting on a stone bench much favoured by Libbie, my late mother's friend told me for the first time about her searching the Holy Land for some sign of her husband. A pilot in the Israeli Air Force, for six days he'd fought only to perish on the seventh – the day of victory. She was determined to believe that his plane or something of it – perhaps something of *him* – would still be out there in the desert somewhere, and she told me that her searching would continue until she'd found it.

'And if you do find it,' I said. 'What then?'

'I'll bring him home,' she said. 'Then I'll rest.' Her hand covered mine. She paused. In a while she turned to me. 'I'll bring him home is what I'll do.'

We walked back a while later in silence, each thinking our own separate thoughts. At the door to her block I kissed her on the cheek; she blushed and touched my shoulder. Then, as I was walking away, heading downtown towards my hotel, something made me turn and look back. The breath of a ghost is how I like to think of it now. But who knows? Not me. Indeed, back then, there was so much I didn't know. I didn't know, for example, that my mother's friend was nearing the end of her search – that it would be ended, unfulfilled, within a year by the cancer that was already killing her; nor did I know – nor could I have guessed that night on Park Avenue – that my own search had already begun.

Part One

Saints and Strangers

1

The Long Silence

Fort Abraham Lincoln, Dakota Territories, June 5th 1876: at a little after three a rider appears – just a speck at first, dark and shimmering in the heat off the plains. Far off, a bugle sounds, announcing his arrival. In the parlour of the general's house set on the northern side of the dusty parade ground, the women – the officers' wives – look to each other, their fingers frozen in that moment of quilting, their singing silenced. Then all as one turn to the wife of the general. She sits a while, then sets down her own work, rises from the table. Since her youth – since her wedding on that early spring day back in Michigan – she has lived this moment in her dreams. Slowly she leaves the room, the image of dignity. She stands, then, alone in the hall, aware suddenly of the heat and the long silence to come.

It almost ended before it had begun, this great adventure westward.

She waits by the door for the sound of footsteps.

Men died of scurvy; all but four of the eighteen married women succumbed.

She folds her hands before her, rests them still against her dress.

And this on a 'sweet' ship, the *Mayflower* – a ship not rank with the stink of disease and cattle-shit, but of wine, her former trade.

She waits for the news she knew one day would come.

And by landfall's first winter – that terrible snow-blown winter of 1620 – with fully half the crew dead and half the passengers, what was left to sustain them but the spirit of God and His tender grace?

When she hears the news she just wants to die.

But they were lucky too. The winter, though sharp and violent, was, for the region, mild and the Indians soon dead with the settlers' gift of plague.

Yes.

But death doesn't come.

It could have been worse.

All that comes is a terrible silence.

It could have been ten years ago and Virginia not Plymouth – Virginia with *her* Indians who fought for Heaven's sake as if the land was *theirs*. So, no, here, blessings were counted and prayers offered to a God both cruel and benevolent, and the Pilgrims survived – what was left of them – clinging to the unseeable, unknowable future with the zealous blind grip of believers.

Not that they were all believers – not all 'saints', not all those mad pious fools escaping the English queen's frightened bullying. No, there were others, the travellers, the chancers, the strangers to God and his mercy, who, like Libbie's father Edward Bacon, with his Norfolk farm* failing and three children dead already from the 'general disease', sought escape to a new England where not only was there – so it was claimed and persuasively so – fruit and fish and all manner of other bounty beyond counting, but also those greater bounties – freedom from debt and from the ever-clinging inescapable odour of failure.

'You mean it wasn't here at all?'

Today, on a stormy day, the coastline where they landed can seem just as it was. What you see today, from the window of a plane, when the winds lash the cold grey Atlantic, you can believe *they* saw *then* from the *Mayflower*'s creaking deck. And from the air, even today, you can see why, exhausted as they were and near half of them corpses, they couldn't stay; for despite its name, there was nothing to sustain them on Cape Cod – nothing but sand dunes and spare battered trees. And so they moved on, aiming for Virginia, but, in the vicious care of winds and tides, finding only Plymouth Harbour.

And of course the famous Plymouth Rock.

* Now part of a famous pre-cooked poultry empire.

8

'I don't know. Say, would you like those books gift-wrapped?'

'So where was it?'

'I don't know. Nobody knows for sure.'

'What do you mean, nobody knows?'

'Maybe nobody except those poor fellas that got to drag it down here.'

'Drag it? You mean the rock? Why would they have to drag it anywhere?'

'To get it to the place people wanted to see it. Where they expected to see it. Where they'd *pay* to see it.'

'But why?'

'I guess somebody was looking to sell some tickets.'

'You mean it's a fake?'

'*Hey, now —*'

John J. Warton, assistant, Plymouth Rock Visitor Center, flicked his eyes left and right like a spy.

'What's the matter?'

He leaned over the counter, dropped his voice to a hiss. 'Fake's a bad word around here.'

I leaned in to meet him. 'So are you saying that that thing out there isn't the real Plymouth Rock?'

Another glance; a shrug. 'Like I say, I don't know. I'm no expert.'

'But you're saying it's possible —'

The sound of voices — he stepped back, stood upright. 'Now, sir,' he said loudly, 'was it just the books?'

'Books?' I said.

The voices faded, were gone.

'I can't believe it,' I said.

He leaned in again; again I joined him.

'Look, all I know is that somebody I hope got paid a whole bunch of money to do it had to drag something down here and how it took them at least one hundred years of thinking about it to get to doing it.'

'A hundred years?'

'That's what I said.' The door banged. A woman and a small boy

9

stepped in out of the rain. Again he stood upright. 'Look, he said, 'are you buying those books or not?'

'What?'

'In your hand. Those books. Are you buying them or just looking?'

'These?'

'Yessir, *those*. Are you planning to pay for them or should I go fetch Mr Preston?'

Sixty-three dollars and one hour later I was sitting in my room at the Blue Anchor Motel on Lincoln Street, studying for the third maybe fourth time first the index of one book then the other for any sign of Bacon.

No Bacon.

Well, great. Two days into my search and already the trail wasn't so much cold as frozen stiff. I closed the books and turned on the TV. Jerry Springer. *I've got fifteen personalities!* I stared at the screen, thinking suddenly, acutely of home, and for a moment the fantasy lingered awhile before fleeing. Home. *Hey, Jerry, you sonofabitch.* What any more was there left to go home *for*? At home – in the rooms of my own house – I was already a stranger. Everything was changed. Karen was gone now, and my murals painted out; other children were playing now where ours never had. I closed my eyes and sat perfectly still, tried to think for distraction of Libbie. *When I heard the news I wanted to die.* Outside on the highway there were trucks heading east and west.

It was sometime in the middle of the night, halfway through a dream about rollercoasters and Steinbeck (he was riding beside Thomas Wolfe, the two of them holding hands and screaming in agony or delight), that the only piece of advice about the trip I'd been given (this, perhaps ironically, from my father, who thought the whole enterprise absurd and had lost no time in telling me) came back to me. *Don't forget there's always the phonebook.* I sat up, eyes still heavy from last night's beer, and flicked on the light.

At first I could only find the Bible, but then, in the opposite bedside table, there it was. I pulled on my glasses, flipped the pages.

Nothing. Then something. *Bacon, MD*, an address across town. I lay back, my heart thumping with the urgency of sudden wakefulness. I checked my watch: four a.m. I closed my eyes and tried to sleep, but could not. I turned on my side and lay, unsleeping, waiting for dawn.

2

Breakfast at the Aquarium

As widows, in the summer of 1876, the wives of the dead had to leave Fort Lincoln, selling what they could, taking little with them. Libbie took her husband's writing desk, a set of antlers, her silver, china and glass, and, accompanied by her sister-in-law Margaret, boarded a train for the east. Crowds lined the tracks to gawp, some throwing mourning garlands. Arriving at last in Monroe, she shut herself away in the home of her old school principal, Erasmus Boyd. Soon reporters gathered, some throwing stones at her window, attempting to entice her out. Some sent notes, suggesting she visit the capital (and so run their gauntlet of questions and flashbulbs) and there take part in the nation's centennial celebrations. Always, the notes went unanswered.* Principal Boyd knew better than to deliver them. Instead he burned them at night in a brazier in the back yard.

Some nights, Libbie's protector would stand in the hall, listening for sounds from her room. Sometimes there were tears. Mostly there was silence.

The morning when it came was bright and clear, the house neat and white and set back from the wide suburban road, protected from strangers by a wire-mesh fence over which had been trained some kind of thick creeper.

'Can I help you?'

'Doctor Bacon?'

* With one recorded exception. To an enquiry from a Seventh Cavalry veteran, who thought she might benefit from the distractions of Washington, she said, 'No, sir, I cannot go. For I am wounded, and a wounded thing must hide.'

I smiled, tried hard to look less out of place than I felt. I stepped forward. 'I was wondering if you could spare me a few minutes of your time.'

The man behind the mesh gate had his hands in the pockets of his tan-coloured chinos. He was slim and fit-looking – maybe sixty, sixty-five – and, up close, smelled of something I couldn't for the moment place.

'What do you want?'

Above all he looked at ease with himself, satisfied with the world and his part in it. 'Well, as I say, I was wondering if maybe –'

'I'm sorry.'

'Sorry?'

'I can't help you.'

'Oh?'

'Because there's no doctor here.'

'What? But I thought –'

'I'm sorry. Now, if you'll excuse me –'

'But –'

Suddenly a frown. He stepped towards the gate, stealthy in his loafers. 'Look, I've already told you I can't help you,' he said. 'And I'm very busy –'

'Busy?'

'Busy, yes.'

'But not with patients then.'

'What?'

'Well, it says here –' I pulled out the page I'd torn from the phonebook. I paused; the man was shaking his head. He looked suddenly quite weary and older.

'Michael Dennis,' he said.

'Pardon me?'

And then it came to me – the smell. It was fish. The man smelled of fish.

'MD. It stands for Michael Dennis.' He sighed. 'I am not a doctor, never have been a doctor, and never will be a doctor. So if you don't mind –'

'But your name *is* Bacon –'

13

The frown again. 'Look, who *are* you?'

I held out my hand, reached up and over the gate. Slowly, warily, a hand reached up and took mine. I told him my name. 'I'm a writer,' I said. 'I've come all the way from London.'

'So?'

'Because I'm writing a book.'

'Good for you.'

'And I could really use some help.'

'Which explains what you're doing here on my property, I suppose.'

'Well –' I looked down at my feet. Technically speaking, I was still on the public street, but I let that pass. 'Look,' I said. 'Just tell me your name's not Bacon and you're not related in any way to Elizabeth Bacon, wife of General Custer, and I'll go.'

He folded his arms across his chest. 'OK. My name's not Bacon and I'm not related in any way to Elizabeth Bacon, wife of General Custer. Satisfied? Do I get my reward now?'

'What?'

'The pleasure of seeing you walking away.'

'But –'

He shook his head. I turned away. I could feel eyes watching me as I crossed the street.

Back at the motel I sat on the bed and tried to figure out what to do now. I closed my eyes and tried to think hard. Nothing. Right now the whole project seemed absurd. What, after all, did I know about telling the truth – or even *finding* it? My stomach started churning and I felt sick at the thought of all those faces – of how disappointed and then deceived they'd look when I returned to London empty-handed. And it wasn't just that: no, far *worse* than that was the money – money already spent that would have to be returned. My career would join the rest of my life in what felt then like ruins, and for sure I would end up sleeping rough beneath a bridge. My stomach turned again at the thought of such humiliation. I ran to the bathroom and threw up.

★   ★   ★

14

'Yes?'

I was awake and answering the phone before I knew what I was doing.

'It's me.'

I sat up, rubbing my eyes.

'You still want to talk?'

Sleepy still, I mumbled *of course.*

'Well, I have to go to the store. You can meet me there if you want to.' He gave an address – a street, a number. I fumbled with a pen, wrote it down. 'When?' I said.

'Now,' he said.

'Now?'

'Well, if there's something else you'd rather be doing –'

'No, now's fine. Now's good. Really.'

'OK then.'

'OK. There's just one thing, though. How did you know where –'

The phone clicked dead. I sat for a moment, receiver in hand, listening to the humming like a fool. Then I set the thing down, crossed to the bathroom and splashed my face with water. I stared at myself in the mirror, thinking without meaning to of my wife. I felt in that moment so terribly sad – as if, with the shock of the telephone's sudden disconnection, I'd suffered again the pain and dislocation of sudden, though not unexpected, bereavement.

It was maybe an hour later when the cab pulled up outside Frank's Aquatics. The driver turned in his seat. 'It *was*, like, fish you was after, right?'

I peered out of the window. Beyond a small empty parking lot sat a long squat building in the middle of the roof of which sat the upturned rear end of a huge model shark* that appeared to have fallen right out of the sky. 'Are you sure this is it?' I said. 'One twenty-three?'

---

* In one of the many curious coincidences that seem to gather around the Custer story, this shark was created by the local sculptor Edward Potter – a name he shares (though he shares no relation) with the sculptor of the Custer statue, *Sighting the Enemy*, in Monroe, Michigan.

He turned back, looked out. 'Well, I can't see nothing else between one twenty-two and one twenty-four, so I guess it is.'

I paid the man and watched the cab cruise away. I crossed the parking lot, pulled on the screen door and stepped inside.

'Hello?'

The air was warm and thick and moist. It clung to my skin and made me blink. It was both gloomy and bright like a stadium under floodlights, the only light in the deep and broad room the lights in the dozens of fish-tanks that lined three of the four walls up to a height of maybe six or seven foot.

'Hello?'

My voice sounded muffled, smothered, half-buried by the tanks' constant humming.

'In here.'

I turned, squinting hard. In the gloom of the fourth wall, a door.

'Mr Bacon?'

'Can you bring the knife? The one with the red handle. It's somewhere by the computer – maybe underneath?'

'OK,' I said. I looked around. The computer was set on a counter just inside the door. Beside it was a large red-handled gutting knife.

'Got it?'

'Got it,' I said. I squeaked across the floor, stuck my head through the doorway.

He was sitting, his back to me, at a long trestle table that ran the length of the far wall. The room was square – maybe ten feet by ten. I made my way around a large oblong tank of bubbling water that stood waist-deep in the middle of the floor and set the knife on the table beside him.

'You hungry?' he said, not looking up.

'Hungry?'

He swivelled around. His hands were wet, his glasses sitting low on his nose. 'You like fish?'

'I guess,' I said.

'Good,' he said.

★　　★　　★

We ate thick white steaks of marlin fried in garlic and butter and drank beer so cold that it made my teeth ache. I asked him why he'd changed his mind about seeing me.

He shrugged. 'Well, sometimes I just get so tired of even thinking about it,' he said. 'Of going over and over the same old ground. But *then* I start thinking maybe it's right that you shouldn't ever try to forget a war as that means forgetting all the good people that died.'

I was lost. What war? What people?

He sighted, set down his fork. 'Which, I suppose, is where you come in.' He hunched a little forward. 'Are you planning to go there?' he said.

'Go where?' I said.

'Well, *I* don't know. You're the writer. You figure it out.'

'Well, I *did* say I'd try to go everywhere *she* went. But then I found out she went to Russia, and all sorts of other places. So I don't know.'

He frowned. 'You mean you're not here to talk about the war?'

'The war? Which war?'

'The *Korean* War.'

'Well, no. I was *hoping* you could tell me about her ancestors – that is, about *your* ancestors. Yours and Libbie's. Like what happened after the *Mayflower*. How they got to be living up in Michigan. That kind of thing.'

He shrugged.

'What is it?'

'You need Frank for that.'

'Frank?'

'My brother.' He gestured about him, petulant suddenly, like a little boy. 'Half-owns this place. Lives down in Florida. He knows *everything* does *Frank*.'

'Would he talk to me?'

'Sure he will. I'll call him.' He brightened. 'I've got something you can give him anyway.'

It was still early when I left the aquarium, the day still cool but vibrant with the promise of heat. I hailed a cab, rode it back to the

17

motel. In my room I set the small oblong box he'd given me for his brother on the desk and pulled off my shoes and socks. The box was like a shoe-box – only narrower as if it were meant for just one shoe. I turned it over. There, just a name: *Colonel Frank P. Bacon*, nothing more. I set it down, took off my shirt and the rest of my clothes, stepped into the bathroom and turned on the shower.

It wasn't until a day later, when I was standing in line at the United check-in for the ten-thirty flight to Washington, that the box and its contents really started to smell.

'Sir?' said the girl behind the counter, screwing up her face. 'Are you *checking* that?'

It was down between my ankles. 'No thank you,' I said. 'I think I'd better carry it.'

And I did – across the departures concourse and into the men's room. Luckily, the room was empty. I slipped the box under a cubicle door like a man planting a bomb. I've often wondered since what happened to it then. Indeed, for several days after, I found myself checking newspapers for news – for one of those amusing little paragraphs meant to lighten the day – but of course found nothing, for there is always something more important in the world or at least more amusing than the story of a fish left abandoned in a box in a cubicle in a men's room at the back of the departure lounge of a small East Coast airport.

3

Voices from the Plains

They came singly and in pairs, some to gawp at Monroe's most famous widow as if at a freak in a side-show (though they took care to smile and to talk and to dress as if for royalty), while others came with 'news' (this of invariably dubious provenance) of the workings of the town, or – in the case of other widows – to share their own grief.* Her visitors (some from as far away as Washington and New York) would say loudly (thinking this would cheer her) how well she looked (though many thought her, in truth, too pale to survive), and more than several enquired when it was precisely that she planned to visit her husband's last resting-place. *It'll be good for you*, they said (many of them had done so and found it a comfort), and some even offered to accompany her there. But she always told them no. She had, she told them, no plans to go. *Never?* they said. *Never*, she said – meaning it and sticking to it, for, not once – then, or in her long life to come – did she take the train west across the plains to that river and those hills, to stand where so many already had stood (and would stand, myself amongst them), gazing down, bleary-eyed, at the hard and bitter, blood-soaked land. No: for her, the very fact of her husband's absence was enough to bear; to see the actual place where his life had been taken would be, she knew, too much. Such a visit would take, she feared, what remained of her own life and so render her silent at a time when, already – with the bodies of the dead barely cool – she could hear from her room and see from the papers (she tried not to read them,

* Of the six Monroe men lost at the Battle of the Little Big Horn, only two were married – George Custer and James Calhoun, whose wife (and widow) was Custer's sister, Margaret.

but it seemed they would not not be read) that the voices of the bitter, the jealous and the cowardly were rising against him, intent on destroying what had cost him – and them – so much to build. *They say he was a fool*, she heard some whisper in the hall when they thought she was sleeping, and she'd read, despite herself, how others (those who only yesterday, it seemed, were calling him hero) now called him butcher.

'*So what are you reading?*'

Indeed, even President Grant, within a week of the disaster, was telling all who would listen that it was Custer who was responsible – and Custer alone – for the deaths of so many, while, at the same time, and with that same sly brutal callousness that had carried him so far on the corpses of others, he was calling for swift and bloody retribution, and, in so doing, attempting to reawaken in a war-weary public a thirst for more blood that would deflect from him their natural and growing disdain and drive on to completion the hard and bloody work of occupation and extinction.

'Is your curiosity genuine or merely idle?'

'Excuse me?'

'Never mind.' I turned the book over. 'There.' But the stewardess didn't look. She just stood there in the aisle, looking at *me*, as the plane lurched, steadied.

'What?' I said. It was a look that let me know more quickly and precisely than mere words could ever do what she thought of me.

She glanced down at the book.

Which obviously wasn't much.

'Custer,' she said.

And who could blame her?

'You know him?' I said.

She *said* it like she knew him – and not just that she knew him, but that she knew, too, he didn't matter. At least *any more*.

Which pissed me off.

'So did you want a drink?' she said.

Because of course he matters.

'What are you saying?' I said.

She smiled, sly.

'I was *saying* do you want a drink?' She pointed at the trolley like I was an idiot and needed pictures.

'Are you saying –' I started, but then something got in front of me, distracting me, and I heard myself stop. Heard the thumping of my heart in my ears, the blood pumping.

'Are you OK?'

The voice distant, refracted.

I let my eyes close.

It was like some kind of truck – the thing – bearing down on me. I clenched up. Couldn't move. *This is it.* It was like somebody said it. I looked around. But there was no one there.

4

Swinging in the Debris

Once asked, in a game, to describe myself, the best I could manage was to repeat what James Caan (I think) said in some movie – the thing about being an unhappy man leading a happy life. Later that day I repeated it to my wife. *Very good*, she said, *James Caan? Yes*, I said, and then she said that the much simpler truth with regard to my character was I didn't know how to be happy.

'*Well?*'

But this was near the end – she was really ill – and so I didn't take it seriously. I wish, now, I had – as I know, now, that the knack of being happy that looks so mysterious in others can – like driving or bridge – be learned. All of which reminds me, for some reason, of a joke the stewardess on the flight to Washington told me, which goes like this.

An old man walks into a bank and shouts at the woman teller: 'I want to open a damn checking account!' The astonished woman replies, 'I beg your pardon, sir? *What* did you say?' 'I *said*, I want to open a damn checking account!' the man shouts. Upset, the teller leaves the window and goes to see the manager. The manager agrees that such language is inappropriate. They both return to the window. 'Sir,' says the manager coolly, 'what seems to be the problem?' 'There's no problem,' says the man, still shouting. 'I just won fifty million bucks in the damn lottery and I just want to open a damn checking account in this damn bank, OK?' 'I see,' says the manager, 'and is this bitch giving you a hard time?'

'Well what?'

We were lying on the bed, Tanya and I, in my room at the

Watergate Hotel. She was still wearing most of her uniform. 'Good joke,' I said.

'What are you doing?' she said.

'Getting under the covers.'

She hitched herself up on her elbows. 'What's the matter?' she said.

I said I was cold.

'No. I mean what's the *matter*?'

Which was true. It *was* cold – November, for Christ's sake.

She shrugged, turned away, started doing up her buttons. She arched forward, eased on her shoes. Her uniform was blue with yellow details – yellow name-badge, a blue-on-yellow wing motif on her blouse. She stood up. I watched her, glad that she'd soon be gone.

'Where are you going?' I said.

'Detroit,' she said.

'Oh,' I said.

She twisted, doing something with her belt. 'Why? Have you got something to say all of a sudden?'

'Like what?'

'I don't know. Like what you're doing here maybe.' She paused. She looked tired – but not the kind of tired to be ever cured by sleep, and for the first time I wanted to touch her, soothe her. 'In fact, what *are* you doing here?'

'You mean in this room?'

'I mean in Washington.'

'I told you,' I said. 'Research.' But it was too late: she was dressed now and really I was glad.

'Oh yeah. I remember.'

'Well, don't sound so interested.' I was glad too that I'd not seen her naked. Women are too strong – too complete – when they're naked.

She sat back down on the bed. I felt the start of slow panic. 'Changed your mind?' I said.

She turned. 'No. About what anyway?'

'I don't know. Detroit?'

23

She turned back. The gazing down at her folded hands, the slightly hunched set of her back, said there was something on her mind.

'What is it?' I said.

Another shrug.

'What's the matter?'

'Nothing.'

'It's not nothing.'

'Well –

'Well what?'

She turned to face me. 'Well, I was thinking about that golfer,' she said.

'What?'

'Payne something. You remember.'

'You mean Payne Stewart? The guy with the plus-fours? What *about* him?'

'I was just thinking about him.'

Jesus Christ.

'About him flying round and round in his plane with his pilot and that friend of his – all dead. Just flying round and round over Montana someplace waiting for the fuel to run out. It was on the news. They reckon there's maybe enough fuel for maybe two, three hours max. And then –' She dropped her eyes, lifted them, tried a smile. 'Anyway. I was just thinking,' she said. She stood, picked up her bag from the floor.

'You OK?' I said.

She nodded. 'It's just a weird thing to think about,' she said. 'Don't you think?'

'It is,' I said.

She sighed. 'Anyway –'

'Take care,' I said.

'Uh-huh,' she said.

'Say hi to Denver.'

'Detroit.'

'Right. Detroit. Anyway, say hi.'

She lifted her flight bag from the chair, heaved it over her shoulder, crossed the room. She paused at the door. 'I was thinking about that woman,' she said. 'The one you were talking about last night. The Custer one.'

'What about her?'

'I was thinking, you *do* know she's dead, don't you?'

'What?'

'Oh, it doesn't matter.' She twisted the handle and opened the door. Musak – the Carpenters, 'I Won't Last a Day Without You' – drifted in from the hallway. 'It's nothing,' she said. And then, without a look back, she was gone.

It was during the cab ride to the National Military Archives that the news came through on the radio.

'Say, what about that?' said the driver, twisting in his seat. 'You hear that?'

I shook my head. 'Hear what?'

You do know she's dead, don't you.

''Bout that golfer guy.'

'What about him?'

'I mean of all the fuckin' places!'

I leaned forward. 'You mean he came down?'

The cab driver nodded in his mirror. 'Came down all right.'

'Where?'

'Right in the middle of that Custer park. The Last Stand place.'

'You mean the Little Big Horn?'

'Uh-huh.'

The cab slowed. The driver cursed the traffic and flipped in a tape. Sting, 'Desert Rose'. The driver eyed me in the mirror. 'Say, you English?' he said.

'English,' I said.

'You like Sting?'

I looked away, out at the thick morning traffic. She'd been right: it was a weird thing to think about – the three of them flying around in some great looping arc, all dead, one man in plus-fours, the whole world down below looking up, craning their necks and waiting for them to fall.

★   ★   ★

25

Back in my room at the Watergate, I discovered that the Stewart plane hadn't come down at the Little Big Horn at all – not even, in fact, in Montana. Apparently, having finally run out of fuel, it dropped from its escort of National Guard F-16s and came at last to earth with a crash in a field in South Dakota. Watched by the TV millions, the plane exploded on impact; the bodies of the victims were consumed by fire. Debris fanned out across the neighbouring fields; an eight-iron and a putter were found on the roof of a barn three-quarters of a mile away, tangled up like lovers along with the strap of a golf-bag. A reporter at the scene for the CBS midday news spoke to a man (the brother, it turned out, of the barn's owner) who claimed to have seen the whole thing. It was, said the man, just like the war again – just like standing on the deck of the USS *Yorktown* and watching the Japanese kamikazes approaching. 'There was nothing you could do,' he said, his eyes filling with tears.

And then a strange thing happened.

At least on my TV.

When the man had stopped talking and the interview was over, the camera panned away to take in the scene and there – I swear it – amongst the wreckage was a man in a uniform (one of the rescue workers – a policeman, maybe, or a firefighter) practising his golf swing – arching his back and raising a burned-black club head high above his shoulder, then bringing it down in a very graceful arc.

The following day, on my way by cab back to the archives, I mentioned what I'd seen to the driver. The driver just shrugged and smiled, obviously thinking me drunk or crazy. That afternoon, sitting at my desk, I told myself it had just been a trick of the light – that no one – least of all a man in a position of authority – would do such a ghastly thing. I dismissed it then from my mind and went back to peering at the documents and pictures as they passed before my eyes. *The Custer family on the steps of Fort Lincoln, May 22nd 1875. Official Records of the Custer Court Martial. Mrs Custer visits Japan.* I slipped down into my chair.

Japan.

In the picture (it was a grainy thing, the blacks and whites just different strengths of murky grey now), she was standing in mourning black before a delicate-looking building that was all sweeps and carvings, an old lady made to seem broad and tall by the group of small, dark-suited, top-hatted, wing-collared figures gathered around her. All were smiling, the men grinning hard, their faces emerging from the gloom and the years like the faces of schoolboys unexpectedly released from school.

'*Everything OK?*'

I looked up. A pale man in a tan suit was smiling down at me. In his arms he held a short stack of books; on his lapel was fixed a badge: *Mr Turner, Chief Assistant Librarian*.

'I'm fine,' I said. The man nodded, drifted off.

I turned my eyes back to the pictures. *The widow considers the beauty that is the Meiji Shrine.*

By four o'clock my eyes were aching, my head overloading with Custeriana. I switched off the machine and squeaked my way through the corridors and out into the street. Dusk was falling already, the air already chilled. I walked back to the Watergate and had a drink, then another, at the Century Bar.

5

A Hollow Centre

Scarcely anywhere in the world can there be a city centre as empty of the living as the centre of Washington at night. Each night, when the government has fled across the river and into the trees of Maryland and Virginia, what is left is a tidemark of poverty and cripples – those who cannot flee – a circle with a great vacant hollow centre stalked only by the slow-moving, never-moving monuments to the dead.

Washington.

Lincoln.

Kennedy.

'Are you visiting someone?' I said. The old man was all shadows in the early-morning light.

'I'm here to visit with my son.'

The 58,000 Americans – the name Bacon amongst them – so uselessly slaughtered in the hills and flooded fields of Vietnam.

'Do you visit often?'

Each name shallow-carved now with a neatness, calm and care at such odds with the blood, fear and chaos of individual inglorious death.

'Yes, sir. Every year his mama and I come to visit with him on his birthday.'

'Today's his birthday?'

'Yes, sir. My boy is forty-nine years old today.'

The old man slipped the United travel bag from his shoulder and reached inside. He pulled out a photograph in a frame, held it shakily beneath the engraved name of his son, the frame's metal hooks clicking against the high-polished Indian granite.

I leaned forward. The picture was of a clear-skinned smiling boy in cap and gown, a diploma clutched tight like a relay baton in his hand.

In a while he lowered the picture, returning it to his bag. He looked about him. Despite the early hour we were not alone: maybe two dozen other fathers, sons, mothers and friends were standing in contemplation of the names of their loved ones, some tearful, hands holding other hands or covering their eyes, others up close to the granite, finger-tipping like blind people the shallow-cut names.

'Except this year,' said the old man.

'Pardon me?' I said.

At the angle of the stone a large man in a fishing vest was down on his haunches, tracing a name with pencil and paper, his tongue lolling out of his mouth in concentration like a child's.

'This year she couldn't make it. For the first time. I had to leave her back at the motel.'

'Is she OK?'

The old man shrugged. 'It's Alzheimer's,' he said. He shook his head, turned his gaze from his son to me. 'You know the worst thing?' he said. 'The worst thing is not when she can't remember, but when she can't forget. Me, I *know* it's thirty years gone, and there's a kind of numbness – a kind of hollowness – to be had in that. A kind of self-preservation. But for Pammy, *Jesus*, Da Nang either never happened at all or it's happening today – *right now* – and she's losing him again just like before –' He paused; a siren, far off, cut the air then was gone. The old man's shoulders rose and fell. 'Anyways,' he said, weary now.

'I'm sorry,' I said.

You do know she's dead, don't you.

For a moment, a parade of pale faces passed by me; then, with the swiftness of a dream, the parade was gone, cymbals clashing, drums beating, all fading to nothing.

The old man sighed. 'But I should go.' He paused. 'You know, sometimes she wakes up and doesn't know where she is.' He shook his head. 'Lord, sometimes she wakes up and doesn't know *who* she is. And that's when the trouble *really* starts.'

29

I opened my mouth to say something, but again nothing came. There seemed nothing at all worth saying. Instead, I just shook his offered hand and then watched him walk away.

A kind of hollowness.

When he was gone, I stood awhile, just watching the others at the wall. Was this, I wondered, the best that can be done? Build an empty mausoleum to be pawed at and wept over? It seemed, that morning, empty and desperate; indeed it seemed – the monument – on that cool autumn day, exactly what it was and nothing more than it was – just a huge piece of stone half-thrust into or out of the earth – a mute declaration, in its coldness and its ghastly immovability, that we really are all alone, and that there never really was any other life but this.

That night I went walking. After a day of checking papers and squinting at computer screens at the archives, I wanted some air – I needed space and reconnection with the living after hours spent studying the dead. I strolled down Pennsylvania Avenue and peered in through the bars at the White House. There were lights in the windows, but they had the look of those lights that the absent leave on to fool burglars. I watched for some sign of life – a shadow perhaps at a window – but there was none. I walked on.

What it was I don't know, but something drew me back to the memorial. I sat on a grass bank and studied its floodlit form. I listened hard as others, earlier in the day, had seemed to be doing – but there was nothing to be heard. There were no voices – no wisdom of the dead to be gathered – just the low hum of the distant-seeming city. Perhaps, it seemed to me then, the only thing to be learned from the memory in our lives of the dead is that they are there and we are here. Maybe life – death – really is as simple and as final as that.

6

Ichigo, Ichie

Stand, today, where she stood in that picture, and you stand on the site of recovered devastation. Destroyed first in 1923, by the earthquake that levelled just about everything in the city except Frank Lloyd Wright's ghastly Imperial Hotel masterpiece, and then, at war's end, by the vengeful American Empire itself, the Meiji Shrine that stands today in Western Tokyo is, now, a true martyrs' shrine both in history and design. And here, every year, three million Japanese come to visit – some to worship and give thanks, some to ask for good fortune in the year ahead, some to mourn at the war shrine those lives taken and given in brutal savage war.

'*You like a picture, mister?*'

Lives that include, now, the lives of the kamikaze – those spirits made timeless by the flames and twisted metal of exultant suicide.

'Mister?'

I turned away.

The man was smartly dressed, small and slim, a half-dozen cameras hanging from his neck and clattering when he moved, like a fairytale veteran's grotesque bloated medals.

I said OK.

He selected a camera and raised it.

'Here?' I said.

'Of course!'

'But what about that?' I pointed to the sign – a camera in a red circle, a red slash bisecting it.

He lowered the camera an inch or two. 'Don't worry!' he said. He was grinning like the serious Japanese men in Libbie's picture.

'What do you mean, don't worry?'

31

He closed one eye, squinted through the camera. They were all, he said (and it was certainly true), dead now, and so couldn't – even if they wanted to – complain.

She came by ship – a ten-day voyage – landing one morning in early spring in the port of Yokohama, south of Tokyo. The only tourist among a complement of businessmen and soldiers (and the only woman – not to mention the only *widow* – travelling alone), she disembarked and was at once surrounded – a tiny, frail-looking figure in black – by reporters and photographers and men who'd been passing and were keen to watch the show. They stared at her, some of them, some scarcely, apparently, believing their eyes, while others – the braver ones – stepped forward, some with their notebooks and cameras, their arms raised high to gather her attention. What, they wondered, did she think of Japan? Was it what she'd expected? For a moment it seemed as if the crush would overwhelm her – but then the policemen arrived in their strangely shaped hats and they drove her away in some big old grand car, and she watched from the window, childishly amazed that even here, so far away and in such a foreign land, her husband's name – and, so, *hers* – was known and revered, his life and his deeds so wildly, and so publicly, celebrated.*

'Holiday?' he said.

We were standing – the man and I – beside a cherry tree, waiting for the Polaroid to develop.

'Honeymoon,' I said.

He was studying his watch. He looked up. 'Honeymoon?'

Yes, I said, honeymoon.

He shrugged, made a show of looking around. 'Then where is your wife?' he said. He was still grinning. It was like the smile was stuck on his face. It was starting to annoy me.

'How much longer?' I said.

---

* Although many really did know the name, most Japanese knew little more. His fame was his name – not the events which made the name. Also many onlookers assumed that the 'famous American' was *the* famous American – that is, Abraham Lincoln. Which explains their surprise – the man obviously having come back from a very famous (and very public) assassination.

He looked again at his watch. 'Two minutes!' His eyes slid up again, found mine.

Silence. Staring. Grinning.

'She's at the hotel,' I said, 'OK?'

'OK!'

With ostentatious show, he peeled off the picture's backing, turned it over.

I thought suddenly of Karen, nearly two years dead now. Anger at myself rose again, then again drew back.

'There!' he said, triumphant.

The widow considers the beauty that is the Meiji Shrine.

'How much?' I said. He quoted. I paid.

'Bye now!'

I watched him walk away, neat and tidy, his high-polished shoes glinting in the light.

I stood for a moment, again thinking for diversion of Libbie and contemplating the picture (I looked ridiculous – pale-faced and grinning), then moved off, heading for the Meiji-jingumae sub-way. At the station entrance, I tossed the thing into what I thought was an ornamental waste-bin.*

Today, the Boku Seki teahouse takes Mastercard and Visa and any western currency. Then, for the widow of such a famous man, no money was allowed to change hands. Word of the intended visit had reached the house earlier that day, and so, as she stepped down from the embassy's car, the bamboo gate opened, seemingly of its own accord, and low bows were made and an escort provided through the garden. Here, in the link between the real world and the other world of the tea ceremony, she met, for the first time, Tadashi Inoguchi.

By then a government official (within a year, having been transferred to the legation in Peking, he would be one of those rescued by troops during the Boxer Rising, in the course of which he would lose the first three fingers of his left hand), Tadashi Inoguchi, as a younger man, had spent three months at the

---

* This was, I have since discovered, nothing of the sort. It was, in fact, a receptacle intended for written prayers.

academy at West Point, during which time he'd learned (as all do) about the history, in general, of the army in the West and, in particular, that of George Armstrong Custer. Consequently, when, nearly a decade later, he heard of the general's widow's plans to visit Tokyo, he arranged this meeting.

The story has them standing, at first awkward, in the neat, well-regulated garden, then sitting (he on a mat, she on a low wooden chair) in a small cell-like room, Libbie, as custom required, admiring the features of the room and the tea utensils, while Inoguchi, in near-perfect English, responded with memories of West Point. It had been, he told her, one of the most instructive periods of his life, teaching him the valuable lesson (valuable particularly to a diplomat) that Americans, once they start a thing, will carry it through all the way to the end, regardless of cost or consequence. Was this not, he added, the very story, in essence, of the general himself? Libbie, it is said, agreed – adding, then, that there was, though, perhaps another lesson. Which would be? asked Inoguchi. That, said Libbie (and here she anticipated a moment of awkwardness – and was not to be disappointed), an army cast adrift from the people's control will not know when to stop – will not recognise defeat and the time to withdraw. At this, it is said, Inoguchi turned away.

'*So?*'

He knew, as she did, that, beyond the delicate and rarefied mysteries of the teahouse and its neat, nature-trapped garden, the streets of the city were filled every day more and more with soldiers, as the power of the emperor slipped more and more into the hands of their masters.

'So what?'

She was sitting in the armchair by the window, turning the pages of some garish magazine. Beyond her, the lights of Tokyo were rising through the dusk, defeating it. Without looking up, she said, '*So* did you find her?'

I crossed the room, fetched a Calpis soda from the mini-bar, cracked it, took a mouthful.

'What did *you* do?' I said.

She shrugged. 'You didn't answer my question.'

'No,' I said.

'No what?'

'No, I didn't find her.'

She looked up. 'But you stood where she stood.' I thought there was pity or disappointment or something in her voice.

'Look,' I said.

'What?' she said. A challenge.

For some reason, then, I thought of the picture in the Washington archives.

'I'm tired.'

The widow considers the beauty that is the Meiji Shrine.

'Of?'

'What?'

'What are you tired *of*?'

I sat on the bed, lay back. I closed my eyes. A whole year gone – one year of a new marriage nearly over.

'Nothing,' I said.

Beside me, the bed took a dip. A hand, light on my forehead; fingertips on my cheek.

'I saw this inscription,' I said after a while.

'Where?'

The fingers traced the line of my jaw, then down to my throat.

'At the shrine. "Ichigo, ichie."'

'What?'

'"Ichigo, ichie."'

She frowned. 'So are you going to tell me what it means?'

I opened my eyes, studied the splitting plaster on the ceiling. 'It means "One lifetime, one meeting".'

'Wow.'

I turned my head. 'What?'

'Well, doesn't that kind of screw things up?'

'How?'

'Well, doesn't it mean you'll never find her?'

35

I shook my head.

Suddenly she was smiling. 'What?'

'I already did,' I said.

7

Miss Libbie in the Alley

Frank Philip Bacon was born on December 3rd 1922. He graduated from high school in Osprey, Pennsylvania, before studying law and accounting at Hepburn College. In April 1942, he joined the Army Air Force as an aviation cadet. He received his wings in April of the following year, and joined the 348th Fighter Group in New Guinea eight months later. It was the beginning of a career that covered two wars and resulted in seventeen confirmed kills.

He served in the Pacific theatre for nearly two years, seeing heavy action in some of the most vicious air battles of the Second World War. With his outstanding natural flying skill and marksmanship, he became one of the most valued pilots in the group.

On September 28th 1944, Bacon was chasing a Mitsubishi A6M Zero in his P-47 Republic Thunderbolt, nicknamed 'The Miss Libbie', when his point-blank gunfire caused the Zero to explode. He was so close when it blew up, he practically rammed the wreckage. Moments later, he found himself under attack from two more Zeros, gunfire from which riddled his P-47's wings and stabilisers. Despite this damage, and with his aircraft beginning to yawl to the left, he returned fire and so claimed his second enemy aircraft of the day.

At the end of the war, Bacon's outstanding record secured him a job with the Air Force Demonstration Unit. The group toured the air-show circuit, showing off the new F-86 SabreJet to the taxpaying public. Following a short period of service with the 1st Fighter Group, he received orders for Korea, where he joined the 334th Fighter Squadron in November 1951. Here, at once, he christened his new F-86F 'The Miss Libbie II', and so began Close

Air Support and Interdiction operations which, by war's end, would see him established as the air force's equal third-highest scoring ace of the conflict.

It was during the Pukhan River campaign, whilst flying CAS missions in support of the Seventh Cavalry in that unit's attempt to capture the Hwachon dam, that Colonel Bacon's F-86F was struck and crippled by Chinese anti-aircraft fire,* and the colonel, being by then too low to use his parachute, was forced to attempt a crash landing. Finding a clearing, he put the plane down with extra-ordinary skill, and was just freeing himself from the wreckage when a ruptured fuel line exploded, covering both cockpit and pilot in a sheet of flame. Though he managed to escape the inferno, he was so badly burned that, disorientated and in terrible pain, he wandered around for several days before being captured by the North Koreans who took him to a POW camp, where the guards threw him into a cell.

The colonel received no treatment for his terrible wounds. Gradually, the burned flesh on his face began to rot and attracted maggots. They turned out to be a blessing in disguise. The repellent creatures actually cleaned his wounds by eating the decaying flesh. The maggots frequently crawled into his nose, and, as his hands had been so badly burned that he could not use his fingers, he was forced to endure them moving around in his nostrils.

Finally, having somehow survived against terrible odds, Colonel Bacon was released from captivity (across the inaptly named 'Bridge of No Return') as part of an exchange-of-prisoners programme, and returned to the United States in October 1953, where he received medical treatment. He was later awarded the Congres-sional Medal of Honor.

★   ★   ★

* Despite the damage done to the aeroplane by the crash and subsequent fire, much remained intact. What there was was collected by one of the North Korean 'Land Cleansing Teams' and shipped to one of a series of warehouses at Songnim, thirty miles south-east of Pyongyang. Here the remains were crudely reconstructed, and can be seen today alongside similar reconstructions of a British Sea Fury downed in the sea off Inchon and a US Navy F9F Panther.

Today, Frank P. Bacon lives in sheltered accommodation in the Springtime Retirement Home* at Kissimmee, Florida. Now seventy-six years old, he is a thin sprightly man, whose reconstructed face has an almost youthful look, untroubled by the usual lines and wrinkles. He is a keen golfer and the co-owner (though now mostly retired from much active participation) of four cold-water and tropical aquaria – the result of an interest he developed during his long captivity.

'There's great fish, you know, over there.'

We were sitting in his room, either side of a window overlooking the gardens.

'In Korea?'

'Yessir.'

He reached into an inside pocket, pulled out a silver flask. 'Drink?'

'Thanks,' I said. I chugged back a mouthful, felt it racing to my stomach.

Although it was still only nine o'clock in the morning, I was already exhausted. Until a few minutes previously, I'd been sitting in an almost identical room (same pink and grey carpet, same teak-veneered furniture, same elaborately fake flame-effect fire) with the man who'd greeted me in the lobby in his dressing-gown and carpet slippers – a man who had seemed to be waiting for someone (for me, or so I'd thought) – one who, when approached and addressed tentatively as '*Colonel?*', had jumped to attention and had stayed at attention until I'd suggested he fall out and stand at ease. Of course I suppose that when he'd insisted on removing all his clothes and squatting in the corner of his room singing 'Somewhere' from *West Side Story*, I should at once have been alive to the deception – but I was not. Just my luck, I'd thought, and I'd just about given the whole thing up again, when the real Colonel Bacon had come to the rescue.

'Can I ask you something?' he said.

'Sure,' I said.

* One of whose residents, as of February 2001, carries the unlikely name of Bart Simpson. Mr Simpson was, in his former life, an accountant and Methodist lay preacher.

39

'My brother – did he by any chance try to *give* you something to give to me?'

The whiskey at once quit boiling in my stomach. 'Give you something?' I said. 'Like what?'

He shrugged. 'I guess he didn't, then.'

I pictured the package, saw it slip beneath the cubicle door. 'No,' I said. 'Were you expecting something?'

Another shrug. 'It doesn't matter,' he said. 'It's just he sometimes likes to play games with people. Last person he sent down here came with a barracuda head in a box. One before that had a Thermos full of frogs. You see, he likes to see if people will take them – and if they'll keep *on* taking them when they start to smell. It makes him feel like a kid again – before he got to be the dumb one.'

'And you got to be the smart one?'

'Smart enough to get my face burned to hell, yes.'

We sat for a moment in silence. I tried not to look at his hands – tried not to imagine them fighting the controls of his Sabre as it scythed through the tree-tops and then burst into flames – but I couldn't. They were pink like his face and smooth, hairless.

'I understand you're interested in Elizabeth Custer,' he said at last.

I looked up, sprung, guilty.

'I'm writing a book,' I said.

'So what do you want to know?'

'Well, anything really –'

'Anything?'

'About her – your – ancestors. For example, how they ended up in Monroe.'

'OK. But let me ask you something first.'

'Of course.'

He lifted his hands, palms up, pushed them out from his sleeves. 'What do you think of these?' he said. He turned them over; the light caught their tight hairless backs.

'I went to Washington,' I said.

'I know.'

40

'I read your archives.'

He lowered his hands, rested them on his knees. 'Then you know what happened,' he said.

'I know about the crash. Yes.'

'But not after.'

'After?'

'When I got home.'

'No,' I said. 'What happened?'

'Well, I wanted to see my old colonel. Just talk over the old days. But I couldn't find him. No records. Nothing. Well, in the end I found him – through another old buddy of mine used to fly MiG Alley with us. Anyway, he was living at the end of a dirt track in North Carolina. He had nothing – no pension from the air force. Nothing. He was just scraping by. And you know why? Because when he got hit he went down and when he went down they got him. And *he* was whole. They used to like them whole. There was more of you to hurt. Anyway, they tortured him – for two months they tortured him – trying to get him to 'confess' he'd been dropping biological weapons. Well, he didn't say nothing. Not for two months. Not even when they cut off his ears and skinned the soles of his feet. But in the end of course they got him, and he 'confessed'. And then there he was on TV in New York and Los Angeles saying how sorry he was and how germ bombs were a crime against the people of North Korea, etc., etc. Well, bingo. Then the war ends and he's home and what's the first thing the air force do? Dishonourably discharge him is what. So he gets nothing – not even medical. And he can't even get a job. Nobody will hire him. And so he got to living in his own shit and drinking – which is how he was when I found him. And why I sent those bastards back the only thing they ever gave me.'

'You gave back your medal?' I said.

'First-class registered. Sent it straight back to those fuckers in Congress. Told them to spin on it.'

We sat for a while in silence; then, in a while, he stood up. He crossed to a desk, lifted some papers. 'You wanted to know about the Bacons,' he said. 'Well, whatever I know – and it's not much –

is in here. I looked it out yesterday when I knew you were coming. You know, the funny thing is I wrote it, but I can't *remember* writing it. It's like somebody else did it. Which makes it just about like everything else these days. I can't hardly remember doing anything I did. I know I *did* stuff – I just don't *remember* doing it. Except the Alley. I remember the Alley. Man, it was beautiful up there. Just blue. It was like being a boy. Just me and Miss Libbie. It was just like being a boy with his girl.'

8

Snoozing in the Sun-room

Edged by the kind of high-backed over-stuffed chairs you can't imagine anyone ever choosing but which, somehow, always seem to get chosen, the sun-room at the Springtime to which Frank had directed me through a maze of tan-coloured thick-carpeted corridors was, by the time I found it (that is, lunchtime: I'd made several mis-turns, opening in the process a number of entirely inappropriate doors), deserted but for the sleeping presence of one elderly soul – a tiny thin-boned white-haired woman half-hidden in the corner beneath the waves of a smock-like floral dress.

I selected a chair at the opposite end of the room and settled in. Despite the day's mellow warmth, the windows and French doors were shut tight, trapping and stagnating the air within. I got out my glasses and slipped them on, so bringing the world into sudden sharper focus. Outside, beyond the doors and the glass-panelled walls, the lawns were neatly clipped, the unruly growth of bushes and shrubs denied by savage pruning. There was a smudge on the left lens of my glasses; I took them off, polished and replaced them, looked again. Way off, in the shade of some big old tree, a figure (a man – Frank maybe – it was difficult to tell) was gazing up through the branches towards (I assumed) the sky. I eased forward in my chair, followed his gaze, expecting something – a plane perhaps. But there was nothing to see but sky. Just the sheerest palest blue going on for ever. *Like being a boy with his girl.* I thought of Frank and for a moment tried to feel the flames he'd felt in that burning cockpit, but could not. All that would come for me now in these times of peace was the warmth of sunlight, not flame.

A cough in the room; I looked away. The old woman stirred, settled, away, still, in sleep. I looked back. The figure in the shade was moving off and was soon lost in shadow.

A boy with his girl.

I opened the wallet and took out Frank's notes.

The notes were close-typed on an old ribbon typewriter, each *e* and each *m* a little offset and dropped down below the line like crotchets and quavers in a musical score. Here and there, casually preserved on the yellowing paper, were the diary marks of some former long-gone life – a coffee-ring, a jagged sellotaped tear, what looked like the palm-print of a baby. I eased down in the chair, fixed my eyes on the page. *Sometimes an old man would come by . . .* My eyes were heavy. I sat back up, concentrating. *Sometimes an old man would come by and tell her how, fifty years ago, he'd stood on Weir Point and listened to the sound of gunfire over the bluff, and how he'd wanted to go to the general's aid but how Reno was drunk and Captain Benteen had forbidden it . . .*

'You missed lunch.'

. . . how Captain Benteen had forbidden it . . .

I woke to a distant voice, then a prodding in my chest. I pushed up, rubbing my eyes . . . *Captain Berteen had forbidden it . . .* The finger withdrew. Frank's pages were scattered at my feet where they'd fallen.

'And you know what *that* means.'

'What?' I said.

Reno was drunk.

I squinted, shifting in my chair, trying to make out a shape – but the sun was low now in the sky, strung between two far-off trees, its cooling light shining straight into my eyes.

'It *means –*' another poke '*–* that friend Hernandez'll be by any time now, poking his nose in and asking more damn-fool questions, and all because of *you –*'

The silhouette moved, stepping back and straightening – a spare covered skeleton shifting in a great billowing cotton tent.

'Look, I really don't know what you're talking about,' I said.

44

'I'm *talking* about Hernandez.'

'I'm sorry, I don't *know* any Hernandez.'

The old woman huffed. Her white hair was wild, standing up from her skull as if shot through with a high-voltage charge. 'Oh *sure* you don't, mister. Just like *I* don't know how your daddy's been getting them over and smuggling them in and finding them restaurant jobs and jobs driving school buses that should be going to bona *fide* Americans –'

'My daddy?'

'Oh yes, sir. Don't think I don't know about our resident war hero. Don't think I don't know how those wet-backs give him kickbacks. No, sir. Don't think I don't know.'

'I see,' I said, though I didn't see at all. The woman was plainly mad – or at least seriously confused. I stuffed the papers back into the folder and stood, a little unsteady still from the residue of sleep. 'If you'll excuse me,' I said. The old woman glared. 'Don't think I don't know!' she hissed as I eased past her. 'Don't think I don't know!'

Frank was sitting on his bed when I found my way back to his room. I paused in the doorway, tapped on the door. He turned slow. His eyes were blank.

'Who are *you*?' he said.

'It's me, Frank,' I said.

He frowned. '*I* don't know you. Who *are* you?'

I told him, held up the folder of notes. 'I was wondering if I could borrow them,' I said.

The frown deepened.

'To maybe get them copied?'

He was looking at me – but through me too, as if to the open door and beyond.

'Frank?' I said.

But then he looked away, something in him defeated.

'Would you like me to fetch someone?'

Nothing. Deafness. I watched him for a moment – his pink, unlined face – tried to picture the young man lost forever in the

45

flames. But the image wouldn't come. All there was now was this weary old man with the stiff livid mask of a boy, and a youth not given in the service of his country but taken with brutal force and never returned.

9

The Long Walk Home

Whenever people asked him how he got to be where he was – how he'd risen from a farmer's low standing to become, variously, a schoolteacher, a director of bank and railroad, a member of the Territorial Legislature, a (losing) candidate for Michigan lieutenant governor and finally a probate judge – Elizabeth's father, Judge Daniel Stanton Bacon, always said simply that he'd walked. And what is more, he often added, his particular journey from Onondaga, New York, where, like his father before him and his father's father, he'd farmed wheat and barley, to the house of a judge in Monroe, Michigan, had merely been one small step in a much longer walk – a walk homeward begun over two hundred years previously across the ocean in Norfolk, England.

'*English – am I right?*'

Consequently, he was, he would say, worth precisely neither more nor less in the great scheme of things than a single link in a long unbroken chain – a chain, he would boast (and with good reason), neither longer nor shorter than America herself.

'You're right.'

'I knew it!'

'I can't deny it.'

'Excuse me?'

'I said I can't deny it.'

'Deny it? But why would you want to?'

'What?'

'You said you can't deny it. Inferring that you'd want to –'

'You mean implying. And anyway, it was a joke.'

'A joke? What kind of a joke?'

'Obviously not a very good one.'

'Jesus. You English.'

'What about us?'

'Nah – nothing. Say, you flown this outfit before?'

'No, I haven't. Please. Tell me. I'd really like to know.'

'Aaah, well OK. You see, it's like the saying goes, "English people don't remember their history; Americans can't forget." '

'I thought that was the English and the Irish.'

'The Irish? Aah, Jesus, don't get me started –'

'And anyway it's crap. Meaningless.'

'What do you mean?'

'I just said what I mean. Maybe you should try listening.'

'What?'

'Exactly. Now. I'm trying to read. So leave me alone, OK?'

'Jeez.'

'Thank you so much.'

'Jeez – you English.'

Another two hours and we landed in Detroit. Fifteen minutes and I was out on the road heading west. Soon, with the city slipping into dusk-light behind me, I pulled off the interstate and parked in a rest area in the shadow of some trees.

I needed a map but the visitor centre was closed, so I got a Coke from the machine and went back and sat in the car. I tried the radio but the noise made my nerves jangle, so I switched it off. It was getting dark, headlights on the interstate piercing the gloom like fireflies. I started the car up and drove on.

Two hours later and I was sitting on a bed in a room in a Motel Six twenty miles or so from Monroe. I put it off for a while, watching TV, but then I picked up the phone, was dialling, half-trying to figure out what time it was in London, but not really caring.

'Hello?'

I opened my mouth to speak, but for a moment nothing came.

'Who's this?'

'It's me.'

48

'Christ – you again. I told you. You keep calling like this and I'm calling the police.'

'OK, OK – but is she there?'

'Look, I told you. You don't live here any more. She doesn't live here any more –'

There was so much to say and seemed so little time.

'Hello?'

I watched my hand as, with an act of great treachery, it set the receiver back down in its cradle.

I dozed for a while, exhausted (all day I'd been feeling like I was sick – like there was something ill-defined wrong with me), half-dreaming of Karen and half-listening for sounds. A car pulling up; voices. A door slamming, shivering the walls and the light above my head in its dirty fly-filled glass bowl. A murmuring, like the voices of conspirators, a barking dog. Someone out in the parking lot rattling ice from a machine.

It was dark when I crossed the parking lot, the air thick and sweet with the threat of a storm. I climbed a grass bank, eased down the other side. Another parking lot, JB's Family Diner, then another.

I slipped into a booth.

'Hi. I'm Caroline, and I'll be your server tonight.'

A line of spooky trucks, loadless, gleaming.

'Can I get you somethin' to drink?'

If I turn my back, I thought.

'Sir?'

Whiskey, beer, wine, anything. I scanned the menu. No alcohol. Sullen, I ordered iced tea.

'Sure. Would that be sweetened or unsweetened?'

I want a drink I want a drink I want a drink. 'Unsweetened,' I said.

When it came it was, of course, sweetened.

'Will there be a storm?' I said. It was something to say.

'A storm?'

'They said on TV –'

She shrugged. 'Then I guess,' she said. 'Are you ready to order?'

'They said a tornado maybe.'

49

She looked away at the sound of tumbling dishes, looked back. 'Excuse me?'

'On the TV. They said there was maybe a tornado coming.'

Another shrug. Her hair was dark – striped blonde, home-applied. It made her look cheap, undernourished.

'You don't think so?'

'I guess maybe. If they said it.'

'But they could be wrong?'

'Excuse me?' She was frowning hard. 'Look,' she said. 'Can I tell you about the specials?'

I was waiting for her when the place closed at midnight.

'Caroline?'

She turned.

Cheap.

I stepped out – a real spook – from the gloom.

'Oh it's you,' she said.

I looked up at the sky. 'I guess they were wrong.' It was true: though the night sky was heavy still with cloud, it seemed benign enough.

'Want do you want?' she said, and it occurred to me then that maybe someone was waiting for her – a boyfriend, a father, at home or in a car maybe.

'Can you show me around?'

'*What?*'

'The town.'

'You mean *now?*'

'Well, unless there's someone –'

She looked at me as if I was crazy.

'Tomorrow then?'

'No. Of *course* not.'

'Why not?'

She turned away again. 'You're crazy.'

'But you don't know me.'

'No. I *don't* know you. That's kind of the point.'

I told her my name.

50

'Look, I have to go.' She started walking – two steps, three, four.

'But what about the storm?'

I followed, caught her up.

'What is it *now*?' she said, and in that moment, as we walked not so much side by side as on parallel paths, the first drops of rain began to fall.

We sheltered under cover of some trees – the second worst place, she said, if there was to be a storm. She didn't say what the first was and I didn't ask. Instead, we just stood there, looking out at the rain. Across the parking lot, beyond the highway, a wind, far off, was bending distant trees and whipping power lines.

'What should we do?' I said.

She half-turned, said something into the rising wind I didn't catch.

'What did you say?'

She leaned in. 'I *said* are you still here?'

'Of course I'm still here. I can stand here if I want, can't I?'

She screwed up her face.

Way off on the highway a billboard started shaking. 'Look,' I said, 'shouldn't we at least *try* to get out of the way?'

'And go *where* precisely?'

'What about the restaurant?'

She shook her head. 'Closed.'

'What about the motel then?'

'What about it?'

'I've got some whiskey.'

'So?'

'And there's a really big cupboard. We could hide in it.'

'In a cupboard?'

'Is that a bad place too?'

She nodded hard.

'You mean worse than trees?'

'Nowhere's worse than trees.'

'So what *should* we do then?'

But then she was running and I was running too, a step or two behind, splashing across the parking lot, up a grass bank and then down, then out across the motel's crumbling forecourt and under the awning.

'What are you doing?' she said. 'Why are you following me?' She was shaking and so was I from the wind and the rain and the running.

'I'm not. I was going this way anyway.'

She looked away.

'You want that drink?' I said.

She looked back. 'I won't sleep with you,' she said.

'I didn't ask you to.'

'Just so long as you know – OK?'

'OK,' I said. 'And now that that's sorted out, can we get out of this fucking wind?'

'OK,' she said.

'Ready?' I said.

'Ready,' she said, and then, counting down from three, we ran hard across the forecourt and down between the cars, shrieking like children, heading for the anonymous sanctuary of my room.

The morning came, lifting a curtain on the tornado's work. There was debris everywhere: branches and uprooted bushes, an old tan saloon upturned in the diner's parking lot. I stood at the window watching Caroline, a tiny figure now, crossing the highway, heading I guessed for home. I watched her until she was out of sight. Later, standing mute in the shower, I tried to remember a single thing she'd said, but could not. She was already out of reach, already halfway home.

10

The House That Dan Built

When, at the age of twenty-four, seeking his fortune in business, Daniel Stanton Bacon arrived in Monroe on the banks of Lake Erie, it was a town, though still in its first pangs of growth (the first sawmills and tanneries, breweries and distilleries were rising on the banks of the great Raisin River), that was already on its third recorded name. First it had been Raisinville, due to its river location, then Frenchtown, thanks to the language of its first white inhabitants. Finally, in 1817, the town of Libbie's birth took the name of Monroe, following the visit in that year in cocked hat, knee-breeches and fine powdered wig of the suffering-liberal-but slave-owning fifth president of that name. Whatever its name, though, the town was, for Daniel Bacon (as, increasingly, for so many others), both an end and a beginning. It was for him (as for those others – and more – those from the east, from New England and New York State) the chosen location of his own particular American dream – its clear waters, rich soil and broad western skies the elements that, along with the efforts of his own hands, would, he hoped (no, more than hoped – *believed*), make of that dream a distinct individual *American* reality.

'*So it was here – the house he built? On this very spot?*'

And it did – defiantly so – for, within months of buying his first piece of land (paid for with a loan from his father), he had cleared over ten acres, selling the timber at $12 a thousand, and soon there stood on the cleared land peach trees, apple and plum.

'Yes sir, right here. In fact, where you're standing was just about dead in the centre of the parlour – just about where, as a young girl, Miss Libbie used to play the piano. Hey, Cheryl, are you there?'

'So why did they knock it down?'

'Cheryl, if you're anywhere's you can hear me, could you come right through to the front, please?'

'Who's Cheryl?'

'Cheryl? Cheryl Stapper. She's chief librarian. Knows all about places to eat in town.'

'Right.'

'Now, what were you asking?'

'You mean about places to eat?'

'No – I remember. You were saying about knocking it down. Well, the truth is they didn't knock it down. They just moved it. Had to make room.'

'They moved it?'

'Uh-huh. Board by board and brick by brick. It's sitting right over on 7th Street and Cass. Did it to make room for the post office. Excuse me – Cheryl?'

'So this was a post office before it was a museum.'

'Yes sir, that's right.'

'And before that it was the place with peach trees? This was the land he cleared?'

'No sir. The house where Miss Libbie was born was a big house surrounded by elm trees. Of course by then, her father was a judge, not to mention having already been County Supervisor and Inspector of Schools. Say, Cheryl, gentleman here was asking about real nice places to eat in town. Should I send him to McGinty's?'

'Is Tom still in Toledo?'

'Yes, ma'am.'

'You sure?'

'Uh-huh. I ran into Janice. Said she ain't expecting him back until Tuesday.'

'Well, OK then. But tell him to be careful, OK?'

'OK.'

'Careful? What does she mean careful?'

'Tell him, well, you know –'

'I know, Cheryl, I know. I'll tell him.'

'Tell me what?'

'About the war –'

'What war?'

'You know – in Ireland. Cheryl means – and she's right – it's just best not to talk about it. You being English an' all –'

'But there isn't a war in Ireland.'

'Hey, you kidding me? You mean it's over?'

'No. I don't mean it's over. I mean there never was a war.'

'Aw now, come on. It was on the news!'

'So was the moon landing.'

'That's right!'

'And everyone knows that was faked out in Hollywood.'

'What?'

'Never mind. Look – this McGinty's. Will you tell me where it is if I promise not to mention the war?'

Ten minutes later I was slipping into a booth beneath a framed and tattered Irish tricolour.

'How're you doin' today, sir? Can I fetch you a drink?'

Sitting in McGinty's Irish Pub was like sitting in the middle of some hallucinogenic summer field: everything in the place – the walls, the carpet, even the clips in Trudi's hair – was a ghastly puke-toned leprechaun green. I ordered a Guinness.

'Can I ask you something?'

When it came it was cold.

'Sure,' said Trudi. She was tall – maybe six foot – and, what with her long blonde hair and pale blue eyes, about as Irish-looking as the Pope. 'As long as it's not about Custer – OK?'

'OK.'

She lowered her pad, cocked her head like a bird. 'Good,' she said. 'Then shoot.'

'Well,' I said. 'About this war.'

She frowned, suddenly wary. 'What war?'

'In Ireland,' I said.

She narrowed her eyes. 'What about it?'

'Well, did you know it's over?'

'What do you mean?'

'I mean the war. In Ireland. It's over. We decided to call it quits. Got tired of trampling all over our Irish brothers – what with them being such a happy, harmless bunch of people and in no way deserving of our tyrannical rule.'

Trudi shrugged. 'Tom never said.'

'Well, maybe Tom doesn't know.'

'Maybe.'

'Yup. The boys'll be home for Christmas, any luck.'

'What boys?'

'And the fair land of Ireland will forthwith be returned to its rightful, peace-loving, blarney-stone-kissing owners. Great, eh?'

'Well, like I say, Tom never said.'

'But don't you think it's great?'

Another shrug. 'I guess.'

'So will you help me celebrate?'

'Celebrate?'

'The end of the war.'

'I don't think so.'

'Oh *come* on –'

She frowned, suddenly dubious. 'Like do what?'

'Well, I thought maybe we could just stay in. Rent a video. Get a pizza maybe.'

'Jeez, you're *strange* –'

'Oh come *on*, come *on*. How many times in a lifetime does a person get to celebrate the end of a war?'

'Well –'

'Great. That's settled then. I'll meet you at the statue – at, say, seven?'

'I *said* I don't know –'

'OK, listen. *I'll* be there at seven. If you're there, you're there. If you're not, well, I suppose I'll just have to celebrate on my own.'

'OK. Whatever.'

'Then you'll come?'

'No. Maybe. I don't know.'

'Great,' I said, and then I ordered – just for the symmetry of the thing – the Dublin deluxe cheeseburger with the County Cork fries and the Mayo, well, mayo.

The Bacon house, as it stands today, on the corner of seventh Street and Cass, remains essentially as it was a little over a century ago – in all but two significant respects. Firstly, it is, of course, no longer where it was; and, secondly, it is owned today (and not only owned, but *occupied*) – or so I had been told, and by no lesser an authority than Susan Hansan, the Historical Museum's senior archivist – not by a Bacon but a Custer – and not by any Custer, mind, but by the general himself.

'You'll see. Just go take a look. And not only *him* – but her too.'

This I couldn't resist, so I took a short detour on my way back from McGinty's and parked across the crossroads from the house in the shade of some trees, then sat awhile, watching.

'You mean Libbie?'

I replayed her words, scanning them for lies.

'I do.'

'I see.'

'You don't believe me?'

'Should I?'

'Well, like I say, go and see for yourself. It's only five minutes' drive. Although if I were you I'd make an appointment first. The general tends to get a little tetchy with people just come to gawp.'

'He likes his privacy, then – the general.'

'You got it.'

'OK. An appointment. Would it be OK, though, to just drive by, take a look?'

'Sure! It's a free country! He may be a general but he still don't own the roads!'

I eased down a little further behind the wheel. I fixed my eyes on the large white house with its deep-green shutters, waiting (though I knew it was crazy) for the door to open any minute and a golden-haired, droopy-moustached man who'd been dead for over a hundred and thirty years to emerge dressed in deep army blue with two stars on each shoulder, brandishing in one hand a sabre and, in the other, the hand of his new wife Elizabeth.

Well, ten minutes passed, twenty, a half-hour – and nothing. I slid down a little further. Another ten minutes went by, fifteen. Then, just as I was getting ready to head back to the motel, sure enough – as if my reaching for the car keys had cued him – out stepped the general, his wife at his side. I sat up at once, forgetting I was hiding. I stared, not quite believing the evidence of my eyes. It was them – really them. I watched as they strolled hand in hand in my direction down the path and got into a blue four-wheel drive Toyota. What I must have looked like that afternoon last summer as I watched them drive away I cannot now imagine – nor, now, can I guess how I managed, in my surprise, to start the car and find drive, nor how I managed to follow them for as long as I did, before going through a red light at the end of South Benton Street right in front of an officer from the Monroe County Sheriff's office who, only that morning (I was later to learn), had discovered his wife had closed both their current and savings accounts in preparation for a night-flit with her lover to Georgia.

I *do* recall, however, how he motioned me over, stepped out of his vehicle and pulled on his hat. He fingered his gun as he walked towards my car.

'Officer,' I said. 'I know what you're going to say –'

One hand on the car's roof, he hung his face like a lantern before me through the open window. I could see my white face in his shades.

'You do?' he said.

'Yes,' I said. I tried to smile. 'You see, I'm just so excited –'

The officer sighed. 'I see,' he said. 'And why would that be?'

'Well,' I said. 'You see, there's been this war and, well, now it's over –'

Another sigh, a slight shake of the head. 'English?' he said.

'English,' I said.

He stepped back, moved away. 'On your way,' he said.

'Thank you,' I said, and, with shaking hand, I stuck the shift in drive and moved into the traffic, not daring to look back, lest in doing so I were to see a man in my mirror – an officer of the law – raising his pistol and taking deadly aim.

11

Cranks in the World

Just as Custer, on that long-ago Sunday in June, could not escape the Sioux (and they, in the end, of course, could not escape the wrath of an outraged nation), so today, in Monroe, you cannot, however hard you try, escape the name and most often the image of General George Armstrong Custer. Buy a tyre, for example, at the Custer Lube and Tire Shop, or a sports bag in the Custer Sports Emporium, and he's there, looking down, stern and forbidding. Or rent a movie downtown at the Last Stand Movie Parlor and he's there, gazing at you disapprovingly, that long slender nose, flowing locks and hollow face seeming to watch you with disdain, his flesh forever sepia, as you try to decide between *Dances with Wolves* and *Dude, Where's My Car?*

Or you try, as I did, that afternoon in Monroe, to rent any one of the dozens of movies that have featured, in so many disguises, the likeness of that brave and foolish man.

'Custer?'

'Custer, yes.'

'Would you have a title for that, sir?'

'How about *Custer of the West?*'

'OK, sir. One minute.' A tapping on a keyboard, a pause, then a frown, a shaking head. 'Sorry, sir. Maybe it's too new.'

'I don't think so. It was made in 1967. It's a classic. It's crap, but it's classic crap.'

'I'm sorry. Is there maybe anything else I can get you?'

'How about *They Died with Their Boots On?*'

More tapping. Another frown.

'*Son of the Morning Star?*'

Another blank.

'Have you tried a search?'

'A search?'

'Of the database. Try typing in "Custer", then click Search and see what happens.'

More tapping, a click, tapping, click click.

'Well?'

Again the frown gathered and was just spreading like a shadow – but then a yelp and it fled.

'Did you get something?'

And was replaced in a second by the face-flooding smile of complete and unexpected victory. 'There,' he said, spinning the monitor and pointing. '*Little Big Man.*'

'Oh great,' I said, trying to hide my disappointment.

'And look, it's got three stars!'

'What does *that* mean?'

'It means it's, like, a real top movie!'* He peered a little closer. 'OK now,' he said, tapping the keyboard once, then again. 'That's . . . aisle three, row two.' He looked up. '*Now* who says I ain't smart enough to tie my own shoes?'

It was a little after three when I got back to the motel. There was a note thumb-tacked to my door. *Dear Sir*, it read, the words looped in an elegant copperplate hand. *The general has instructed me to advise you that he will not tolerate being pursued as if he were some kind of a animal. Should you continue to do so, I have the general's authority to tell you that the consequences will be both swift and severe. That is all. Yours sincerely. J. Frost. Scout.*

I looked around me. Nobody – at least nobody I could *see*. I let myself in, fetched a beer and sat down. I looked again at the note. *Swift and severe.* For sure it was crazy, but something about it gave me the creeps. It was partly the over-neat spidery writing (and what that said about a most likely obsessive kind of nature), but mostly it was wondering how they knew where I was staying. *Will not tolerate*

---

* Whatever its merits as a piece of drama, as an historical record, *Little Big Man* is nonsense; it is, indeed, more hysterical than historical.

being pursued. But then I balled the thing up and tossed it across the room. Maybe it was just crazy. I finished the beer and took a long shower.

As it is, at any time, with General Custer, so it is with America. At any moment, as the nation's estimation of its own private moral worth rises and falls, so does its view of George Custer. He stands – that is, his *memory* stands – for the nation, ready to suffer any unjust abuse or receive any praise (this often equally unwarranted) as the nation's endless cycle of flagellation and gratuitous self-congratulation goes on.

'I'm sorry, but the general's not in. May *I* help you?'

But, hey, don't just take *my* word for it.

'And you would be?'

Take his, or – next best thing – hers.

'I have the honour, sir, of being the general's wife.'

Of course you are, I thought.

'May I ask, sir, who it is I am addressing?'

So I told her, and I mentioned the note. What, I said, was meant by 'swift and severe' consequences?

Silence, a sort of sniffling.

'Hello?'

The phone clicked dead.

I called again.

'Who is it?'

'It's me again. Why did you hang up?'

'What do you want?'

Good question: what *did* I want? I drew a breath, aware suddenly of the weirdness of it all. 'An interview?' I said.

'No.'

'No?'

'No.'

'Why not?'

'You should know why not.'

'You mean because of the following thing?'

'Maybe. But look, it don't matter anyhow. Like I told you, the general's not here.'

'But I don't want to talk to the general.'

A pause.

'Hello?'

'Then what *do* you want?'

'You. I want to talk to you.'

'Me?'

Another pause.

'Well?'

'Why?'

'Well, I'm writing a book —'

'A book? About what?'

'About Eliz — About, well, *you* —'

'No, I'm sorry. I can't help you.'

'Look, can I ask you why you're so, well, suspicious?'

'Because, mister, there are cranks in the world.'

Cranks.

'And when people hate America they take it out on the general.'

'People?'

'In I-ran. Somalia. Cuba. You name it.'

'But I'm English,' I said. 'I don't hate America. In fact I *love* America! And, besides, I just want to talk, maybe ask a few questions —'

'No, I'm sorry —'

Again the phone clicked dead in my hand. I redialled the number, but now there was nothing — just dead, empty air. I set the receiver down and lay back. I closed my eyes, but they wouldn't stay closed. I sat up. *Mister, there are cranks in the world.* Barefoot, I padded quiet across the floor and eased open the door. I looked left, then right, then left again. Nothing. Then something: a glinting in the trees that bordered the motel. *Oh shit.* This could only mean one of two things: either I *was* being watched or I really *was* going crazy.

12

'I Am His Only Comfort'

As with the state, so with the man. In 1837, the year that Michigan officially entered the Union, Daniel Stanton Bacon, now thirty-nine years old, a man of some means and standing in the community, and a man in need, consequently, of a wife who would bear him a son and heir, met and found suitable for this role Miss Eleanor Sophia Page, the 23-year-old only daughter of Grand Rapids nursery owner Abel Page. Following the most formal of courtships, during which the judge was pleased to discover that his initial feelings as to her suitability had 'undergone no change', the two were married in September of that year. Both, at first, found the change in their circumstances troubling: Sophia, being separated for the first time from her family, admitting to loneliness in letters to her sister, while her husband, having 'been so long a boarder in a publick house', found the transition from bachelor to married man a sterner challenge than he'd imagined. Indeed, it was only with the arrival of their first child, Edward Augustus, on June 9th 1839, that the marriage, for both partners, gained a certain uneasy equilibrium – a state made more permanent with the birth three years later of a second child – a girl – at eight-fifteen in the morning of Sunday April 8th.

Although named Elizabeth Clift in honour of her paternal grandmother, the girl was always Libbie, and from the very start she exhibited the even temperament and 'wonderful disposition' that would not only stand her in good stead in a future filled with change and often danger, but would also prove a blessing to her parents for whom her birth would be the high point in a marriage henceforth blighted with the death in infancy of a third child, Sophia, and a fourth, Harriet, who died at six months. And so there remained just Libbie and her brother Edward, the judge's son and heir, the one upon whom so much depended.

According to his father, Edward Augustus was, at six, 'a large child, destined to be as tall as myself and one of the healthiest children I ever saw'. However, he was also a handful, 'wild and ungovernable', and his father feared that '. . . he may fall from fences, trees, into the canal or lake'.

'I thought you weren't coming.'

And so, as if cued by such a premonition, during a visit to Grand Rapids with his mother and sister, the boy fell through a broken step and suffered serious spinal injuries. From these he recovered, only then to be struck down by cholera from which he died on April 11th 1848.

'I said I would, didn't I?'

And so Libbie was alone – an only child – the only survivor of four.

'Well actually, no.'

'Well, anyway I'm here. So what now?'

'Did you know,' I said, looking up to the statue* overhead – Custer on his horse at the Battle of Gettysburg – 'that he had a pet pelican?'

'What?'

'Custer. He had a pet pelican. Used to take it everywhere on the plains with him. Not to mention dogs and snakes and even a couple of racoons.'

'Right.'

* *Sighting the Enemy* by sculptor Edward Potter was dedicated on June 4th 1910, during a ceremony attended by President William Howard Taft. Mrs Custer, then sixty-eight years old, watched the dedication from the dais in Loranger Square, at the junction of Washington and Sixth Streets, within sight of the church in which she had long ago been married. Declared a traffic hazard in 1923, the statue was moved to a park along the south side of the Raisin River. This being a far less prestigious location, the widow announced she would never set foot in the town again. In 1955, it was moved to its present site on the south-west corner of Monroe street and Elm Avenue. The statue depicts Custer having just seen Jeb Stuart's rebel cavalry on the third day of the Battle of Gettysburg, a day that would end in the south's defeat and open the way for the north's eventual victory in the war.

Trudi glanced away, as if checking her path of escape. 'Look,' she said, 'maybe this wasn't such a good idea —'

'And a wife,' I said. 'Elizabeth. Did you know he had a wife?'

The lights changed on Elm Avenue. Traffic drew to a stop, faces peering out over steering-wheels in the slow-falling dusk-light.

'Trudi? Are you OK?'

She was still looking away, but now with less conviction, as if she'd pictured her sanctuary and found it wanting. She turned back. 'I don't know what I'm doing here,' she said.

'Well, we *were* here to celebrate —'

'Oh, that's right — the end of the war.'

'Right.'

She cocked her head and smiled a mean sort of smile. 'Except it's not over. I asked Tom. He said the Brits are still there. So you lied.'

'Well, that's the damned Brits for you.'

'That's what Tom said.'

'And yet you still came.'

'I nearly didn't.'

'But you *did*. Why — if you knew I was lying?'

She shrugged.

'Trudi?'

Nothing. She looked up at the statue arching high overhead. 'Did he really have a pelican?' she said. 'Or was that another lie?'

'Really,' I said. 'And a wife.'

She sighed.

'Elizabeth,' I said. 'Her maternal grandfather was the first man to grow tomatoes in America.'

Despite herself, a smile. 'Tomatoes?' she said. 'Are you serious?'

'Absolutely,' I said. 'He called them "love apples". People thought they were poisonous. They weren't, of course. Except to me.'

'What?'

'I'm allergic to them. Come out in a rash. Can't sit down for a week.'

The smile broadened. 'Truth?' said Trudi, sceptical.

'Truth,' I said.

We stood then in silence – just the hissing of traffic at the junction of South Monroe Street and Elm Avenue. Then a voice across the street turned her head – it was boys playing catch-up on their bikes – and something in her turning seemed suddenly familiar. But from where I couldn't think.

'Look,' she said, turning back, 'I should go.'

And then I could.

'Do you have a sister?' I said.

She frowned. 'No,' she said.

But she did. I knew it.

'I'm going,' she said, and she started walking. I followed – just as, before, two days ago – I was certain – I had followed her sister through the first winds and rain of a storm.

'What are you doing?' she said, neither stopping nor looking back.

'I want to ask you something.'

'Ask me what?'

She was passing the three war memorials – the world wars, Korea, Vietnam – then so was I.

'About Caroline,' I said.

She slowed.

'She *is* your sister, *isn't* she? Trudi?'

'What?'

'Well, *isn't* she?'

Slowed, then stopped. I stopped too. She turned. 'Just leave me alone,' she said, 'will you?'

'But –'

Then she moved away and I watched her go – watched her walk the long straight road until the dusk and the distance embraced her and she was gone.

'Hello? JB's Family Diner. How may I help you?'

On August 27th 1854, Eleanor Sophia Page died, probably of dysentery, at the age of only thirty-two.

'I'd like to speak to Caroline.'

'Oh why,' the twelve-year-old Libbie confided to her diary, 'did

67

they put my mother in that great black coffin and screw down the lid so tight?' Then she went on, 'I hope that the good Lord will spare me to my father for I am his only comfort left.'

'Did you say Caroline? You mean Caroline Downey?'

'Caroline – yes.'

And so, by the age of twelve, everything that had once – albeit briefly – seemed, for Libbie, so certain was changed for ever.

'I'm sorry. You can't. She left.'

'What do you mean she left?'

'What I say. She left. Quit. Didn't even take her coat.'

'So what happened? Did something happen?'

'Look, mister, I only just came on. I don't know if something happened, and I don't care. Now, was that all?'

'Just one other thing.'

'What now?'

'Does she have a sister called Trudi?'

'A sister? You're asking me if she had a sister?'

'Well, did she?'

'I don't know. Maybe. Maybe, yeah. Why do you want to know?'

'Nothing. No reason.'

'Look, mister, who the hell are you?'

And within a month, then, her father, considering himself incapable of raising a child – especially a girl – alone, sent her to lodge with her aunt in Grand Rapids; then, when this was done, he closed up the house on South Monroe Street and moved into the Exchange Hotel.

13

Buffalo Bill and the Girls

Usually, when he was sober, my father would have no idea – no memory at all – of what he'd told me when he was drunk. This was a situation which, as a young boy, I found both exciting and bewildering. It was exciting because, once forgotten, whatever he'd told me would become a secret that I alone knew – and bewildering because I discovered early on that, contrary to what seemed most likely, it was only when he'd been drinking that he was moved to tell the truth, and that, consequently, all his sober talk was lies.

Amongst the truths that slipped unawares from his loose tongue one day was the fact that, as a young man in North London just before the Second World War, he'd taken a job with a private detective. This man (whom he always referred to simply as *Lowen*, or sometimes *Lower*) was mainly involved in 'matrimonial' work – which meant, of course, checking up on cheating partners and serving court papers and then scarpering quick. This last bit – the scarpering – was where my father's expertise lay.

Anyway, the point of this is that it was my father who taught me the importance of the phonebook as an aid to any search. 'Give me the phonebook,' he used to say, 'and I'll get you the Queen.' Certainly it wasn't much of a lesson for a father to hand down to a son, but I have never forgotten it. Indeed, whenever I think of those big fat books I think of him.

'*Yes?*'

For the rest of the time I just try to forget him, which is fairly easy, believe me.

I cupped my hands to the screen door, trying to see in. 'Look, you don't know me –' I said.

'You're right there, mister. So why don't you just fuck off?' The door inside closed hard, buffeting the screen door and making the porch tremble.

I stepped back, checked the number and street against the page from the phonebook – *Cleveland Downey, 1645 W Mercer St* – then knocked again. Nothing. I moved along the porch, picking my way through a bunch of old paint-pots and a bicycle wheel and all sorts of other useless stuff, and peered in through the window. It was dark inside – nothing to see but the vague shapes of chairs and a table and something big on legs, maybe (but this seemed unlikely) a piano.

I tapped again.

'I told you to fuck off,' called the same voice – but further off, as if from down a hall.

I leaned forward, until my lips were just touching the mesh. 'I was looking for Caroline Downey,' I said. 'Or Trudi.' I listened. Nothing. 'Hello? Mr Downey? Are you there?'

Somewhere out back a door slammed, followed by the revving of an engine. I moved down the porch steps, and was just heading round towards the side of the house to see what was happening – to see who was there – when a car swept by me down the alley to the road, its fender striking the gutter as it turned with a swerve, tyres squealing, and was gone.

'You're lucky he didn't shoot you.'

I turned.

'Excuse me?'

A man with a paunch – maybe sixty – with a beer in his hand was leaning on the wire-mesh boundary fence and smiling. 'I said you're lucky he didn't shoot you. Shot the last one who came by. Least he tried to.'

'The last one?'

'Uh-huh.' He tipped back his pale jowly head, drained the beer and belched. He tossed the bottle over his shoulder. 'Too drunk to shoot straight, though,' he said. He laughed. 'Buffalo fuckin' Bill.'

'You mean Mr Downey?'

'I mean Buffalo fuckin' Bill is who I mean.'

'Are you serious he tried to *shoot* someone?'

He scowled. 'What's the fuckin' matter with you? Ain't you got no fuckin' ears? Didn't I say he tried to shoot the fucker?'

'Who *was* it?'

'Who? Jesus fuckin' Christ. I don't fuckin' know. Some guy.'

'So why isn't he in prison?'

Another belch, this one from way down. 'He was!'

'But they let him out?'

'Couldn't hold him, man. They just couldn't hold that fucker.'

'You mean he escaped?'

'Who?'

'Buffalo Bill. Are they still looking for him?'

'Is *who* still looking for him?'

'Well, I don't know. The police? The FBI?'

'Lookin' for him? Are you kiddin'? They's tryin' to *avoid* him.' He shook his head, rueful. 'Jesus,' he said, turning away. 'That fucker. Him and them poor fuckin' girls —'

'You mean his daughters?'

But then he was gone, shuffling across his rubbish-strewn front yard and in through a banging screen door. I thought about following him, maybe asking him some more about the sisters, but I decided against it. Instead I crossed the street and got into my car. Sometimes you just know life is going to be baffling whatever you do; sometimes it's best to walk away, still not knowing — not understanding. Sometimes, something inside tells you that ignorance really is the better bliss.

Larry at reception was waiting for me when I got in. He was excited — hopping from one foot to the other like a chicken on a hotplate. Apparently, while I'd been out there'd been a phone call.

'A phone call?' I thought at once, *It's Karen.*

'From the *general*,' he said, his voice hushed with a private's reverence.

'What did he say?'

'Say?'

'Yes, *say*. You know – like, "Can I speak to so-and-so," or "Hi, it's the general here." That kind of thing.'

For a minute Larry Pegg seemed quite thrown, as if the idea of such an elevated soul actually *speaking* to some mere un-starred civilian was bizarre.

'Larry?'

'What?'

'The general – did he *want* something?'

'The general?'

'Yes, Larry. General Custer. Did he want me to call him back?'

But then the eyes blinked, so returning their owner from the rarefied heights of command to his desk in reception at a Monroe motel. 'Yes,' he said, frowning.

'Yes?'

'Uh-huh. He said – that is the *general* said – for you to call him. But not until eighteen hundred hours.'

I looked at my watch: five past six.

In my room I picked up the phone, found the number and dialled.

'*Hello?*'

It was Custer's maid – or rather the pretend-Custers' pretend-maid, all rolling-eyed vaudeville, all *Gone with the Wind*.

'Mrs Custer?'

'Nosah. This is Eliza here talking. Who's you?'

I told her – said I'd got a message to call.

'Oh yes,' she said. 'Jus' a minute, sah –' There was shouting then – at a dog maybe, or a cat. She came back. 'Now, where was I, sah? Oh yes. This evening,' she said. 'Miss Libbie told me to tell you the general's hosting a small supper-party, and would greatly *appreciate* your attendance.'

'He would?'

'Yes, sah. She said to say round about nine o'clock. And she said to say it's a sure' nough full-dressin' occasion –'

'It is?'

'Yes, sah, there being company –'

'Company? Who else is coming?'

72

'No, sah, I cannot say. Miss Libbie, she got me swearin' to keep my big ol' black mouth closed tight. Anyhow, is you comin' or is you ain't?'

'I'm coming,' I said.

A click. The connection gone. I lay back on the bed. *Full dress.* Did that mean uniforms? Uniforms with swords and rows of medals? I fetched my bag from the cupboard, tipped it out. No uniform. No sword. Certainly no medals. *There's always the phone-book.* I stuffed everything back in the bag, made a couple of calls. By eight that night I was ready. *Round about nine o'clock.* I flicked on the TV, killing time.

14

Deliverance

If any move from Grand Rapids can be said (as it *should* be said) to be a kind of deliverance, then for Libbie it was doubly so, for, with her father's enrolling her at Erasmus Boyd's Young Ladies' Seminary on the shores of Lake Erie, it meant also a homecoming – a return to Monroe, a return to all that was familiar. But it meant, above all (or would *come* to mean), entry into that charmed pre-war circle where a young lady's education was a thing to be sought, indulged, then put away upon marriage like childhood dresses – a good marriage being that happy state for which all of life was preparation.

'*The gennel's been called away to the war, sah – the president too –*'

Especially for a girl like Libbie Bacon – a girl adrift with a mother dead and a father always travelling.

I looked up from my New Balance sneakers. It was ten past nine. 'Excuse me?' My sneakers were old and scuffed and didn't sit at all well with the fancy-dress uniform of a US army captain.

For her, as for all women then, subsumption in marriage was the future and the only future.

'– and, oh Lord, I ain't *never* seen 'em so awful jumpity –'

And she just had to read her books, smile, blush and wait for it to come.

A hand grabbed my arm.

Wait for a man with position and a future – wait for someone older and wiser, someone settled – someone to protect her from the cruelties of life. Someone to guide her towards old age and death.

'*Jumpity?*' I said. I felt suddenly, in that moment on Custer's verandah, unaccountably weary.

74

'And cussin' and prayin' like the Devil in daylight –'

I could just turn and go, I thought.

'Just stompin' those floorboards, waitin' and worryin', worryin' and waitin' –'

I could get in my car and just drive away. I could drive and drive until I'm home. 'Waiting for what?' I said.

The woman rolled her eyes.

I could start again, leave everything bad behind.

A poke in the ribs and the fantasy fled. *I told you. You don't live here any more.* I squinted at the woman before me. *She doesn't live here any more.* She seemed huge – as broad, stout and black as she was in all the pictures I'd seen of Libbie's maid Eliza – her vast hands, as in the pictures, as large and as leathery as a pair of end-of-season baseball mitts. 'For *what*?' she said, scowling. 'What do you mean for *what*? For the *doctor*, sah! For *you*, sah!'

'Doctor?'

A hand pulled hard on my arm; I resisted. *This isn't your home now.* I felt in no mood for absurd make-believe. 'Look, I'm sorry,' I said, 'I don't understand. I'm just here for dinner. At least I thought –'

The hand gripped tighter, the great black sweating face looming near. 'Ain't no use now what you *thought*. What's use now is you get up them stairs and do your doctorin' –'

I felt suddenly nauseous.

'She's sweating like a nigger and turnin' blue –'

'Blue?' I said, scarcely hearing my own voice. *I'm going to be sick, I'm going to be sick.* 'Who's blue?' In my mind's eye, I saw a distant, familiar house, strolled in my head down a path, up some steps, along a hall to a bedroom bathed in light. I felt myself standing again and staring at a bed, at its covers turned back, feeling again the comfort to be found within – all the certainty and permanence, in fact, so recently lost – lost and replaced by what? By my standing here in a hall in a house in the back end of nowhere with a seriously strange woman, not only – and quite absurdly, it seemed now – *dressed* as a soldier (and, it seemed, a *doctor*) but expected to *act* like one too –

'*Well*, sah? Is you comin' or not?'

– and at once, then, with the greased-up kaleidoscope tumbling of the mind, all the ghastly 'fun' of childhood was returned to me; returned to me, also, was the churning in my stomach and sweating that the prospect of all those eyes upon me as I mugged and ridiculed myself for the pleasure of adults had always unerringly produced. I pushed myself back, tried to breathe low and regular. 'Look,' I said, 'I don't mean to be rude, but maybe I should go –'

'*Go?*'

'I'm really just not in the mood – and, besides, if they're not *here* –'

But the woman just gripped my arm tighter, drawing me in. I resisted – or tried to – but it was no good. 'The *mood*, sah?' she said. 'The mood? Why, you think Miss Libbie's in the *mood* for *dying*? You think she wouldn't rather be ridin' out with the gennel or having lady-talk with Mrs President?'

'*Who?*' I said. '*What?*'

But the woman had already turned to the stairs and was climbing – and so, as a consequence, was I, my arm smarting from her grip, my thoughts spinning back again to times that though only recently departed seemed now so distant as to appear less like a catalogue of events with cause and consequence and more like the strange jarring fantasy of dreams.

'Well, sah – ain't you got no medicine? Ain't you gonna *do* nothin'?'

The air in the sick-room was thick with breathing, the lights low, curtains drawn against the day.

Another poke in the ribs. 'Well, sah? *Ain't* you?'

Back at the motel, waiting again for Karen, I'd let the telephone ring twenty times, maybe thirty. *Ten more rings*, I'd told myself, *and I'm putting it down* – but then, as if cowed by the threat, a click on the line then a voice – a woman's, sleep-heavy – said '*Yes?*', and for a moment I was frozen, words trapped and backing-up in my throat.

'Doctor?'

The voice in the bed was tiny, sickly-sounding.

'*Hello? Hello? Look, who the hell is* this?'

'Is that you, doctor?'

'*Do you know what time it is here? Hello?*'

Another poke. I squinted in the darkness, my eyes raging at the gloom. The figure in the bed was bundled up under thick, heavy blankets –

'Doctor?'

– in fact, all that was dimly visible were the eyes and hands clutching the covers, drawing them up tight. Then a hand broke away, reached, trembling, ghost-like out towards me.

A push from behind. I raised a hand, took hers in mine. It was warm and smooth – tiny like a child's hand.

'Well, sah?' hissed Eliza, a dark, looming shape in the gloom. 'Is she gonna live, sah?'

'Well –' I said, aware in that moment, more than ever before, of the bizarre tidal lapping of fantasy and truth – and how one supports the other and is crippled without it, and how both are necessary – vital – if a life is to be (temporarily at least) survived.

'Well, sah?'

I closed my eyes, heard again the scuffle then silence then the sudden change of voices on the phone – a man's this time, sleepy also, but waking fast.

'Sah?'

'Right. That's it. I'm calling the police.'

I peered at the bed. 'Look, this is crazy,' I said. '*You're* crazy, all of you –' I tugged at my hand, but the hand gripping mine tugged back.

'You mean,' said the voice from the bed's dips and folds, 'that there's madness in the house?'

'What?' I said, pulling harder.

But the hand gripped tighter still. 'And my baby – are you saying that my baby will have the madness too?'

'Your *what?*' A final wrench and at last I was free. I backed away, found the door, turned and scuttled down the stairs, my fake sword rattling the banisters as I fled.

15

Lucky Man

If it's true that the lucky man grows into his skin and comes to feel it in time as comfortable and forgiving as a fine bespoke suit, then seldom can there ever have been a luckier or more well-tailored soul than the George Armstrong Custer who died nearly a century and a half ago now one hot June Sunday on a Montana hillside overlooking a clear, sparkling river. And if, then, the trick of it is to slip the thing off before bones grow brittle and flesh shrinks and the suit grows slack with grotesque age, then he was doubly blessed – for death embalmed him, lying naked and so white on that hillside – froze him in the heat of monumental catastrophe as ever-whole and gorgeous as some pharaoh in a tomb.

But then let us not forget that even pharaohs start out awkward and poorly fitting their lives. Generals too.

Like Custer.

Especially like Custer.

He sprang from German stock – the Kuesters – Emmanuel Henry Custer, his father, being a bright and outspoken, genial, blond-haired blacksmith who lived beside his shop in the village of New Rumley, Ohio. A widower, a father to two surviving sons (two daughters having died within a year of their birth), a justice of the peace and a most forthright Jacksonian Democrat, he met and married Maria Kirkpatrick (herself a widow and mother of two), and together they had seven sons and a daughter, the first two of whom – James and Samuel – died in infancy. The third, George Armstrong – born December 5th 1839 – survived, and was followed, over a thirteen-year period, by brothers Nevin, Thomas and Boston. The final child, Margaret Emma, entered the world on June 5th 1852.

Despite the enduring, unquestioning love of his parents and adulation from his siblings that would last until death, the young Autie Custer (he couldn't say Armstrong and so garbled it to this) comes down to us as a quick-witted and boisterous, though largely unremarkable boy. Bright though a poor scholar, his father's 'Yellow-Haired Laddie' knew, however, the value of education – especially to a poor boy – and was determined to get himself one. As for the future, he was non-specifically ambitious, except insofar as he knew above all that he would not become a farmer. Following a failed and quite inappropriate apprenticeship with a furniture-maker in Cadiz, his parents sent him to live with his half-sister Lydia-Ann in the south-eastern Michigan town of Monroe, from where, at the age of sixteen, having applied himself hard, he qualified as a grammar-school teacher, and from where he left in 1855 to take up a position at the Beech Point School in Athens Township at a monthly salary of $28.

It was during the summer of 1856 that George Custer decided to apply to West Point, although it is by no means clear even then that he planned to commit himself to a military career. For a young man without family funds on which to draw, the Military Academy was a way of gaining a first-rate education at the government's expense.

All he had to do was get in.

In those days, appointments to the academy were almost exclusively in the gift of politicians, and so, coming not only from a family whose means were modest but also one whose politics, in a Republican state, were decidedly Democrat, the young Custer's hopes were at best slim. However, with the luck that would follow him for so much of his life (and desert him only at the end), he had, by chance, met and fallen in love with a Miss Mary Holland, daughter of prominent Republican Alexander Holland. Fearing, then, the loss of his only daughter in marriage to such an ill-suited suitor, Holland drew the attention of Congressman John Bingham to the undoubted strengths of the young man's application, who, in turn, wrote to secretary of war Jefferson Davis requesting the appointment.

In January 1857, the secretary of war approved the appointment, and on the twenty-ninth, Autie Custer accepted. The two-hundred-dollar admissions fee was found, and in June of that year, in Scio, Ohio, he boarded a train for New York.

The West Point Military Academy is a two-hour drive from Newark Airport – except if you get a flat halfway there (oh, this was years ago now, but still seems like yesterday) and you can't find the wheel-brace and then you *can* find the wheel-brace (it's under the spare) but the wheel-nuts are so tight (gunned-on at high speed) that nothing can shift them and all you can do is go find a phone (in the middle of nowhere) to call toll-free for assistance.

But can you find a phone?

You cannot.

And all this on your honeymoon – an opportunity *to really get things right – to really start as you hope to go on.*

Some (as it turned out) opportunity.

'Well?'

For there was more: suddenly there was rain – really really *wet* rain, the kind that fills storm drains in two seconds flat, the kind you can't see through and trying to is useless and you end up just standing there and letting it all come down and wondering what you did that was really so bad as to deserve such a totally fucked-up life in return.

'Well *what?*'

And then you remember, and suddenly you can see God's point and it doesn't seem unreasonable at all.

'Well, what are we going to *do?*'

In fact, it is, you decide – all *this* – nothing more than you deserve. In *fact*, you're getting off *way too lightly*, which is what makes you want to take off every stitch you're wearing and just dance about like a crazy man and to hell with the consequences, to hell with everything –

'*Well?*' said Karen.

80

'I don't know,' I said, and then Karen said nothing – except it was the kind of saying nothing that says all kinds of things and none of them good and all of them something to do with all the things I'd done wrong and for which (I thought) I'd at long last been forgiven.

'Maybe I should try and find some help,' I said. I looked at her. She was looking away.

Nothing.

'OK then,' I said. I made a show of looking left then right – up the road then down. There was nothing to distinguish one way from the other. 'I'll be going then,' I said.

Still nothing. A shrug maybe.

I started walking. A few steps, then something made me pause. Without turning I said, 'I'm sorry about everything,' but the wind and the rain whipped my words away. I walked on, into the darkness, not caring at that moment if the rain kept coming and the world and everyone in it was once and for all swept away.

16

Freedom, a Hat and a Horse

That night, following my exit at speed from the Custer house, I drove with little care for where I was going, and in an hour or so I was sitting in a rest area on the highway maybe forty miles out of town, just staring out into the darkness and wondering how on earth I'd ever got here from there. I closed my eyes, thought about sleep – but sleep wouldn't come. All that would come were voices – one voice in particular – clear but distant now, like a voice heard in summer across a lake or a field. *You don't live here any more.* I opened my eyes. Before me, in the trees, nothing stirred but the wind. *She doesn't live here any more.* Then I felt the tears gather, and then – like a child – I just let them come.

It was close to midnight when I got back to town. Pausing at the lights on the corner of Monroe street and Elm Avenue, I looked out at the Custer statue. It was grey and just stone now – heavy and quite dead. The lights changed; I sat a while longer, then drove on.

The Custers' blue Toyota was parked outside McGinty's. The bar itself was dark, the blinds drawn. I pulled over. A light was on upstairs, figures moving slow, casting grotesque shadows on the curtains. I sat for a while just watching and trying not to think. At one o'clock I flicked off the lights, locked the car and crossed the street.

At first there was no answer to my knocking, but then the sound of boots on the stairs.

'Yes?'

The voice was close-up, muffled by the door.

'I saw the car,' I said.

'Who is it?'

I said my name.

'Who?'

'The . . . *surgeon*,' I said, aware but uncaring of the foolishness of it all.

The rattle of a handle, the turning of a key. The door swung in. Sweat on warm air spun out into the night's chill.

President Abraham Lincoln, though hatless, was still immensely tall. His face had the gaunt look of the battlefield photos, though he'd only half a beard still attached, the other half hanging down. He leaned out, glanced up the street, then down.

'What's the matter?' I said.

He screwed up his face. 'Ssssh.' He lowered his head. His whiskey breath was warm on my ear. 'The Mrs President,' he whispered.

'I see,' I said, though by then I neither saw nor cared to see.

He closed his eyes, nodded earnestly. He was, I noticed, swaying. 'Can't be too careful,' he hissed. Then suddenly the great hooded eyes opened wide, the face bunching up in a scowl. A hand grabbed my jacket, pulled me close. 'Say −' a belch from way down, 'you ain't one of them Johnny Reb spies, are you, mister?'

I shook my head; the moment passed. He stepped back unsteadily, bowing deep, 'Then won't you come in, sir?'

The stairs were steep and dark. The president led the way, stumbling now and then and cursing. On the landing he paused a moment, as if lost. Then, remembering (and illustrating the remembrance by tapping with one finger on the side of his thin pointed nose), he crossed the landing and rattled a door. The door was locked. 'Hey!' he called out. Nothing. He rattled again. 'Wasgoinon?' He banged with his fist. 'Hey, Custer!' he shouted. 'What's going on in there?'

'Whoozat?' The voice was distant, muffled by sleep.

'What do you mean whoozat?'

'Isityou, Mister President?'

'Well, of *course* it's me. Now open up −'

The sounds of stumbling, the turning at last of a key. The door swung back and there was Custer, golden locks and all, bleary-eyed from sleep, the tails of his cavalry shirt hanging low like an apron. Behind him was a table spread with playing-cards and stacks of plastic chips. He squinted, scowling, first at Abe Lincoln, then at me.

'Whoozat?' he said.

'This,' said the president, 'is the surgeon.'

'Look –' I said, and I meant to go on – was really meaning to once and for all put a stop to this increasingly ridiculous charade, when the president raised a pale solemn palm, and too easily my resolve bled away.

'Say nothing,' he said.

'OK,' I said, beaten.

'Nothing, that is, but the truth.'

All I wanted then was to lie down – to close my eyes and let go the reins.

'Well?'

I opened my eyes.

'Well what?'

'What news, sir?'

'News?' I thought of the woman back in town – of her pale child's hand and darting frightened eyes.

'Of the war, sir, of the war –'

You mean that there's madness in the house.

'The war?' Suddenly weary beyond telling, I leaned back against the wall. Across the room, General Custer was slumped now on the table, his head on his arms and snoring.

'Yes,' said the president, his face reddening, 'the war, the *war*. What news, sir? What *news*?'

'Look, I don't *have* any news, OK?' I said.

At once the face drained, became that of a ghost. '*Defeated?*'

'*What?*'

'And Washington threatened? Our men in disarray? Oh my Lord!'

My heart – having long since sunk – sank further. I watched as the president edged his way like a blind man to the table. He scraped back a chair and sat down. He'd the look of all the troubles of the world in his face; he lifted a hand, as if to sweep them away, but the hand stalled, fell back. He turned, raised his eyes to meet mine. 'Do you know what this means?' he said.

I couldn't hold back a sigh. 'No,' I said. 'I don't. But I'm sure you're going to tell me.'

'It *means*,' he said, ignoring (or not hearing) my tone, 'that the war is lost. It *means* that we have no choice but to sue for peace.'

'I see,' I said. 'Ah well. *C'est la vie*, I suppose.' I pushed off from the wall.

He frowned. 'Well, *doesn't* it?'

'Absolutely,' I said. 'Now, if you and the *general* here will excuse me –'

'Unless –'

Oh Lord.

'Unless . . . *no*. It's too wild –'

I took a step, then another, towards the door and deliverance. Suddenly a thin bony hand was gripping my arm, the president in his frock-coat having sprung up beside me. His face was up close, his sunken eyes wild. I snaked my hand behind me, found the handle. The face drew closer still. 'Do you think,' he said, 'that he'd fight for us, if we let him – if we promised him something?'

I tried to smile, reassuring, but it came out the grin of a madman. 'I don't know,' I said. I gripped the handle tight: it turned. 'Who are we talking about?' I said. I pulled; the door opened.

'Why, the black man!' said Lincoln. 'Do you think he'd come and fight for us if we gave him, say, a hat?'

'A hat?' I said.

The face fell. 'You don't think so?'

I eased the door open. 'I don't know,' I said.

'Or a horse?' said Lincoln. 'Do you think that would do it? Or maybe a horse *and* a hat?'

'How about freedom?' I said, tensing, ready to spring.

'Freedom?' said the president, stepping back, as if away from the dread word's infection. 'For the black man?'

And then I was moving, three stairs at a time, then rattling the front door, then swinging it open and crossing the street without looking, without caring, just fumbling – all thumbs – with my keys.

It was time – past time – to get out of town.

17

Gardens of Stone

'What I'm trying to tell you, ladies, is that, right from the start – from her very beginnings – Libbie Custer was special –'

'Rubbish.'

'Pardon?'

Three days after fleeing Abe Lincoln and the general, I was standing with a tour group in the cemetery at West Point in upstate New York, looking down at the grave of Libbie Custer.

'Oh, nothing.'

Our guide – Miss Stoney from her name-badge – tried, unsuccessfully, to disguise her weariness. 'Yes, quite,' she said. 'Anyway –' She paused, resetting herself, her brows gathered, as if she were searching for her place in a book. 'You see, even with her father's remarriage in February of 1859, Miss Libbie, when faced with the arrival of her stepmother, couldn't help but *charm* –'

'*Smarm*, you mean –'

'*Couldn't help but charm* the widow Wells Pitts, until the two became firm friends – confidantes even –'

'Was she a Yankee too – this *widow*?'

'Mrs Pitts, I believe, was from a New York family of some renown.'

'You mean she was from the Pitts of New York?'

Flustered, Miss Stoney swallowed hard. Again, she straightened herself, again clearing her throat. 'Now then,' she said, a hand raised to her temple as if – too late – for protection, 'where was I?'

'You were saying she was *special*, this *Libbie Custer*.'

'Oh yes. Well. For *example*, ladies – and gentlemen –' here she

looked at me (with eyes, I swear, that said *Help me, I'm drowning* '–
on her first Christmas morning at Doctor Boyd's Young Ladies'
Seminary, while the other girls were dressed entirely in white,
Libbie – still in mourning for her mother – descended from her
rooms overlooking Lake Erie, her face deathly pale and her long
dark hair fixed with elegant black ribbons –' A huff from her
audience; she pressed on. 'You see, though still only thirteen, she
already knew the power of drama and symbol; and, what is more,
being already a beauty – grey-eyed and auburn-haired – she knew
the *value* of that beauty: when, for example, her dancing-partner
tried to kiss her at a New Year's Eve party, she stepped back and
slapped him – but didn't flee. Later that evening, forgiven, he
returned to her dance-card and thence to her arms –'

'So what are you saying?'

'Pardon?'

'Jesus, Lord. I *said*, what are you *saying*?'

'Well –'

'*Well?* Well *what?*'

'Well, I'm *saying* she was, well, strong –'

'It sounds to me – to *us* – like you're saying she wasn't a real nice
person at all –'

'What?'

'Well, *doesn't* it, ladies?'

A murmur of assent from the Bush–Cheney Daughters of
Dixieland tour group.

'Well, *no* –'

'No?' said their leader (a woman dressed for skirmishing in steel
hair and track pants – and name-badged, too: Mrs E.V. Shelby, of
Lickno, Ohio, Colonelette). 'Well, it seems to *me* that's what
you're saying.'

'No, no, not at all –'

She shrugged imperiously, loudly unimpressed. Taking her lead,
the ladies about her shrugged too. Miss Stoney, her always scant
powers really failing now, swallowed hard and looked about her as
if searching the cemetery for some route of escape.

'And it seems to me you're saying she got what she deserved –'

She looked back. 'Deserved?' she said, haunted now and increasingly desperate. 'I don't know what –'

'For marrying a Yankee.'

Again, the approving murmur, the stealthy gripping of camera straps by red-tipped outraged southern fingers.

'And a *murdering* Yankee at that –'

A whelp, then, as, as if encouraged by an unseen signal or an order inaudible to those not from Dixie, the Bush–Cheney ladies advanced and Miss Stoney stepped back, losing her footing on the wet grass as she did so and nearly tumbling but not quite. Grasping the corner of the Custer obelisk, she raised a shaky hand. 'Please, ladies,' she said. 'Please! Remember where you are!'

The colonel paused, causing her ladies to bunch up behind her. 'What?' she said, scowling. 'Is that it? Are you saying it's over?'

'Over?' said Miss Stoney. 'But of course! We're all brothers now – or at least sisters –'

Sighing, the colonel shook her head. 'I meant the *tour*, stupid,' she said. 'I *meant* don't we get to see the rest?'

'The rest?'

'Of the *cemetery*.'

A moment then of silence – just the birds in the trees – as Miss Stoney drew the first gorgeous breaths of unexpected survival.

'Well?'

'The rest,' she said at last, as if the words were exhibits in some dusty old cabinet. Then, their meaning slowly dawning, she brightened. 'Yes,' she said; then: 'Absolutely!' Then, stepping back on to the path with all the ersatz confidence of a soldier stepping out into an uncharted minefield, she advanced a few paces, paused, glanced back. 'Ladies?' she said. Another huff from the colonel; then she, too, advanced, followed one by one by the sports-casual belles of her coiffured command.

This, then, the fifth anniversary of my wedding.

Odd, perhaps, but not the oddest.

I once knew a man who took his new bride to Poland – to the beautiful city of Krakow with its yellow-walled castle rising high above the Vistula and its streets filled with flowers and cheap

Russian watches and bicycle races on the cobbles in spring. 'Oh it's beautiful here,' she said, and even on the bus when the driver – '*Oh sorry, forgive, forgive*' – touched her calf as he reached, his hand wandering unsure like a blind man's, for the handbrake, she smiled and was smiling still that homely stupid smile when the bus pulled up, spewing diesel and dead leaves, and they were there, stranded like school children, on a grey scrubby dismal road, behind them a factory that had once made something that somebody once had wanted, before them rusted gates and a long sweeping drive.

'Where are we?' she said.

'Auschwitz,' he said.

Like I say, an odd place to celebrate, West Point – but not the oddest.

'Well, *don't* you?'

We were watching them go, the ladies and their guide; we watched them rounding that Winfield Scott's great brick of a tomb, watched them until they were gone.

'Don't I what?'

'Think it's strange.'

I turned back. 'Don't I think *what's* strange?' Steve from Charleston, South Carolina was looking down at Libbie's grave – at the flat eight-by-six piece of Pennsylvania stone – looking hard as if he were trying to see beyond it.

'Being buried. Being put in a box in a hole in the ground.' He looked up, around. 'Being a part of all this, I suppose.' He turned to me. 'I mean, is this what you'd want? Lying here for eternity with all these other rotting bodies?'

I thought of the wills Karen and I had once made on a day before flying – how she'd written *I wish my body to be cremated* on the page headed 'Additional Information', and how I'd left that same page blank. 'Do you believe in eternity?' I said 'for me there's first here and now.'

'There is and I don't,' he said.

'So what does it matter then?'

'It *matters* because of the people left behind.'

I asked him why — though I thought I knew.

'Because that's the whole thing about dying. It's the other people who do it really — or rather that have to *keep on* doing it while you've just had to do it once.'

I asked him who he meant.

'I *mean*,' he said, 'the people who survive. The mothers and fathers and sons and daughters who come to places like this and think they're going to find something. The fools who put themselves through all this agony for nothing.'

'Except in this case,' I said.

He looked up. 'What do you mean?'

'I *mean*,' I said, 'in *this* case, by the time *she* was gone, there wasn't anybody. For either of them.'

'Nobody? No children?'

'No children. Nobody. No mothers or fathers or brothers or sisters —'

'Why didn't they have children?'

'Just everybody else, wanting to touch them — or rather her — wanting to know the secret.'

'What secret?'

'Of how to sustain love and not to let it just become the memory of love, and to kid yourself that the two are the same. She could do that — did that, for over half a century. That was her genius. That was what everyone wanted to know.'

He turned away, raised his head, stared up at the sky. 'It's going to rain,' he said.

I looked up. 'It already is,' I said, as the first drops hit the stones, shivering the leaves of the garden's mournful trees.

18

A Soldier Needs a War

Separated by a century but united by a boy's dreams of bloodless death and danger, last-in-their-class cadets George Armstrong Custer (class of 1858) and Steve Philip Brandson (class of 1997) both needed a war to save them from failure. Custer got one (and a big old *civil* war no less – always the best and bloodiest kind); Brandson didn't – or at least it seemed then unlikely he would. And time was running out. For him, the likelihood was that failure in maths and way too many demerits (but still far fewer than Custer) would see him leave the Point and soon, his sights forcibly lowered, and that he'd drift, in his own estimation a half-soldier, perhaps into the lower-ranks army or back into the wholesale grain business (his father's) and thus into tedious inglorious obscurity.

'He won't understand. Mama says he will – but he won't. Not when it comes down to it.'

'Your father?'

'My father.'

'Maybe he'll surprise you.'

We were sitting in the bleachers overlooking the vast grass parade ground. The rain had moved off. An army of grass-cutters was moving in one long row now, left to right, preparing the ground for some mid-term parade.

'He won't surprise me.'

'But you haven't not made it yet. There's still time – isn't there?'

'Sure.'

'Well then.'

'There's still time to make the *infantry*.'

'And that's bad?'

'It's the *worst*.'

'But isn't it important – the infantry?'

He shrugged, staring out at the grass-cutters – at the West Point precision of their work. 'May as well be counting grain,' he said.

We parted at Thayer Gate. He saluted, turned away, the very model in aspect of a soldier.

'In which year did the Korean War begin?'

I watched him until I lost him amid the belts and buckles and dress greys of other cadets.

'1948?'

That afternoon, as I lay back on my bed watching *Who Wants to be a Millionaire?*, I could not have guessed that within three days he'd be dead – his body found hanging from a beam in a local hotel, his bags already packed for the long journey home.

'1949?'

'Fifty,' I said to the empty room.

'1950?'

'Yes.'

'Or 1951?'

'No.'

'Is that your final answer?'

'For Christ's sake *yes*.'

A pause, anxious music, a smile, a break. 'Back after these messages,' said the man. I flicked the remote. Again. A man sitting nervous in a car. He glances in the mirror. He is sweating. Suddenly from nowhere a shot, the ringing of a phone.

My phone.

'Hello?'

'It's Steve.'

'Hi, Steve.'

'Look –'

A pause.

'What is it?'

'You want a beer?'

'Now?'

'Sure now.'

But I'm comfy, Steve. And it's raining. 'OK,' I said.

'You sure?'

'Sure. Ten minutes?'

He was standing at the gate when I arrived, talking with the guard. I tooted. He turned, waved, crossed the road. Slipping into the car, he seemed to bring the wind and rain in with him.

'So where now?' I said. The car was idling.

'I'll show you,' he said.

We drove out of town, following signs for Bear Mountain. As we started to rise, the pine trees grew thicker, the afternoon darker. 'Here,' he said at a sign for the Bear Mountain Lodge. I eased off the road, steered up a smooth narrow track.

The lodge was set at the end of a long sweeping drive, crouching low at the foot of a sheer mountain of pine. Built entirely from logs, it seemed to have crept forward from the mountain and to have assembled itself without the help of man. Also, it seemed to be scowling, squinting out from beneath its overhanging eaves.

'This the place?' I said. It gave me the creeps.

'Pull up over there.'

It was like something out of a movie (it reminded me at once of the hotel in *The Shining*) – the back-end-of-nowhere deserted kind of place that travellers fetch up at on some dark and windy night.

'Drink, then?' said Steve.

The lobby, the bar, the wide shallow staircase – all were made of the same heavy pine. Even the barman was so impassive, his movements so neat and so restricted as he poured two beers, that he too could have been made, oiled and hinged, from the region's great resource.

'Busy?' I said, as he slid the beers slow across the bar like chess pieces.

'Busy, sir?' he said.

'Tonight,' I said, looking around me.

'No, sir.'

It was true: the place was deserted – the table-lamps lit, each spilling out its light, but for no one.

'I suppose it's out of season,' I said.

'Out of season, yes,' said the barman.

I turned to Steve. He was smiling, but trying not to show it.

'What is it?' I said.

'Nothing,' he said. 'Hey, you want to see something?'

'What?'

'Just something.'

I followed him across the bar, through a pair of double-doors that gave on to the dining-room. The room was set – one long central table, maybe forty, maybe fifty places – as if for a banquet, each setting a creation of white linen, glinting glass and high-polished cutlery.

'Looks like they're expecting someone anyway,' I said. Steve said nothing. He stepped beyond the end of the table – to the pine-panelled wall and a row, head height, of gold-framed black and white photos. I stood beside him, beneath a long low beam, peering at the images.

'See?' said Steve. He was tapping the glass with the tip of his finger.

I leaned forward. 'Is that Custer?'

He nodded. 'And look.'

'Jesus,' I said. It was Libbie.

'Yeah. And look where they are.'

They were standing shoulder to shoulder against a dark panelled wall, their faces half-striped by the shadow of a beam.

'Is it *here*?' I said.

'Exactly here,' said Steve. 'She's standing where you're standing. I'm standing where he's standing.'

'When was it taken?'

'June of 1862. Three weeks before Gettysburg.'

'Do you know what they were doing here?'

He shrugged. 'I guess they were at the Point for something.' He turned. I could feel his eyes on me. 'Did you know,' he said, 'that Custer didn't drink?'

'So they say.'

95

'You don't believe it?'

'Well, they also said he was faithful to Libbie. At least *she* did. And they believed her – at least they *said* they believed her.'

'You mean he wasn't?'

'Let's just say it's possible, but unlikely.'

Steve looked back to the picture. 'You don't like him much, do you?'

'Like him? I've never really thought about it. Chances are I wouldn't have liked him if I'd met him – and he wouldn't have liked me.'

'Why not?'

'Because I'm not a soldier. And he only really liked soldiers – and in particular one soldier.'

'Custer?'

'Custer.'

'And what about her?'

'What about her?'

'Would you have liked her?'

'I don't know.'

'You don't know?'

'Well, how could I know?'

'Just by looking at somebody you can tell.'

'You think so?'

I peered again at the picture – at Libbie, at her calm level smile. *Karen*, I thought.

'Well?' said Steve.

I shrugged. 'Maybe,' I said.

'Not maybe. For sure.'

'You mean Uncle Steve can tell these things?'

'Of course,' he said, smiling. 'Don't you know I'm the last in a long line of mediums?'

'The last? Why the last?'

The smile bled away. He looked back at the picture.

'Steve?' I said.

'What?' he said.

The room breathed a chill. 'Oh nothing,' I said. Outside, unnoticed by me, a storm had come up. 'You want another drink?' I said, just as the lights in the dining-room flicked off then on, then buzzed a moment brightly, then died.

19

War (and Peace at Last)

The talk in the New Year of 1861 was all of war. By mid-January, Florida, Mississippi and Alabama had joined South Carolina in departing the Union. Within a fortnight, Georgia, Texas and Tennessee had joined them. In Monroe, while the town's churches held special prayers for peace, men waited for news; at the Boyd Seminary on the shores of Lake Erie, the blackboard was edged in black. At West Point, southern cadets left to rejoin their states, saluting friends as they passed through Thayer Gate – friends who would soon become enemies. War was coming, and Cadet George Custer rejoiced – for, for him, war, not study of war nor the endless polishing of boots and buttons, was soldiering.

'Hello? Are you there?'

Graduating last in a class of thirty-four, he joined the Second Cavalry just in time to witness (but not contribute to, the Union cavalry, then, but not for long, employed simply as guards and couriers) the north's first defeat at Bull Run – just in time to watch the ladies, out for a summer day's spectating, fleeing north in panic, their hampers left strewn on the hills with their parasols, the wheels of their broughams raising thick blinding dust-clouds.

'Yes I'm here.' It was my sister.

It was close to midnight, a bottle of wine on the bedside table, *ER* on TV.

'Are you OK? You sound weird –'

The child's dead, Dr Greene.

'I'm OK.'

Dr Greene? Are you listening to me, Dr Greene?

Hearing her voice on the line made me think *I'm just dreaming –*

'Have you been drinking?'

'Maybe. A little. Why?'

A pause.

'He had a heart attack.'

'What?'

There's nothing you can do, Dr Greene.

'Did you hear what I said?'

'Dead,' I said.

'What?'

Mark – the kid's dead.

'He's dead,' I said.

'*Jesus*,' said Janey, 'how did you know?'

On the screen there were tears – a mother in a corridor trying to take in the news, a man in a white coat, a stethoscope round his neck, hunched over and holding his head in his hands. I pointed the remote, touched a button, killing them all.

'Hello?'

'When?' I said.

'Last night.'

'Your time or my time?'

'What?'

'Last night your time or my time?'

'My – *our* – time. Why?'

'How?'

The screen was black now – a black mirror. I raised a hand, turned it slow like a man waving in space.

'I told you. It was a heart attack.'

My palm was pale, a ghostly white.

'Was he drinking?' I said.

'Drinking?'

I flexed my fingers, stretched the muscles in my face like some terrible ghoul.

'Look, are you *sure* you're OK?'

'Sure,' I said.

A pause on the line. Breathing.

'Janey?'

Another pause.

'Yes?'

In my mind's eye, I saw her standing in the hall, dressed in blue and ready for work at the hospital, her keys in her hand and the minutes ticking by.

'What is it?' she said.

I knew she'd be thinking, *I'm going to be late.*

'You're going to be late,' I said.

'What?'

'For work.'

'I'm not going in,' she said. 'Of course I'm not going in. Not today.' A rustling, then, on the line. 'Look,' she said. 'Are you coming home?'

'Home? You mean for the funeral?'

'Well, there's things to do. Things that have to be done.'

He's dead, Mark. There's nothing you can do.

'Janey?' I said.

Far off, breath expelled, perhaps in a sigh. 'What is it?'

'Have you seen her?'

'What?'

'Sorry,' I said.

'Sorry? What for?'

Everything. I'm sorry for everything.

'Nothing,' I said. 'It's nothing.'

'Look –'

'Yes?'

'Well, I need to know. About the arrangements. I need to know if you're coming home.'

'Home?'

'I mean back. I need to know if you're coming back.'

Unseen by a soul (except me) I nodded; the figure in the TV nodded too.

'Well? *Are* you?'

'Yes,' I said. 'I'll call you.'

'OK then.'

Silence.

'OK then,' I said.

'Bye then.'

I set down the phone, lay a while, tried to think what I should think. But nothing came. My mind was quite blank – my life imploding, folding in on itself. But I couldn't feel it. *He's dead, Mark. There's nothing you can do.* All I could feel was how I needed a drink. I twisted on my bed, checked the bottle. The bottle was empty. I called room service and ordered another.

20

The First Time She Saw Him

He was drunk the first time she saw him – home on leave and heading for his sister's house. She watched him from her window weaving this way and that between the trees on South Monroe Street. He was scruffy, unkempt, his boots thick with dust. For a girl whose latest beau was a preacher prone to fainting, he was just about the wildest, most disturbing example of a man she'd ever seen. She watched him moving away until he was gone, then turned and put him out of her mind. The following day, in an effort at endearment, the pale preacher Dutton presented her with a book containing his late wife's recollections of their dead only child.

That night, and several nights thereafter, Libbie Bacon had a dream. She dreamed she was standing in the hallway of a large clapboard house. Outside, beyond the dusty windows, lay the great western plains. The house, in her dream, was quiet – quiet, save for the beating of her heart and for the muffled weeping of women.

21

The Furnace and the Fire

'Let us pray.'

I once knew a man whose job it was to stand behind a thick velvet curtain and unscrew the handles of coffins for recycling as they passed by. These – the handles – he would slip with a light *chink* into the pocket of his apron, then he'd light up a cigarette and watch with suitable reverence as the box and its contents trundled on its rollers into the furnace.

We lowered our heads. I studied the crease in my trousers, the ludicrous shine of my shoes, scarcely listening to the minister's words. An itch began just over my kidneys. I reached around to scratch; the man to my right sssh'd me. I glared; he glared. I scratched anyway.

'Amen.'

Grateful, we rose from our knees.

In all my life I have only ever been to two funerals. The first was Karen's; the second, this, my father's.

The itch started up again, again I scratched.

'I said *sssh*.'

'Well *sssh* to you. I have an itch. I have to scratch.'

'Well, scratch outside.'

'It doesn't itch outside.'

'What?'

'And besides, what difference does a little rustling make now?'

'Are you drunk?'

'A little, maybe.'

'You're disgusting.'

'Me?'

'There he is lying in his coffin and you've been drinking.'

The minister reached under his lectern, his hands moving as if independent.

'Ooops – here we go!'

With a hum like the hum of an air-conditioning unit, the velvet curtains drew solemnly together, and I could feel something moving in – pressure like hands on my temples. Unseen then, the coffin started moving, and in a moment was gone.

Oliver Wendell Holmes: 'In our youth our hearts were touched with fire.'

Libbie, on the eve of marriage: 'Every man is so ordinary beside my own flaming star.'

Fire, flames, a shooting star.

They finally met at a party at the Boyds' house. The young man, a captain now with the Fifth Michigan Cavalry, had reddish-blond hair and fierce blue eyes, and a reputation already for fearlessness in the field. True to a promise made to his sister, when offered a drink he declined. When Libbie offered her hand, he kissed it. She smiled. His advancement in the army, she noted, had, according to her father who followed such things, been rapid. He noted, in return, his good fortune.

And then they parted.

Such was it then, their first meeting.

At first Libbie Bacon – to her friends at least – was unimpressed. She disliked, she told them, his yellow hair and the gaudy yellow lining of his coat. In her diary, however, she wrote that 'with the critical and hard eye of a girl, I decided I would never like him'. She would, she determined, never care for him except as an escort, and on this she would never be moved. Besides, as an obedient daughter who sought above all her father's approbation, she knew how he feared she might marry a soldier, and in such dangerous times be left a widow in weeks or even days. No, for her, George Custer, with his garish golden hair and satin-lined coat, would remain just another in the long and growing list of her careless girlish conquests.

But then he started standing in the street – sober this time – and she'd watch him, leaning against a tree, removing then replacing his calf-skin cavalry gloves or just staring at the house as if he thought he could draw her from it with determination alone. Day after day, she'd ease back the curtain and there he'd be, the soldier – General McClellan's aide, no less – whose name was appearing now in all the Monroe papers, and in those as far away even as New York and Washington.

And he was waiting for her. She'd draw back the curtain with a scowl, pleased to be appalled.

And then one evening after dinner, Judge Bacon mentioned, in the course of his daily report on the war, that the young Captain Custer would be leaving at midnight to return to the Chickahominy and the war. That night, Libbie told herself – but not her diary – that there had been others who had shown great devotion, and that there would be others still. To her diary, though, she confided her fear that she'd 'had something to do with his going', and that, consequently, should he not return – should he be 'consumed by the fires of battle' and lie dead on some desolate field – she would be in some way to blame.

And so she added the young man who she'd determined to dislike to her prayers – praying for his survival, praying for his safe return.

'Did you know him well?'

The man curled up on the grass is me. He makes no move, gives no sign that he's heard, can hear.

'You know you can't stay here.'

His eyes are open wide, not blinking; he is staring towards the trees and the river, as if he can see something beyond them but isn't telling.

'Here, let me help you.'

But he is rigid and will not be helped.

The closeness of shoes. At last he blinks. They are black, the shoes, and high-polished. He can see his own eyes in them. He blinks again.

'Look –'

And the grass crushed beneath them is outrageously green. Green and, he thinks, moist.

'Come on. What do you say? Shall we go and join the others?'

Moist. *Moist.* It's a funny word when you think of it. When you say it over and over again. Like *scabbard.* Like anything if you say it often enough.

'I can't just leave you here.'

Karen, he thinks, then he thinks, *no, that's another one.*

'What was that?'

The shoes twisting as if in a dance then, knees cracking, a face looming low.

'Did you say something?'

And then he is speaking so much but he cannot seem to make himself heard. And then they are carrying him, over grass, over tarmac and then he's strapped in tight and moving on rollers into a dark enclosed space. He cranes his neck and the minister is smiling, and then the door closes but he keeps on moving, and then someone is screaming right there in his ear and he tries to sit up but cannot sit up and he tries to call out but there's this screaming and he cannot be heard.

I was admitted to Aldernorth Hospital on Monday 4th July. I had my own room – one of many identical rooms giving off a long waxy corridor. From my window I could see a courtyard, once neatly kept but now scrubby, across which, maybe two or three times an hour, a nurse or sometimes a doctor would scuttle hurriedly on his or her way to some unknown (to me) appointment. At night, the courtyard was completely dark and could have been the darkest jungle. I used to stand at the window asking my reflection the way to the toilet. I never made it in time. In time, I took to trying to eat the ashtray that someone had carelessly left by my sink – the kind with an old model car fixed to it. I broke two teeth. The ashtray was removed.

About all this, and the speed at which I came to it, no one is more shocked than I.

Part Two

The Genius of Love

22

Chickahominy

My first day on the ward started early. Later, when the routine of the place had become as familiar to me as the constant unthinking beating of my heart, I would wake as if as a consequence of some unheard alarm (we weren't allowed clocks – why, I don't know) and be sitting on my bed, my hair – like a little boy's – neatly brushed, and my slippers on my feet, ready for the short walk down the corridor to the TV room. Here, my fellow inmates and I would take our places around the large central table, our gazes, as one, drawn to the TV set on a high bracket on the far wall. The TV was never switched on (I never once saw it on) but still we gazed at it, only looking away now and then in order to balance some cereal on the end of our spoons or to respond to the voice of Louise if she called out our names.

But back to my first day.

That day, being only a novice in these things, I was still lying in my bed (it was six o'clock and I'd been awake for what seemed like hours) when someone banged something hard – something metal and sharp-sounding – on the door. I waited, expecting some instruction, but nothing came. All that came was the squeaking of shoes along the corridor, then a pause, then a banging on someone else's door. This would be repeated seventeen times after me and twice before me.

Louise was tall and skinny, the flesh drawn taut on her face so revealing the shape of the skull beneath. She smiled a lot and always seemed to somehow make things better. It was Louise, after all, who showed me (by standing on a chair), on the day of my leaving, that the TV was in fact just a box with no innards and so couldn't have been switched on even if someone had tried. 'See?' she said that day, easing the thing around and prising a plastic flap off the back with a screwdriver. 'But why?' I said. She withdrew the screwdriver and let the flap flip back into place. 'I don't know,' she said, stepping down, then putting the chair back against the wall. It was like that, she said, when she came, and that was ten years ago. Later that morning, as I made my way out to the taxi that was waiting to take me home, I looked back and up, scanning the hospital's roofs.

'You ready?'

I turned away. It seemed fitting somehow that a man who has wasted so much of his life watching television should have spent seven months in a place without even so much as an aerial.

The first thing I did when I left the hospital was to return to my father's house. It was just as I remembered it. I walked around the rooms – the living-room with its huge dead fireplace, the dark-tabled dining-room, the kitchen with its chipped and scratched cupboards, the garden room with the murals of a jungle and a South Sea island scene I'd painted as a boy – aware at every turn of the absence of the departed. There was no sound in the place now unless I made it. I climbed the stairs and pushed on my father's study door. The floorboards creaked as they had always creaked.

His desk was just as it had been at the moment of his death – the papers he'd been working on still awaiting the attention that now they would never receive. Even his pen lay just as it had fallen – uncapped, ink spilled and dry now on the carpet. I picked it up, set it down on the desk, and was turning away when something – a word – caught my eye.

Chickahominy.

The sheet was closely typed, the word just one amongst hundreds. I patted my pockets like a blind man, searching for my glasses. Nothing. His were lying on the desk's far edge, precariously balanced as if set there on a dare. I slipped them on, bringing the world into some kind of focus. I sat down in my father's chair and started to read.

Custer rejoined McClellan's army as it made its way in leisurely fashion up the Peninsula. On May 21st 1862, advance elements reached the Chickahominy River, a stream that flowed in a south-easterly direction across the region, eventually giving on to the James River. Because of the recent rains, the river was swollen and had burst its banks. On the southern bank, only five or so miles from Richmond, the rebel capital, Confederate sharpshooters lay hidden in the woods and in the branches of the trees.

McClellan ordered his command to halt a mile away from the river's northern bank. Engineers were sent out to reconnoitre, charged with the task of finding a way across. George Custer volunteered to accompany Brigadier General John G. Barnard, the army's chief engineer, in one such detail.

The enemy positions notwithstanding, the most immediate problem was the depth of the river. In its present state it was impossible to tell whether it was possible for a man on horseback to ford it without drowning. General Barnard sought a volunteer to attempt a crossing and thus determine the river's depth and the feasibility of such a crossing. The task was dangerous; the volunteer, of course, Lieutenant George Custer. Without hesitation, he plunged his chestnut mare off the bank and into the water – and into a hail of sharpshooters' bullets. Not a single one struck him, and he returned not only having crossed the river and so ascertained its depth, but also with a plan of attack which he was then instrumental in carrying out. Later, the man in charge of the raid, Lieutenant Bowman, noted in his report that 'Lieutenant Custer, Fifth United States Cavalry, was the first to cross the river, the first to open fire on the enemy, and the last to leave the field.' For this action, Custer was summoned to the general's headquarters and promoted to the rank of captain. Thus it was here, on that day and on that river, that the phenomenon that came to be known as 'Custer's Luck' began. Although constantly, recklessly exposing himself to danger, it would be another fifteen years and during a completely different war that the first shot would strike him, and this shot – a shot to the temple on a bluff overlooking the Little Big Horn River – would be the shot that killed him.

I took off my father's glasses, set them down on the desk. From overhead, in the loft, came the scrabbling sounds of mice. I sat quiet, listening, aware as I did so of something approaching – something far off but getting nearer. Then, from out of nowhere, like a sudden gust of wind sweeping over a barren field, a coolness drew over me, encircling me, and I closed my eyes tight against it, the better not to see.

Your father's working and cannot be disturbed.

But sometimes, no matter how tightly shut one's eyes, no matter how dark the day, there are things – sights – that will not stay unseen.

I opened my eyes.

Your father's working.

I looked down at the papers on his desk. Those in the larger, left-hand pile were face down. I turned the top one over. *A Life of General Custer*. 'Oh Lord,' I said, the words spinning out – just a whisper – then failing, unheard in the empty unlistening house. I sat up, pushed back, tried to stand – but something told me *no*. I closed my eyes. Nothing: no sound. Even the mice in the loft had stopped moving.

All his life he'd been obsessed with General Custer and the west. This obsession was like a virus (one for which, I know now, there is no cure) – one of many he passed on to me. For hour after hour as a boy I would sit and listen to the story of the great man's life – and of the life of his sweetheart Libbie Bacon. On winter afternoons, when the pain in his head was distracted and gathering itself for the evening assault, we would replay the battles – Chickahominy, Antietam, Gettysburg, Appamatox, the Washita and Little Big Horn – covering his desk with companies and regiments of tiny plastic soldiers. Sometimes I was Reno, the 'cowardly drunk' who'd abandoned the general at the Little Big Horn and fled to the hills, and sometimes Benteen who had long wished him dead, and lived to get his wish; never, though, did I get to be Custer himself. This role was always reserved for my father. Only *he* was allowed to stand defiant, circled by Indians, last man to fall, pistol in hand, and only he was allowed to lie still and white, his body stripped and mutilated, as the afternoon faltered and the night chill came on.

Above all, though, in my memory of those days, there was his 'work' – the Custer book he said he was writing – the book that nobody saw, and the existence of which we all, in no time, came to doubt. He would shut himself away, engaged in his 'writing', a *Please Do Not Disturb* sign stolen from some swanky hotel fixed to the door, and there he'd stay, sometimes for four, five, maybe six hours, until at last the floorboards would creak and he'd emerge blinking like a mole into the light. He'd remove the sign from the door – cursing, all thumbs – then make his way down the stairs, where he'd find us, my mother, my sister Janey and me, watching TV, each one of us trying not to breathe, each one of us knowing but never sharing the knowledge that his writing was a sham and his book just a fantasy born of pain and medication.

Until now.

Now, like something risen from the ashes, here it was, just as he'd left it – the book that we'd all thought a phantom – two piles of pages that together were maybe an inch and a half high with holes neatly punched, ready for binding. I know I should have been proud to see it – such evidence of a fight, even some kind of *victory* – but I was not. I was, and am still, bitter. It was so typical of him – so selfish. What he should have kept to himself he passed on, and what he could and should have shared, he did not. Instead, by not doing so, by not handing on the tools that someone had handed him, he condemned me to have to fight the same fight with little chance of victory – to have to suffer the same bouts of madness and the same searing pains without even the most rudimentary means of defence. A victory? Perhaps for him. To me it was all just another lesson lost – just another in a long list of gifts ungiven.

I left the house that day and posted the key to my sister. Two days later, still drunk from the night before, I was back on a plane and heading for Vienna.

23

Like a Freak in a Circus

'Excuse me.'

She wore white and silver and carried myrtle blossom; her crown was studded with opals and diamonds. Following an interminable ceremony performed by the Cardinal Prince-Archbishop of Vienna, the other Elizabeth, now empress, withdrew to the Hofburg to begin a life of restrictions and courtly denial – a sentence only lifted over forty years later on the shores of Lake Geneva by an assassin's rusty knife.

I opened my eyes. 'Yes?'

The plane was descending, the child across the aisle still buzzing and beeping on his GameBoy. Beside me, Darren from Chichester (whose wife was a lesbian) was leaning towards me, his shoulder jammed hard against mine, his breath, sour and sickly, rolling over me like some fine putrid fog.

'I couldn't help noticing,' he said.

'I was asleep,' I said. 'Didn't you notice that?'

He was nodding at the papers on my tray.

'May I?' he said. He reached over, picked up the top sheet, sat back.

'No,' I said, grabbing it back again.

The boy across the aisle turned his head, his thumbs for a moment suspended.

Beside me, Darren shrugged.

The sheet was scuffed now, a tear across one corner. I tried to flatten it with the edge of my palm.

'Sorry,' he said, though he clearly was not.

I said nothing.

A shuffling beside me. 'It's just –'

It would need taping up now – or maybe retyping altogether. Which meant I'd have to match the paper somehow – and how would I ever manage that?

'Just *what?*' I said.

It being – the paper – unlike any other I'd ever seen – a sort of in-between weight with a watermark of some kind of bird – a raven, maybe, or a crow.

'Well, I was thinking, what with you being a writer –'

'Who says I'm a writer?'

He nodded again at the papers. 'Well, *aren't* you?'

I thought at once of my Libbie Custer book – of all there was to do. 'No,' I said. 'I'm not.'

Darren frowned. 'Are you sure?'

'What do you mean am I *sure*? Wouldn't I *know*?'

'Well, I *suppose*.'

'You suppose.'

He sat back a moment, quiet, as if thinking. I looked down at the papers and tried to read, but I was worked up now and the words wouldn't settle. I closed my eyes. For a moment, in my mind's eye, I saw a man advancing, eyes narrow and wicked. He was wearing a cloak and carrying an old rusty knife in his hand, raising it as he was walking until it was high above his head –

'*Hello?*'

– and he was just about to plunge it deep into my chest, when a jolt at my shoulder froze the image and it fled. I opened my eyes. Darren was in close again, his face again too close to mine, his breath again foul enough to wake the dead.

'What is it *now?*' I said.

'Sssh –'

'What?'

He glanced about him, narrowing his eyes like a spy. 'Have you noticed?' he said, his voice just a whisper.

'Noticed *what?*'

He edged closer still. 'Look.' He gestured slyly with his eyebrows to the boy across the aisle. 'No ears.'

'What?'

'Take a look.'

I turned. It was true. The boy had no ears – just a curious redundant curling of flesh. I turned back. The lights overhead winked on.

'Ooops, here we go then,' said Darren, settling back.

I put on my seat belt, glanced again across the aisle. The boy was looking straight at me and smiling. Moving his lips like a fish, he mouthed the words *Darren's a wanker*, then went back to his GameBoy, frowning hard.

When she arrived in Vienna in the spring of 1891, Libbie Custer, famous widow, found the city in thrall to Empress Elizabeth's weight. The empress was fasting to the point of exhaustion and collapse, regularly fainting when her magnificent hair was brushed, and then sinking into gloom and shutting herself away if the hairs, when counted, that had fallen from her head, totalled more than a hundred – so signifying, if only to her, the beginning of the inevitable onset of baldness.

'*You mean Diana?*'

She was, people were saying in the cafés and coffee-houses, becoming quite mad (she was taking hay baths, no less, at Gastein), what with her obsession with black and her visits, unaccompanied, to the city's sprawling slums.

'No. Not Diana. *Elizabeth.* Empress of Austria and Hungary.'

The cab driver shrugged.

'Lots of hair. Dressed in black. Went crazy. *Hello?*'

He was leaning forward, elbows over the wheel, his eyes fixed like a hunter's on a figure up ahead.

'*Hey!*'

The cab lurched to a halt. Pressing his palm on the horn, he wound down his window, stuck his head out and started cursing in German. Before him, on a crossing, a woman who was wearing what looked to be a half-dozen coats turned her grizzled head and gave him the finger. He revved the engine, all the time creeping forward.

'So that's a no then,' I said.

Then, with the old woman gone, and the driver still twisting and cursing, we lurched forward and into the traffic on Mariahilfer-strasse, heading for the centre of town.

She motored across the continent, her name travelling before her like a president's outriders, announcing in the newspapers her imminent arrival. Suites were prepared and flowers ordered; in Lille, the owners of two rival restaurants came to blows in the shadow of the cathedral as they vied for the prestige of her patronage. Men and women would pause in the street and stare at the small erect sprightly woman dressed in mourning black as she climbed a hotel's steps or stopped to admire a particular view, the name of her famously dead husband on their lips – though for the most part, of course, they couldn't have told you when he died or even why. But such was the power of celebrity – the draw of such a famous, tragic name.

'*You stay long in Vienna?*'

It was a name that opened doors, both metaphorically and literally (the latter by grave-looking porters in braided suits and caps), so allowing the widow to escape from the loneliness of conventional widowhood and hide with her husband in the great bustling world.

'I don't know,' I said. 'It depends.'

The receptionist at the Hotel Orient smiled. 'Then you wish your end to keep open?' she said.

Yes, I said, smiling back, I wished, if at all possible, my end to keep open.

That evening, after dinner of boiled beef and potatoes at a restaurant near the Hofburg, I took a walk through the quiet streets to the main square, the Stephansplatz. The square was still busy – people criss-crossing the cobbles this way and that, heading home or out or nowhere in particular – and, despite the hour, the cathedral at its centre was still open. I picked my way through the walkers and slipped inside.

High-vaulted and gloomy, the Stephandom has always been a

great target for men and their guns but – like St Paul's in London – has never been hit. It stands today, just as it has always stood, immense and unyielding – a celebration, if ever there was one, of man's will to deny his own need for destruction.

24

The Proximity of Bones

By Christmas of 1863, Brevet Captain Custer was back in Monroe, ready to resume his campaign. Once again Libbie would watch him passing the Bacon home in full uniform 'perhaps forty times a day' – and on Sundays there he'd be, standing outside the church, waiting – rain or shine (and that winter it was mostly rain) – to escort her home. 'Whenever I put my nose out of doors,' she wrote to a friend, 'there he is.' To another, she said coolly: 'It's pleasant to have an *escort* to rely on.' To her diary, however, she confided, 'Dear C – try as I did for six months to suppress the "fancy", it has done no good. The *fancy* is no more. It is *love*.' There were, however, still her father's wishes to consider. She would, she determined, talk to him that night – and if he said no, then that would be that.

But he did not say no. Instead, impressed with the young man's extraordinary advancement (he was now, at twenty-three, a brigadier-general – the youngest general in the history of the United States army, no less), and reassured by the couple's evident devotion, he gave his blessing, for – despite his earlier misgivings – in the end, he said, all that mattered was Libbie's 'present and future happiness, for which I have lived'. To Custer, he wrote, 'Your ability, energy and force of character I have always admired, and no one can feel more gratified than myself at your well-earned reputation and your high and honorable position.' For the judge this was high praise – the expression of an admiration of the older man for the younger which, once established, would never waver, even in the dark days to come.

But those days, then, *were* still in the future. Then, that winter, with the war's and the south's back broken at Gettysburg, there were plans to be made – a date to be set.

The couple were married at the First Presbyterian Church on South Monroe Street at a little after eight o'clock on the evening of February 9th 1864, the groom, his long hair trimmed, wearing his full-dress uniform and sword, his bride, with orange blossom in her hair, an elaborate gown and train, in her hands a bouquet of roses tied with yellow silk, the cavalry's colour. The ceremony was conducted, of course, by the Reverend Erasmus Boyd, and attended by over two hundred guests, with several hundred onlookers gathered outside in the street.

'So it was here – the funeral?'

It was, by all accounts, just about the finest wedding the state of Michigan had ever seen.

Oskar Kirchner, said yes, it was here.

'And then?' I said. He and I had been schoolfriends – the two of us and Charlie inseparable.

'Then?'

'Where did they take him then?'

He frowned. 'To the cemetery, of course,' he said.

'Can we go there?' I said.

'Of course,' he said.

And so we did.

Today, the cemetery of St Marxer Friedhof, with its neat paths, trimmed edges and grand stands of trees, gives nothing of the secrets of its past away. There is nothing there now of how this graveyard built outside Vienna's city walls must have looked one bleak winter's night in 1791, when the body of a young man not yet thirty-five was tumbled into a mass grave, unnamed and unmourned, his final, pathetic, irrevocable fall witnessed only by the grave-diggers to whom the genius of Mozart was unknown, his music, to them, unheard. No records were kept as to the contents of this or any other of the city's mass graves (they were, after all, emptied every eight years or so – the bones dug up and scattered to make way for new tenants – so what anyway would have been the use?), no help provided for those mourners who'd a need to be close to those departed — no guidance for a wife, even — for Constanze — or even an empress — no means of saying and being sure *Yes, this is it, he is here*, and so gaining, as people do, that strange comfort to be had in the knowing proximity of bones.

'Did I tell you she came here?'

We were standing, Oskar and I, before the quite randomly placed Mozartgrab with its broken pillar signifying the great man's early death.

'Who?'

'Elizabeth Custer.'

'The empress, too.'

'She did?'

'Well, it's mostly just rumour. No one knows for sure. And anyway, if she *did* come — and I think she did — she would have been in disguise, so no one would have known it was her.'

'Disguise? What was she frightened of?'

'Oh, only assassination to start with — but then, towards the end — everything. You see, there was madness in her family — and suicide — and she feared that in time she too would go mad.'

'And did she — *was* she?'

'Well, if travelling from one end of Europe to the other and then Africa searching for an antidote to madness is evidence of madness, then, yes, she was. Oh, and she had a tattoo of an anchor on her arm —'

'A tattoo?'

'— and if a storm blew up while she was on one of her voyages, she'd insist on being strapped to the mast in case a wave swept her overboard. Not that that was necessarily madness.'

'You mean perhaps she was just taking reasonable precautions?'

Oskar shrugged, half-smiling. 'Well, no one wants to get swept away — right?'

'Right.'

'And *everyone's* got a tattoo —'

'Of course.'

'Even you — right?'

'Maybe.'

'Maybe?'

'Well, have *you*?'

'Of course.'

'What is it?'

Oskar rolled up his sleeve, pushed the bunched fabric over his elbow. 'So what do you think?' he said, flexing.

I leaned forward, peered at the blue-black design on his bicep. It shifted with the shifting of the muscle beneath, distorting what looked to be the features of a face.

'Who is it?' I said.

'Jorge Haider,'* said Oskar, his tone set somewhere between challenge and pride. He looked up; he was smiling, eyes direct. 'What about you?'

'Me?'

A deal, he said, was a deal.

I shrugged, wishing suddenly I was back in that old dentist's chair at Big Bob's Tattoo Hut with the choice to make again.

He frowned. 'Problem?'

'No problem,' I said, lying, cursing myself for not having chosen Nelson Mandela or Martin Luther King.

He leaned in towards me. 'It's OK,' he whispered. 'Nobody's looking.'

'No, I can't,' I said.

He scowled. 'Why not?'

I would, I said, have to lower my trousers.

'So?' said Oskar.

'*So?* So this is a *cemetery*, Oskar. For Christ's sake, it's the cemetery where *Mozart* was buried. I can't just drop my trousers.'

'You think he's watching?'

'No, Oskar. But *somebody* might be.'

Another shrug. 'Who cares? I can do what I like.'

'What?'

'It's ours now.'

'What is?'

* Jorge Haider, present governor of Austria's Carinthia state and leader of the neo-Nazi Freedom Party.

124

He looked around him, spreading his arms wide. '*This,*' he said.

'You mean the cemetery?'

'I mean *everything*. I mean the *whole fucking country*.' He lowered his arms, stepped close. 'Shall I tell you something?' he said. His breath was like smoke now. 'Shall I tell you how they burn?' He was smiling.

'What?' I took a step back.

'What's the matter?' he said, matching my step with a step of his own. 'Don't you want to hear it? Don't you want to *know* what we're doing for you?'

'I don't know what you're talking about,' I said. 'And anyway, I didn't *ask* you to do anything –' I felt sick, off-balance, as if I'd been struck.

A sigh, a smile. 'What I'm *talking* about is getting back what's ours – yours and mine. What I'm *talking* about is at last getting rid of these fucking Jews and niggers. And fucking Turks. Jesus, those fuckers. Did you ever see them? Did you see their fucking *women*? Like fucking dogs. Or pigs. Jesus fucking Christ –'

I took another step back. This time he didn't follow. This time he just stood there, looking suddenly exhausted – suddenly pale and small like some hard-time distant cousin of the funny, clever boy I'd known at school.

'Where are you going?' he said.

I turned, half expecting him to follow. He did not, and I did not look back.

That night, alone in my room at the Orient Hotel, I tried to settle, but could not. Oskar's face kept appearing – up close then drifting back – snarling then smiling, his breath on the cold air spreading around me like a mist.

Sometime after midnight, still unable to sleep, I flicked on the TV. Football. I watched for maybe ten minutes – staring at the screen like an idiot or a drunk – then flicked it off. In a while I sat up, swung my legs off the bed.

The bathroom was cold. I reached for the light. It flickered at first – ricocheting like bullets off the chrome and the tiles – then settled. I squinted at myself squinting back in the mirror. I screwed up my eyes, tried to focus – but could not. All there was now – all I could make out where once there'd been a face – was an indistinct blur, blue-black and ugly like a birthmark or a bruise. Giving up the struggle, I went back to bed, turned out the light. I must have slept then (though, waking, I had no memory of sleep – in my head no fragments of dreams to account for the hours), for when next I opened my eyes the room was filled with light, the cleaners down the corridor outside already hard at work.

I closed my eyes, dozed a while, was woken by a tapping on the door.

'*Entshuldigung?*'

I pushed up. 'Who is it?'

The rattling of a chain; the turning of a key in a lock. The door eased inward.

'Hello?'

A face edged its way round the door. It was Anna from reception. The smile I'd thought permanent was gone. 'I'm sorry –' she said.

'What is it?'

She was pale now, her face like the face of a little girl. 'Can you come, please?'

'What's happened?'

'Police.'

'*What?*'

'Please?'

And then she was gone: the click of the door, the sound of hurried footsteps in the hall growing fainter.

25

Eine Kleine Kristallnacht

'Is this you?'

'*What?*'

'This is your floor – no?'

There is madness to be found in the most unlikely places. It's there in the corner of a field on a clear summer's day, as the most loving husband and father of two digs a grave with his bare hands (the ground is hard – mostly stones – and he curses), and there buries, unwitnessed, his brother's builder's tools; it's there, too, in sleep, in the movement of fingers as they twitch like a cat's ears, gathering lint beneath the nails; and it's there, boxed but breathing, in a woman's gentle humming as the cables stretch taut and the wheels start to turn and the lift sinks with some grace to the mezzanine.

No, I said, it wasn't.

The woman smiled; the doors closed. She resumed her humming.

The lift slowed, sinking to a stop.

At first glance, the reception area and the area of seating opposite seemed just the same – no busier than they'd been the day before and the day before that. Sure, there were a few people milling about – a group of businessmen, I guessed – standing at the far end before an open window – but what was unusual in that?

Nothing, I told myself.

I let go my breath, uncurled my fingers.

Until I saw that the window wasn't open, but broken, and the group standing before it weren't businessmen but policemen.

'*Hello?*'

I turned. The man before me was short – only a shade over five foot – and had to tip back his head to address me. His face was thick and jowly and red like a drinker's face is red; what remained of his hair he wore long and swept back. He slipped a hand inside his sports coat and withdrew a tarnished and chipped silver badge. This he held out before him like a shield. *'Polizei?'* he said, as if asking a question.

'What happened?' I said.

He shrugged, all the time not taking his eyes from mine. 'Do you not see?' he said.

I told him I saw that the window was broken.

He nodded, looked down for a moment as he slipped the badge back into his coat. 'Yes, the window is broken.' He looked up. His eyes were dark-ringed: an insomniac's eyes. 'So are many other windows.'

'When?' I said, though I knew.

'When?' He looked away at the far-off sound of footsteps crunching glass.

'You don't know?'

'I know,' he said, turning back.

'Was it last night?'

He nodded.

I drew a shallow breath, tried to keep calm. 'Was anybody hurt?'

'Hurt?' He shrugged again, pushing out his lips this time as if to indicate he neither knew the existence or extent of any injuries, nor did he care.

'So do you know who did it?'

A smile broke over his face. 'Oh yes,' he said. 'We know who did it.' He paused. 'Do *you?*'

'Me?'

The smile dipped. 'Don't you know him?'

'Know who?'

'Oskar Kirchner.'

'Oskar?'

'Because *he* knows *you*. In fact, he keeps asking for you. He says you were schoolboys together. He *says* you'll know what to do.'

'He does?'

'He does, yes. *Do* you?'

'Do I what?'

'Know what to do. In such a case as this. Should he, for example "come clean"?'

'Well –'

The smile re-emerged. 'Then you'll tell him this?'

'Tell him?'

'Splendid.' He turned away then, walked a step, a second, paused, turned back. 'Will you follow me, please?'

He was sitting – Oskar – on the floor of a cage in a van, his knees drawn up, his arms around his knees, his head buried in his arms. His hair was mussed up – matted in places and shiny. He looked up at the rattle of keys, the creaking of the van's rear door.

'Oskar?'

He was pale in the harsh morning light, his face puffed up, a bruise beneath his left eye glowing yellow and blue. He squinted hard. He didn't seem to know me.

I told him my name – said I'd been asked to talk to him, to get him to tell the truth. I heard myself saying it would be all right. He dropped his head, buried it back in his arms.

'Oskar?'

He mumbled something I couldn't hear.

'What?'

He lifted his head. He opened his mouth. His mouth was full of blood. He pushed out his tongue and the blood overflowed his swollen bottom lip and ran down his chin. He pulled back his lips, revealing stumps where his teeth had so recently been.

'Jesus, Oskar –'

He leaned towards me.

'What the hell *happened* to you?'

'Deal's a deal,' he whispered, grinning, through the mesh.

'Oh, Jesus –'

His tongue flicked out, touched the wire, withdrew. Beyond his eyes he looked distant, disengaged.

'Oskar? Can you *hear* me?'

129

He cocked his head, as if listening like a bird. He whispered something, barely making a sound.

'What *is* it?' I said.

He moved his head sharply, beckoning me forward. I edged my ear towards the mesh.

Nothing – just the rasping of a tongue over cracked and swollen lips.

'Oskar? I can't *hear* –'

The rasping ceased. '*Libbie Custer, Libbie Custer,*' he hissed through his stumps, his breath falling warm as a baby's on my cheek.

Ten minutes later, I stood in the hotel lobby amid what was left of the broken glass and watched the van and its escort leave the scene. It whooped and wailed and then was gone. I ground my way back across the lobby to the lifts, pressed the button, waited.

According to the uniformed officer who had slammed shut and bolted the van's heavy doors, Oskar would, if convicted, be liable for a fairly substantial fine (maybe even as much as two thousand schillings – that is, approximately two hundred pounds) and a year's (maybe eighteen months') prison sentence – this most probably suspended. It was, he'd said, banging his gloved fist on the doors then stepping back as the engine started up and the van moved off, after all just a little glass – and besides, he'd no doubt learned his lesson and wouldn't be so foolish again.

'Foolish?' I said.

He smiled.

'What are you smiling at?' I said.

He said nothing. Instead, he just went on smiling, then turned and walked away. I watched him idle across the street to his car, pause and light up a cigarette, aware as I did so that I'd somehow just witnessed something unseen and unseeable – that something unhealthy had just passed between us – though I wasn't sure quite what. In a while, feeling weary and like I'd never slept, I too turned away, but something made me pause and look back. *Just a little broken glass.* Across the road, the car started up, indicated, moved off, disappeared then into the early-morning traffic.

26

The Empress and the Widow

They met in secret, so goes the story, in a small café on the Singerstrasse: two ladies in black – one in mourning still for her long-dead husband, the other in disguise behind a thick mourning veil. They ordered chocolate cake – of course the famous *sachertorte* – and sipped coffee with gloved hands from small china cups. The American (so the story goes on) drank little and ate less; not so the empress, who, though pathological about her weight (she suffered, in today's terms, from both anorexia and its grotesque bloating cousin, bulimia), was by then half-starving, having fled after ten or so minutes, as was her usual custom, the Hofburg dinner table, so dull and enervating that evening (as every evening) had she found the emperor's dreary talk.

'*More coffee, sir?*'

So while the empress ate, the widow watched her.

I said no. The waitress drifted off. I watched her go. I took out my notebook and pen, turned a new page. My hands were shaking. I flattened the book with my palm; the binding cracked like old bones. *Libbie Custer*, I thought. *Libbie Custer, Libbie Custer.*

Just exactly what she was thinking as the empress, her veil partly lifted to facilitate the bingeing, her pale and drawn face thus in part at least revealed, gobbled up the sweet and sickly chocolate in preparation for that chocolate's later agonising expulsion, remains (even in the story) unrecorded. What *is* recorded, however (and gleefully by those to whom any kind of privilege is anathema), is that the empress was by now quite the prisoner of her misery, and could no longer find solace even in those things that once had soothed her. Indeed, by the time she was hiding with Libbie Custer in that café, there was no longer, she knew, for her, any hope of escape; all there was for her now was the oncoming inexorable madness that she had for so long feared. All there was for her now was to sit in her state rooms in black pearls and gown and wait for that madness to call.

Back at the hotel, Anna at reception said a message had come for me.

'For me?' I said. 'Are you sure?'

She said yes, she was certain, she had taken it herself.

'But no one knows I'm here.'

She started searching again through the pile of small yellow slips, scowling hard.

'Can you remember the name?'

But she didn't seem to hear me: she just went on scrabbling.

'Shall I wait then?' I said. Nothing. I crossed the lobby, took a seat by the window.

The lobby was back to normal now, save for a sheet of opaque plastic covering the broken window. Outside, up and down the street, there were other, similar sheets protecting other, similar stove-in windows. Aside from that (that, and a single round-backed man sweeping glass into the gutter), the street now was just as it had been – people passing by, no longer turning their heads, their eyes quite blind now to the damage so recently done. I took out my notebook, fished around for my glasses. The shapes – at first just blue blurs like veins on an arm – merged, coalescing, settled at last into words. I flipped to the page marked, *America when she left it – reasons for leaving*. I slipped down in the chair and started reading.

'Hello?'

America, I read, *when she left it, was no longer the nation for which her husband had died. The railroads, for whose progress so many had been slaughtered, were crossing the land now unhindered, all sacrifice forgotten, carrying men and women of all colours and tongues to new western cities, while in New York factories were being built on the open fields of Harlem –*

'Excuse me?'

— and the country that her husband had known was changing out of all recognition —

'Sir?'

I looked up. My eyes were heavy. Anna was standing before me.

'You found it?' I said.

She shook her head. She was, she said, so terribly sorry. It was, she said, all her fault. She started to cry.

Oh Christ.

'I'm so sorry —'

'Look,' I said, standing up, 'it doesn't matter. Really —'

'So sorry, so sorry,' she said through her tears. Her make-up was running; people were starting to look. I put my arm around her shoulders and led her back to the desk. She leaned heavily against it.

'All this for a message?' I said.

She shook her head.

'Then what is it?'

'I don't know,' she said, then she straightened up, started rubbing her face with the backs of her hands. 'I'm sorry,' she said again. She reached over the counter, pulled a tissue from a box, blew her nose.

'Is it the glass?'

She lowered her hands. Her eyes were red, her cheeks streaked with tears. 'I must go,' she said.

'Will you be all right?'

'Yes,' she said.

'*Was* it the glass?' I said.

'It's nothing,' she said.

I watched her walk away.

The lift came at once, the doors opening before me as if cued by my approach. In my room, I turned on the shower. I sat a moment on the edge of the bed. I felt so terribly weary. I lay down, let my eyes close.

When I woke the room was full of steam. In my dream I'd been kneeling in a cemetery at dusk, arm-wrestling with my father, our elbows grinding hard on a chest-high stone tomb. My father was dressed in a powdered wig and breeches, the rings on his fingers huge and gaudy. *It was me who did it*, he kept saying, and I kept saying *Did what?*, but he wouldn't tell me. *What won't you tell me?* I said. *I won't tell you*, he said, *that it was me that swam to shore and changed the O to an S. What do you mean?'* I said *What are you saying?* – but at this he just grinned, and was grinning still when the stinging of sweat running into my eyes woke me.

I pushed myself up, bleary-eyed.

It was me that swam to shore.

I stood, unsteady, made my way to the bathroom. I filled the sink, splashed my face with cold water. I saw Oskar's face again in the back of the police van – how he'd seemed so lost, his purpose in life so utterly spent. Then I thought of the policeman, felt again the pollution of his smile. I sat on the edge of the bath – for how long I've no idea. In a while came the sound of a tapping on the door.

The message was lying on the carpet just inside the door. I opened the door, checked the corridor. Nothing. No one. 'Anna?' I said. Silence. I stepped back inside. I fetched my glasses and flicked on the desk-lamp. There was a name – *Herr Taschenbach* – and a local number written in a sloping elegant hand on the small yellow square. This I set down on the desk beside the phone. I crossed the room and lay down on the bed. I closed my eyes but couldn't settle. I flicked on the TV. Black and white. An old movie. *Step out of this room, deputy, and they'll shoot you dead*, said a cowboy in a hat. *That's OK*, said the deputy with a smile, *dying's my job.*

27

Reasons for Leaving

Next morning at ten I was waiting in the lobby of the Spanish Riding School deep in the Hofburg. The lobby was grand – all marble and stone – a vast sweeping staircase at one end, a kiosk selling guidebooks and postcards set into the wall at the other. At the foot of the staircase were two guards in fancy outfits. They glanced at me now and then (I was the day's first visitor – the show didn't start until eleven) as if they knew my recent history and what had become the recent history of those around me and were half expecting trouble. I tried to smile, attempting reassurance.

'Hello there!'

But they just narrowed their eyes, resetting their hard martial gaze.

'I don't think they like me,' I said.

'No?'

'But then I'm not sure I blame them.'

Herr Taschenbach – a thin, dark-suited man with the face of a schoolboy – offered his hand. We shook. He drew close. 'Between you and me,' he said, 'I'd count that as a bonus.'

'A bonus?' I said. His cheeks, in fact, were so smooth you'd swear they'd never seen a razor.

'Gay,' he said, nodding.

'Both of them?'

He nodded again, this time closing his eyes for a moment as if to spare himself the pain of unpleasant contemplation.

I sneaked a look. The far one was scowling.

'It's the horses,' he said.

'The horses?'

Another nod: enough, obviously, had been said.

'Anyway,' he said, straightening, 'shall we begin?'

In his position as assistant curator (porcelain and glass), the riding school was not, in normal times, Joachim Taschenbach's concern. These were not, however, it seemed, normal times. For three weeks now the city had been struggling (and, he said, failing) to cope with a vicious Asian flu said to have blown out of the east across the vast Russian steppes and over the mountains into Austria. The virus was, he said, as we climbed the marble steps (I didn't dare look at the guards, and they didn't alter their staring), bringing with it a degree of chaos not seen (or so he'd been told) since the nation's collapse at the end of the Second World War. Some people, he said, were not leaving their houses for fear of breathing in contaminated air, while those (that is most) who had no choice but to sit side by side on a tram or in a car did so in silence like condemned men on the eve of their scheduled execution. Indeed, he said, just that morning on the Heldenplatz, he'd seen a fit-looking middle-aged woman simply crumple without warning as if her bones had suddenly turned to salt – and had anyone stopped to help her? He shook his head sadly. At the top of the narrow winding stairs, he pushed on a door. 'Not a soul,' he said. 'Not a soul.' He held the door for me. I passed through and on to a balcony. 'You see,' he said, 'it's a kind of madness.'

'Madness?' I said. Down below – maybe thirty, forty foot – was an oval dirt arena, the size of a hockey pitch.

'Lack of oxygen,' he said. 'People don't want to breathe and so they don't get enough oxygen. And what happens then? The brain is starved. And when the brain is starved that's when people get desperate, and when they get desperate they go mad. Quite mad.'

'But it'll pass,' I said.

'In time,' he said, 'in time.'

'And so will the madness.'

Herr Taschenbach shook his head. 'Madness,' he said, 'never passes. It just changes shape and colour. It just steps aside for a while, counts its pocket-change and waits. But still –' He smiled, turned away. 'Do you see that?' he said. He was pointing down at the arena.

'What is it?' I said. I could see nothing but dirt.

'Dung,' he said, and he touched my arm; I flinched. His fingers curled, gripping my jacket. 'And shall I tell you something?' he said.

'What?' I said.

He drew a breath to speak, but then changed his mind. His fingers loosened their grip, slid down my forearm to my hand.

'What are you doing?' I said.

His grip was tight. 'Come with me,' he whispered.

'Where are we going?' I said.

'Sssh.'

'What?'

He tapped the side of his nose like an old-time stage villain. 'Showing's better than telling,' he said, and then he was off and I was following, heading down some narrow steps and into an ever-deepening gloom.

'Well?'

Horse-dung as a healer: to me (as, no doubt, to Libbie) the notion seemed absurd. Dung, after all, is dirt – something expelled as useless, unwanted – perhaps (I didn't know, though the smell was giving clues) *toxic*.

'This is a joke – right?'

Herr Taschenbach shook his head. 'No joke,' he said. He offered the palm-shaped patty in his hand. 'Feel it,' he said. 'Feel all the goodness.'

'It's OK, thanks. I believe you.'

He frowned. '*She* did,' he said.

'Who did?'

'Your Elizabeth.'

'She *did*?'

He nodded. 'She did as the empress requested. She stood exactly here.'

'And talked about dung?'

'No, no, no. Not just *dung*. *Special* dung.'

'Dung that can heal. Right.'

'You don't believe me.'

'Well —'

'Here —'

'What?'

'Take some.' He held out his hands, palms up. 'Go on.'

'I don't think so,' I said. 'In fact, I think I should go.' I looked around: the Dung Room (for such, truly, is it called) was lit but only dimly, the shelved walls with their regiments of air-tight china pots half-buried, half-gleaming, in shadow. 'If you'd just point out the way —'

Herr Taschenbach sighed, quite clearly disappointed. '*She* did,' he said.

'I know. You said.'

'And do you know what she did then? She took it all the way to St Petersburg and gave it to the tsar!'

'Look —'

'Go on,' he said, 'take it. Compliments of the school.' He looked about him. On a shelf to his left and just behind him was a line of jars, their tops flipped open. he took the first of these and, with great care, pushed in the dung on his palm. He sealed the jar with a click. 'There,' he said, handing it over, 'no mess — no smell! You could take this anywhere!'

It suddenly seemed pointless to resist. 'Thank you,' I said, accepting the gift.

'Splendid!' said Herr Taschenbach, and he led the way then from the gloom of the Dung Room, up the narrow twisting stairs and out into the lobby. The lobby was filled now with people. The guards had changed.

'Can I ask you something?' I said, as we stood beside a pillar, out of the way of the tour groups and day-trippers.

'Anything,' he said.

'OK. Can I ask you why you wouldn't tell me on the phone what it was you had to show me? Did you think I wouldn't come?'

He shrugged.

'I would have, you know.'

He smiled. 'And you did,' he said. 'And now, like me, you'll never catch the flu.' Then he closed his eyes, pushed out his chest and breathed deeply, filling his lungs with the city's contaminated air. He breathed out, long and low. 'See?' he said, his eyes sparkling. 'See?'

'I see,' I said, feeling suddenly then a vague and absurd sense of comfort.

We shook hands, parted. I watched him go. Next morning, at first light, my jar of sacred dung buried safe in my bag, I caught a cab to the airport, then a plane heading east to St Petersburg.

28

Libbie and the Soldier

The honeymoon couple headed first for Cleveland, then on to Onondonga and thence Howlett Hill. Here, when introduced to his new bride's aunts Eliza and Charity, the groom, it is said, made an impression so favourable (despite having been shorn, for the ceremony, of the long golden locks made famous by the New York papers) as to never be forgotten. He was, people said, even more dashing and handsome than had ever been reported – the very image indeed of the cavalry officer. Lean and gracious, with a roving wicked eye, he was the fearless hero all the men wished in secret they were, and the husband all the women wished they had. 'I am,' Libbie told Eliza, several days later, as she boarded the train with her husband bound for West Point, 'quite the envy of all. Oh how is it possible,' she said as she embraced her family and friends and waved to the curious onlookers come to gawp at this golden couple, 'that I could be so fortunate and yet so undeserving?' Back then, on that sharp spring morning, with disaster still so distant (though every day drawing, unseen, ever nearer), it must surely have seemed as if the life that lay ahead was as endless and as certain to endure as the steel glinting rails beneath the train's spinning wheels.

A bump. *It was me that swam to shore.* I opened my eyes. The voice of my father bled away. 'What is it?' *It was me that climbed the hill. It was me that scrubbed out the O and painted in an S.*

'Sir –'

I didn't know Tito was on our side.

I looked around, squinting in the harsh light. The cabin lights were on, the plane rocking, the stewardess bracing herself in the aisle. A shudder; the plane shifted left, bumping down, then again, like a pushchair on a step. 'Are we landing?' I said. Somewhere up ahead a woman shrieked.

'Please,' said the stewardess – she was pale, her voice weak – 'your . . . *seat*. Is to be *straight*.'

The large man by the window leaned across the empty seat between us. He'd been drinking all flight: Bloody Marys, no ice. 'American?' he said.

'English.'

'*Sir, please* –'

I pushed the button; the seat-back flipped up. 'Jesus Christ,' I said. 'Is this *normal*?'

He raised his shoulders in a shrug, slopping as he did so the contents of his glass. 'Normal?' he said. He pushed out his lips. 'What is normal?'

I suggested that surviving a landing was normal.

He leaned closer, all booze and sweat. 'Orlando,' he said, covering my face in a light vodka shower. 'Is it normal to snow on Walt Disney? On Mickey Mouse, is it normal? On ET phone home?'

I looked out of the window. The ground was frozen, tiny figures scuttling about in mufflers and greatcoats, and I suddenly wished I was home.

A big sigh. He slumped back. He turned to the window as the wheels touched the ground. 'In Russia,' he said, 'fucking snow fuck fuck fuck.' He closed his eyes. His chest heaved. In a moment we were taxiing and he was snoring, his head on his chest, his Aeroflot cup upturned in his lap.

'*Can I help you, sir?*'

While my father was in the Mediterranean upsetting the Yugoslav partisans (and so leading to official representations in Whitehall – Churchill, no less), my father-in-law – Karen's father – was up in the Arctic, flying Wildcats off aircraft carriers in protection of Russian convoys. Sometimes it was so cold that the planes would stick, frozen, to the carrier's deck, preventing take-off, and if a man baled out and ditched in the sea, he would live for one minute before the cold stopped his heart – unless, like my father-in-law, he was a New Zealander, in which case, statistics have it, he'd live another minute, maybe two. Anyway, the convoys carried everything from corned beef to tanks – aid of all kinds for the enemy's enemy. That the majority of (at least) the food found its way not directly (if ever) into the mouths of the starving, but passed through the hands of gangsters and black-marketeers and thence into the bellies of the Party's Most Faithful, was of little importance in the great scheme of things – the great scheme of things having, in this case, as in so many others, less to do with saving the starving and more to do with the assertion of power and prestige.

'Yes,' I said. 'The Hermitage. Is it far?'

Symbols, that is, like Leonardo's *Adoration of the Magi*, returned to an embattled and starving nation during that desperate winter of 1942 (returned thanks, in large part, and with perhaps even larger irony, to the efforts of that smoothest of fascist anti-Semites Lord Halifax) to its home at the Hermitage on Dvorcovaja Street, from whence it had been sent the year previously for safekeeping.

The desk-clerk shook his head. The distance, he said (his voice taking on that slight disengagement that comes with a phrase's too-often repetition), from Summer to Winter was no more than a mile. He sighed and smiled together. 'When speaking, you understand,' he said, 'of palaces.'

'I see,' I said.

'You walk?' he said.

I said I thought I would.

'Like Henry Kissinger,' he said. 'But not,' he said, 'like President Jimmy Carter.'

'I suppose he jogged,' I said.

'Jogged?' he said.

'Never mind,' I said. I thanked him for his help. I crossed the lobby, swung my way through the doors and out into the street.

For Libbie, the city of St Petersburg, with its sweeping grand façades and golden cupolas, must have seemed that winter like some strange ancient city. With the streets ankle-deep in snow and the Neva River frozen so hard that children and adults could skate on it, and even carriages could cross it from the Admiraltejskij Gardens on the south side to the university on the north without fear of breaking through, it must have seemed a whole world and more away from the dry baking plains, from Monroe, from all that she had lost.

I sat on the steps and looked out across the river towards the fortress of Peter and Paul.

Which is not to say that even here she was alone, or felt herself to be.

The fortress seemed so benign now – so artfully cleansed in the bright spring sunshine of its terrible past.

For he is always by my side, she wrote to a friend. *Here as everywhere, here as always.*

I watched the tiny figures crawling over the ramparts within which had been committed unspeakable acts of degradation and torture, city guidebooks in hand, the sun glinting from their cameras.

I turn and he is there.

It was, she said, the city, 'a city of ice' – even colder than Kansas in winter. Several times she nearly fell, and once – here on the steps of the Hermitage – was only saved from tumbling by a soldier on leave who had paused at the top to consider the view.

I looked down at the stone step between my feet.

Boots.

He offered his arm, she wrote to her friend. I looked up.

Despite the mild weather, the soldier before me was wearing a greatcoat and gloves. He was scowling, pale and thin-faced beneath the peak of his olive-green cap. He was wagging his finger.

'Hello,' I said. *The young man led me inside.* His face was that of a boy, his cheeks pitted with acne.

'*Navyerkhoo*,' he said.

'Excuse me?' I said.

'*Navyerkhoo. Navyerkhoo.*'

Heads were turning. He leaned towards me. 'No . . . *to sit*,' he said.

'No?'

'No.'

I pushed myself up. *He'd the general's way of walking, but not, of course, the general's eyes.* He stood back, tense, both hands on his rifle as if he was expecting trouble. I smiled; he didn't. I turned away, tensing up (I was half expecting the crack of a rifle butt on the back of my head, but nothing came), and crossed the stone entrance, aware as I did so of his child's eyes upon me. I pushed on the heavy doors and stepped from his sight into the cool and the gloom.

Libbie's escort was, it turned out, no ordinary soldier. He was, she discovered, a lover of art, and a painter of some talent. They crossed the marble hall, the young man talking all the while. His full name, he said, was Vasiliey Zimmerman.* He had been born a peasant's son in a small village near Odessa. His choice of a future had been from birth a stark choice of two – the soil or the army – and even this hadn't lasted. Thanks, he said, to the great floods of 1884 and the consequent winter famine, if he'd wanted to eat (and to see his parents eat) there really had been no choice.

And so, reluctant to leave his home and his family, he'd joined the army.

At first, along with all the other recruits, he'd dug ditches and learned to swing a sabre and fire ancient carbines. After a month, though, having shown unusual dexterity, he'd been assigned to the cartographers' tent, where his duties included sharpening pencils and preparing the various coloured inks.

It was during an inspection of the camp on the banks of the Neva River by the Grand Duke Alexis that the sixteen-year-old Vasiliey first discovered, quite by chance, his talent for drawing. Having just returned from a visit to the United States, the grand duke (third son of Tsar Alexander II and himself only nineteen) was carrying with him a number of his own pen-and-ink sketches composed during the great Nebraska buffalo hunt of 1872 (work exhibiting, it was said – though always, of course, sotto voce – a great deal more enthusiasm for the medium than ability) – an event staged in his

* According to one (unreliable) source, the great-great-grandfather of Bob Dylan.

144

honour by no less a figure than that famous (even, by then, in Russia) American general, George Armstrong Custer. The sketches, though little more in fact than childlike despatches from some simple stick world, had been much praised (in the same way, that is, and for much the same reason, that the young man himself had been variously described by previous hosts as being a fellow of great charm and even greater intelligence, when, in truth, the truth lay elsewhere) – so much so, indeed, that the prestigious Renfrew Gallery in New York (owner, Eustice Renfrew, millionaire steel magnate and, it was rumoured, once the lover of the grand duke's father's first wife, Maria Alexandrovna) had requested that a selection be sent for exhibition. However, reluctant to have such priceless originals leave his side, the grand duke demanded that a copyist be found *that day* and that *these* be the pictures sent precariously east for exhibition. So, an officer was despatched right away to the cartographers' tent, where only present that morning was a boy called Vasiliey Zimmerman, whom the officer discovered sitting hunched on a barrel sharpening pencils with a field knife. 'You have pencils and paper then?' said the officer. 'Yes,' said Vasiliey. 'Good,' said the officer. And that, pretty much, was that. The copies were made (the originals improved upon no end) and subsequently sent east where they remained for six months on the walls of the Renfrew Gallery.

For a year and a half, Libbie and the soldier exchanged letters. He talked about art, and she talked about the general. She talked about West Point, how those first days following her wedding had been her 'happiest time', and she told him all about Nebraska and the buffalo hunt – how the scouts had been led by Buffalo Bill Cody, and how the hundred or so Sioux who took part had included the niece of Crazy Horse himself – and how the general had charged the herd, so scattering them in order that the grand duke could get close enough to a target for a shot and a kill. Then one day his letters stopped. She wrote, asking why, but received no reply. What she didn't know – what she would *never* know – was that Vasiliey Zimmerman, the peasant boy from the Ukraine with an eye for the beauty in paintings, was dead – having, ironically perhaps, not been killed in battle by bullet or sabre, but beneath the wheels of a new steam tractor given to his father by a grateful, but always anonymous (though, it was rumoured, royal) benefactor from St Petersburg.

29

Seasons of Silence

West Point, in that spring of 1864, was at its most beautiful. The tree-covered hills that ran down to the banks of the Hudson River were a thousand shades of green, the river itself majestic – as untroubled now by man's fleeting and petty war as it had been in the days before he'd first gazed with envy on its vast sweep and power and dreamed like a fool of controlling it and making it bend to his own hollow will.

For Libbie, the academy was quite the most splendid place she'd ever seen. So familiar was it from her husband's stories that their arrival was almost like a homecoming, and she understood at once his wish to be buried there. For him, it really *was* home. Even the dogs remembered his scent and followed him around, and those professors whose marks had once predicted such a dim future for the boy now jostled with each other in their wish to be seen to be near such a hero. He sought out his old haunts, while his new bride was entertained by a group of that year's raw cadets, their tour including a walk down Lovers' Lane. When, later, on the train to New York, she told him of this (telling him, also – as it turned out unwisely – that one of the older professors had even stolen a kiss), he was far from amused. Indeed – despite her protestations that the whole thing had been quite innocent, not to mention the fact that it had been *him* who had left *her* alone and at the mercy of others – he sulked all the way to Penn Station, only speaking when the train's whistle blew and those waiting on the platform saw his face and started waving.

'*Hello?*'

It was Libbie's first experience of what she would later come to call her husband's 'silent seasons'.

'*Is Charlie there?*'

It was to be the first of many – preparation, perhaps (though she'd not known it then, and could not have believed it if she had) for that longest and most silent of seasons that would begin a decade later with his death and only end, in the end, with hers.

'No. He has a class. Who is this?'

I told her my name.

'Is there a message?'

'No, no message.'

'OK then.'

'OK. Are you a friend of Charlie's?'

'A friend, yes.'

'Is he OK?'

'OK?'

'Never mind. I'll call again. Nice talking to you.'

'Bye then.'

'Bye.'

I put down the phone and sat at the table. I looked out of the window at the city of St Petersburg below. I flipped the pages of my notebook. *1891. Libbie carries dung to Tsar in St P. Time of famine and cholera. Typhus.* Everything seemed distant now. Everything was silent. Just the whisper of the turning pages, the crack of the book's breaking spine. Too lazy or weary to go to my coat, I searched the drawers for something to write with. Nothing. I picked up the phone, punched the buttons, asked for a pen, a pencil, anything. Then I lay back and waited, counting down minutes in my head. The bed was hard – like lying on a table. I closed my eyes. But all I could see was Karen's face, then Libbie's. I opened my eyes; the image remained, frozen, upturned on my retinas like a face in a fun-house. I turned my head on the hard pillow, lay gazing at the picture on the bedside table.

I was trying to jimmy the window when a porter arrived with a pencil. He knocked; I was ready. We stood in the doorway, him trying to look past me for the cause of the room's freezing temperature (I'd given up on the window lock and just cracked the glass with my elbow wrapped in a towel), me just grabbing the pencil and stepping towards him, so bullying him back out into the corridor. I shut the door in his face, then waited a while, listening. Nothing. Then footsteps receding.

By the window the carpet was crunchy underfoot. I was glad I'd thought to put on my shoes before breaking the glass.

I stood before the broken pane, felt the sharp, biting cold on my face. The snow was falling hard now, as if it was already winter. I closed my eyes, felt it settle a while on my face before melting with the warmth of my blood.

Once, when I was a boy, I saw a child falling through a hole in a frozen-over river. I crept over the ice and peered in. The child was struggling. I reached in, took his hand, hauled him out. He lay there on the ice and I watched him, and when he'd finished gasping like a fish, I asked him if he knew anything about Russia. It was my homework: the life (in three hundred words) of Tsar Alexander III. But the boy said nothing. He just moved his head *no*, his eyes staring up at the white sky, quite blind.

30

The Dark Corridor

Tsar Alexander III was six foot three inches tall, a robust, vigorous man who, it is said, believed in the necessity of thinking hard about things about as much as he believed in the need for sociability – which, largely speaking, was not at all. Of limited – strictly military – education, and referred to even by his own father as 'the bullock', his favourite pastimes are said to have been bending pokers and breaking roubles with his teeth – which activities would presumably have continued indefinitely and without interruption had it not been for the death, in 1865, of his elder brother Nicholas (and his consequent ascension to the role of heir apparent), and his marriage shortly thereafter to the Danish princess Dagmar, a tiny, beautiful woman whose charm impressed the sceptical St Petersburg nobility and compensated for her husband's distinct lack thereof.

'*And so we ending the White Hall.*'

Which is not to say that even *she* could compensate sufficiently.

'And now to move forward, please?'

Indeed, when, thanks to his father's assassination (the last of several attempts), Alexander became tsar of all the Russias, all the Russias were really in trouble. Instinctively and immovably resistant to any change, except that which served further to widen the gap between rich and poor, the serf and the nobleman, or to further disempower the nation's already much-abused Jews, he appointed a whole series of ministers, each one of whom, on identifying and then articulating the nation's desperate need for reform, was summarily dismissed and replaced by another – a process that went on and on, until the country was tumbling into anarchy and famine.

'Please, sirs and ladies –'

We shuffled on, heading as instructed for the Gold Drawing Room, bunching then in the doorway like a herd of nervous cows at a cattle-grid, waiting for Katarina, our guide, to lead us in.

When Libbie arrived in the autumn of 1891, Tsar Alexander III was forty-six years old, and suffering already from the cocktail of ailments that would, in time, see him dead. Aside from chronic backache and a limp (the results not only of the train crash at Borki three years previously, following which he is said to have saved the lives of his wife and son by shouldering, literally, the weight of a collapsed roof, but also, indirectly, his excessive drinking, the result of which was, invariably, his rolling around on his back, waving his arms and legs in the air), he had trouble with his kidneys (Bright's disease) that made pissing bloody murder and hunting on horseback even worse. All of which troubles only served to make him more like his old self than his old self had been – that is, still more doubting and distrustful of the outside world and change (which, to him, were one and the same); and, as a consequence of *this*, even shyer than hitherto he had been – so much so, in fact, that when Libbie took her seat in the Gold Drawing Room, it is said that the tsar remained for over an hour in an anteroom, just peering at his famous visitor through a hole specially cut in the doorframe, and that it was only when he feared she might get up and leave that he was persuaded to make an appearance.

'The Gold Drawing Room is here to the tsar when meeting important peoples. Note will you the all-over gildings and ceiling. Also gems.'

I squeezed the dung in my pocket and thought of Libbie. Along with her own dung (as it were), she'd brought with her a nugget of Black Hills gold, fashioned in Minneapolis into a tiny bear's head.* I peered into the nearest cabinet, half expecting to find it there glinting back at me.

* A replica of this can be found at the Miners' Museum, Medora, North Dakota.

'Please –'

I looked up.

'Do you have questions?'

The rest of the group was already moving off.

'Well, I was wondering,' I said, 'if someone brought a present for the tsar – some famous person, say – what would happen to it? Say it was a gold nugget, maybe in the shape of a bear's head –'

Katarina cocked her head, frowning, sceptical. 'A bear head?' she said.

'Really small,' I said. I circled my thumb and first finger. 'About this big?'

She glanced to the group, some of whom were looking back and scowling, impatient.

'Do you think it would still be here?'

She turned back.

'I have to go now,' she said.

'But *do* you?'

She shrugged. 'I don't know. Perhaps in the . . . *archiva?*'

'Archives?'

'Archives, yes.'

'Can you show me?'

Another glance across the room. 'I have to go.'

'Later, maybe?'

'No. I cannot.'

'Why not?'

'I'm sorry. I have to go. And you must come.'

'Maybe tomorrow?'

'You must come, please.'

She turned away and crossed the room, her rubber soles squeaking on the high-polished floor. The tour group parted, engulfing her, and then she was gone, leading her flock from the brightness and gold of the sunlit drawing room and into the gloom of the Dark Corridor.

They talked of buffaloes and the west (about which the tsar knew nothing, thinking as he did the buffalo a kind of stumpy-legged horse and 'the west' to be located where any map would place Ireland), and, of course – *of course* – they talked of the general and of his famous and glorious death. The tsar tugged distractedly at his beard, his eyes filling with tears, as the widow spoke of duty and of her determination that such a sacrifice should not be forgotten. He listened grave-faced as she described how, upon the death of her husband, she felt she had entered a dark corridor, a place as long as it was black – a place whose only light was the clear light of duty. It was, she said, a darkness so deep that she feared were it not for the hand of the general to guide her, she would certainly have stumbled and fallen long ago. At this, leaning forward, the tsar nodded and touched the widow's hand. He knew, he said, the burdens of duty and the sacrifices demanded by God of the great. It is said, then, that he took her to the window and pointed out at the vast sprawling sickly city that lay beyond the gates. It was, he told her, a guilty city full of murderers and Jews – a city drenched in the blood of his father (blood that had been revenged with blood, despite calls for clemency from that liberal, Mr Tolstoy) – a city upon which, in payment for the crime, had been visited the current and terrible twin retributions of famine and disease. It was, he said, his duty to stand firm; to remain, against all odds, a reminder of all that was right, and not falter – for to do so would be to let the gates open and the savages triumph.

The interview ended with an exchange of gifts. On Libbie's part there was the bear's-head nugget and, of course, the dung. In exchange, the tsar promised a big surprise. Then they parted, talking of meeting again one day. But they never did. Within three years the tsar was dead, the monarchy dying. Though it staggered on, in the person of Nicholas II, bitter and repressive for another twenty years, in the end the new tsar finally succumbed, engulfed in war at home and abroad, and the palace – where his father had entertained the wife of the famous American martyr – was stormed and sacked, the Dark Corridor, between whose tapestries she had walked away, filled now not with the respectful fearful silence of flunkies, but with the ghastly cries of the wounded and dying of the temporary red revolution.

31

The Unembalmed Heart

Following two days in New York spent visiting friends and attending the theatre, the newly-wed Custers arrived in the capital to find it (again) in a high state of panic. With the skittery population thinking (again) a rebel invasion imminent (in fact, General Lee was no closer than Charlottesville, fully two hundred and fifty miles south on the Virginia Central Railroad, and had neither the will nor the means for such a campaign), the unpaved stinking streets beyond the White House were thick with soldiers and civilians alike, the former fighting the desire to flee but mostly staying, the latter, in large measure, while wishing to see themselves staying (it would be something to tell the grandchildren, after all), finding not the courage to do so and at least attempting to flee. Indeed, so thick with uniforms were the streets that spring, Custer observed that should a person, at any point along Pennsylvania Avenue, have decided to close his eyes and throw a stone in any direction he'd have been bound to strike 'at least a half-dozen brigadiers' all hoping to be noticed – all competing 'to look the bravest and most earnest' in the hopes of attaining a major-general's star. Not, of course, that he considered himself to be one of their number (although he was, admittedly, *himself* a brigadier) – on the contrary. Already famous, *he* had no need to seek a higher profile, one that would raise *him* above the bleating mass – just as *his* broadcasted deeds had long since set *his* bravery and dedication to the cause beyond question. Indeed, that spring – as he strolled the sidewalks with his new bride, or swirled her in a polka at some glittering government ball – his star, in life, could not have been higher, and would never be – except, at times, in death. He was, in short, for that briefest and most dangerous of American moments, the absolute apotheosis of all that America most admired: he was beautiful, dashing, brave and quick-witted. He was all this, and one other thing. He was, above all, flawed – beautifully, romantically, *outrageously* flawed – and so, consequently, doomed. For America, with Custer there was never the grotesque, un-American threat of ageing and decay: he was the beautiful, daring boy who would remain beautiful, even in death – the necessary martyr embraced and embalmed by a brand-new, growing nation in need of a noble, tragic, excusing past.

'*Hi.*'

But all that, then, was yet to come. That spring, for Libbie, there was a wife's work of support and consolation to be embarked upon. There were senators and generals to be met and charmed; there was even a president – Honest Abe Lincoln – who wished to meet the woman who had captured such a hero.

'What do you want?'

'Are you busy?'

'I have to go home.'

She started down the steps. I caught her up. It was four o'clock: winter closing time at the Hermitage.

'Ten minutes?' I said.

She didn't stop. 'My father is waiting,' she said.

'*My* father's dead,' I said.

That made her stop.

'A heart attack. But he'd been drinking. Vodka.' It wasn't true about the vodka, but there was a neatness to be enjoyed in saying it.

She sighed. 'What do you want?' she said.

'You said you'd show me the archives.'

She frowned. 'I said no.'

'But you didn't mean it.'

'What?'

'When you said no. You really meant yes.'

'No. I *really* meant *no*. And now I have to go.'

She turned to go. I tried to think of something to say that would stop her, but nothing came. Instead I just watched her walk away. She crossed the road. She didn't look back.

She had seen him once before at the theatre. He'd been sitting in a box with Mrs Lincoln, his pale, lined face half hidden in the shadow cast by the heavy velvet curtains. She (like everyone else) had tried not to stare, and had mostly succeeded – but there had been a look of such terrible sadness in his dark, hooded eyes, that it had been hard not to. For distraction, she'd studied every word in the programme, and, when the lights had gone down and the actors had taken to the stage, she'd tried to lose herself in the story of Denmark and its king. But then she'd found her mind wandering and her gaze drifting over the heads all around her and up to the figure in the box. Even in the lamps' yellow light, his flesh had looked grey to her – grey like the heavy grey flesh of a corpse – and there had seemed to her about him a combination of extreme frailty and enormous, immovable strength. That evening, in the theatre, while uncles were slain behind curtains and kingdoms won and lost, she had come to believe that, should the man in the box only live long enough, then the Union would be saved. It was, she felt certain then, all in him: in his hands and in the beating of his heart lay success or failure, victory or defeat.

They met at ten o'clock, in the Blue Room at the White House, while her husband had an interview with chief of cavalry General Philip Sheridan. She stood in line, and when the usher said her name, she curtsied as rehearsed. The president, tall and thin (seemingly more so when contrasted, as then, with his short and squat wife), took her hand, nodded distractedly, and moved on. But then, moments later, he paused as the significance of the name came to him. He moved back a step or two (so confusing those behind him and causing toes to be stood on and yelps to be uttered and stifled), and regathered her hand. 'So,' he said, 'this is the young woman whose husband goes into a charge with a whoop and a shout.' He smiled that creased smile. 'I doubt, now, he will do so again.'

'Sir?' said Libbie.

'Now that he has much more than himself to lose.'

Libbie blushed and said no – that her husband would not – indeed, *could* not – change the bravery of his ways for anyone.

'Not even for me?' said the president.

'Not even for you, sir,' said Libbie.

'Oh, then you want to be a widow, I see,' said the president – and everyone laughed. Everyone, that is, but Mrs Lincoln, who, it was reported by the Democrat-leaning anti-Lincoln *Washington Observer*, gave a long and weary sigh.

Katarina caught a dirty red, green and cream tram at the end of Malata Morskaya Ulitsa and rode it all the way east along the Nevskiy Prospekt. She sat in the window and watched without interest the buildings passing by. She must have seen them all a thousand times, and, consequently, could see them no more. Just past the canal the tram paused outside the Silver Rows Arcade to change rails; the driver opened the passenger door (he'd tried his own, but something had defeated him, causing him to curse good and hard, his voice rising like cigarette smoke in the sharp air), and there followed some sort of slightly comical business with a pair of long sticks. At last (more cursing), he got it done and the tram up ahead moved on, its place at the rail change point taken by my own. The process was duplicated (even down, curiously, to the stuck door and the curses), and then we, too, moved on, the second and third trams (there were four in all) rumbling one after the other along the dark and pitted road.

I kept my eye on the tram up ahead, ready to get off when she did – and then she did, and I was up and out and standing, as if naked, on the street.

She was gone.

'Are you following me?'

I spun around, my heart suddenly banging like a steam hammer.

The collar of her coat was up high, giving her the look of someone buried up to the neck in sand. There were dark circles like bruises beneath her eyes.

I couldn't think of a lie.

She asked me why.

I shrugged, though I knew of course. And it wasn't (though I *said* it was) the archives business and the nugget in the shape of a bear's head.

'I told you I couldn't,' she said.

'I know,' I said.

'And now you follow me.'

'I know. Where are we going?'

'We?'

'Sorry. I mean *you*.'

'I told you. I'm going home.'

'My father was a private eye, you see. It's like a habit.'

'A habit?'

'Following people. That and steaming open letters. Looking for secrets.'

She shook her head. It was cold: she was starting to shiver. 'I don't know what you are saying,' she said.

'It doesn't matter.'

We stood then in silence, watching a tram approach, pause, hissing. The driver got out. Another man was waiting, stamping his feet. The two men embraced. The new man waved, climbed up into the cab. Some more hissing, a series of electrical clicks, then the tram swept on by.

'What will you do?' said Katarina.

'I don't know.'

She sighed, looked away.

'What is it?'

It was as if she was turning something over in her mind. She looked back. 'You can come to my parents' home,' she said. She shrugged. 'If you want.'

'To your home?'

'If you want.'

'Are you sure?'

Another shrug.

'Won't your father mind?'

'If you want,' she said. She nodded across the road to an approaching tram. 'This one,' she said. She started walking, glancing this way and that, edging her way through the traffic.

It took two more trams and then the ancient stone city gave way to one that was all scrub and stained concrete. Shoddy-looking towerblocks rose above the wasteland like the hollow useless chimneys of a bombed-out Kiev or Dresden.

'Here,' said Katarina, as the tram hissed and slowed. We stood, swaying side to side as the tram shuddered and stopped. There were a dozen or so of us left on board – mostly old people wearing either too many or too few clothes; all rose and shuffled to the exit as if answering some unspoken command, then, once released by the doors into the dull evening light, they scattered, bent over, huddled closely to the land, heading for this block or that and whatever sparse comfort lay within. 'Come,' said Katarina, and, following the others, we moved down the shallow incline from the road, placing our feet with some care upon the brittle yellowed grass and stepping round the oily pools and the shards of jagged wire that rose in our path.

The lift in Katarina's block looked clean enough (the doors were open – permanently, as it turned out), but whatever it took to run it – to clench the cables and drag it up – had long since run out. So we took the stairs. They were concrete, rough-edged, and echoed our footsteps. I lost count somewhere between two hundred and two hundred and fifty. Every landing looked the same, and every door on every landing. Someone, somewhere, long ago had decided the doors should be turquoise. Katarina paused before one, found the lock with her key, turned it and pushed. The door opened on to a dark narrow hall. She called out something; from somewhere, muffled, someone – a man – responded. 'Wait here,' she said. She moved off down the hall, disappearing into the lighted room at the end. I looked around – there was little to see: a cheap-looking, spindly-legged table, a yellowed print on the wall of round-cheeked girls playing in a meadow filled with flowers.

'Hello?'

The floor was bare, save for a narrow worn rug.

She was standing in the door way, a dark shadow against the light. She beckoned me forward.

Her father was sitting at a small yellow table, before him a bowl of what looked to be some kind of soup. He had his forearms on the table, either side of the bowl, and bunched fists. He was looking straight ahead towards the small grimy window.

'My father,' said Katarina.

The old man moved his head, turning towards the sound. He was staring, blinking, blind.

'Pleased to meet you,' I said, then to Katarina, 'What's that in Russian?' She translated. The old man nodded.

'Do you want something to eat?' she said. When I said no, she shrugged. She went to the old man, touched him on the shoulder, said something. The old man unfurled one hand, found his spoon and started eating.

'Have you lived here long?' I said.

'Twenty-four years,' she said. 'I was born to here. My father was thirty years old on the day I was born. My mother was twenty years old on the day I was born.'

'That's quite a coincidence,' I said.

She frowned.

'Lucky,' I said.

'Lucky?'

The old man set down his spoon, said something. His daughter replied, then said, 'My father wants to know why if you come from such a rich country you have such *shoes*.'

I looked down. 'What's wrong with them?' They were Nike trainers, still in good shape despite all the miles and the mud and the stones.

'He says they are workman's shoes,' she said. Was she smiling?

'They're comfortable,' I said. 'And they were expensive.'

Katarina translated. The old man turned his head, and there was something in the action – something in the tilt – that made me think he thought me (or at least my shoes) absurd. He said something else.

'He said I'm to show you his . . . *souvenir*.' She scowled. 'Is that right – *souvenir*?'

'Maybe,' I said.

She smiled. 'Will you come?' She left the room; I followed. We went back down the hall, she opened the door nearest the front door and stepped into a small, dark, humid room. From the hall then, the sounds of a door opening and closing; from inside, in the room, a sort of scrabbling in the darkness, then a light flicked on, low and rose-coloured. 'Come,' she said. She was standing next to a small beaten-up metal box, the sort photographers use to carry their equipment. 'Come near,' she said. I did. The box was humming.

'What is it?' I said.

'My father,' she said, 'was a . . . how you say, *embalming*? He worked in Moscow. Red Square. He embalmed Stalin, and when nobody wanted Stalin, he –' She paused, that frown.

'He *un*embalmed him?'

It was a joke, but she nodded. '*Unembalmed*, yes. He took all the . . . *do you say fluid?* . . . into a bucket and threw it into the drain. And then he went home – to St Petersburg. But he take – *took* – with him a souvenir. Look –' She lifted the lid of the box, releasing a heavy cloud of thick sickly-smelling moisture.

I leaned forward, peered in. The box was packed with ice. Somewhere inside, refracted by the shards of frozen water, was something darkish grey, about the size of a man's fist.

I looked up. Katarina was smiling. 'It looks like a heart,' I said. She shrugged.

'It's a joke, right?'

She shook her head. 'No joke.'

'Right.'

'The *joke* is everybody said he doesn't have one.'

'Who?'

She sighed. 'Stalin, of course,' she said.

'Or maybe there's a cow out there somewhere that doesn't. Or a sheep. Or *something*.'

'You don't believe me?'

'I believe it's a joke. I *hope* it's a joke.'

'No. No joke.'

'Well, if *that's* his, then he *did* have a heart. He certainly doesn't any more.'

'Yes,' she said. She nodded towards it. 'Do you see how cold it is?'

'It looks frozen,' I said.

'Frozen, yes.' She closed the box, flicked off the light. We stepped out into the corridor. 'Do you want to eat now?' she said.

'What about your father?'

She was off down the hall, heading for the kitchen. 'We have sausage. You like sausage?'

'Won't he mind?'

She started rattling pots and pans in the sink.

The old man was gone, his bowl and spoon cleared away.

'Where's your father?' I said.

'My father? He is gone now. Every day he plays chess with his friend.'

'He can play chess even though he's blind?'

She glanced over her shoulder, smiling, quizzical. 'Of *course*,' she said. 'He remembers with his hands.'

We ate sausage and cabbage and drank strange, dark, sweet-smelling beer. She asked me about my life and about my books and I told her about Libbie and my search – how it had brought me to St Petersburg, to the Hermitage, to her and her father's cramped flat with its pink light and joke heart frozen stiff in a box. She asked me when I was going home, and I said I didn't know. I told her I longed to go – to *be* there – but that I was no longer sure where *there* was.

Later, as we were standing at the tram stop, she asked me if I had a wife.

'I did,' I said. 'She's dead.'

She touched my arm then, as, hissing like a villain, the brightly lit tram approached. She said something that was lost to me as I climbed the steps.

'What?' I said.

162

'Tomorrow,' she said.

'Tomorrow?'

The tram was moving off. She followed it a few steps, but then stood, her arm raised in a wave. I waved back, watching her until she was gone from sight and the blocks with their water-stained concrete slipped away and were lost in the fast-falling night.

32

The Gift

A light tapping on the door. She stirs, half-waking. She listens: nothing. She closes her eyes again – and again, at once, as always, he is there. *Our children will be beauties, and brave too.* He is lying in her arms, in their warm dipping bed at Fort Lincoln on the plains. More tapping, a far-off scrabbling sort of sound; the image stutters, dips away. She sits up.

'*Hello?*'

'Who is it?' she says – Libbie – here in this room, here in this bed.

I pushed back the covers, pulled on my trousers. I eased open the door.

'Katarina? What time is it?'

'Seven o'clock.'

'I thought we said eight.'

She shrugged. 'Shall I go?'

I opened the door – this door – as Libbie did.

'I have to get changed,' I said. 'Will you wait?'

'I'll wait,' she said.

He was dressed, so the story goes, in a long heavy coat, his large head and whiskers disguised by a poleskin hat and the coat's high collar. Unused to waiting (other than for the crown, for which he'd seemed to have been waiting half a lifetime), he'd spent the hour Mrs Custer had required to ready herself arm-wrestling with his principal personal guard Yasarovich (a huge man, by all accounts, said – not least by himself – to have once knocked a runaway horse clean out with a single solid punch), and, when that had palled as a pastime, he'd practised stepping into and out of his thick winter

164

boots, then rolling his socks down and rolling them up again. That he'd been standing bootless and with his socks rolled down when a call from within had at last admitted him is said not to have embarrassed him at all or given him the slightest pause. But, then, nothing did – not any longer. He was now, at last and after all, tsar of all the Russias (a state of affairs he never failed to point out – often with a riding crop of fine Spanish leather – when faced with any real or imagined lack of deference), and, as such, could not *be* embarrassed, leading as he did the mores of the day and not following. At any rate, he pulled up his socks, stepped into his boots, knocked on the door and entered.

After three months away, for Libbie, it was time to start for home. There was work to do: if she were absent from America for too long the lustre of her husband's halo would fade and tarnish, and would need her attention, her polishing. And so she'd packed her bags and was preparing to go when the tsar appeared, heavy-booted, fur-hatted, and announced that his gift awaited her in the courtyard.

It was, he said, a symbol – both personal and public. It represented, on the one hand, 'a living bond' between the peoples of two great nations, and, on the other – being a *bear* – it stood for her husband's great fortitude and courage.

'*What are you thinking?*'

What Libbie thought, moments later, as she stood in that snowy courtyard, peering in through the bars at such a brave but sad-looking captured thing, remains unrecorded, the image just an artful reconstruction.

'Nothing.'

For, today, the courtyard is a car park for the hotel's residents, and on the cobbles where once stood the poor bear's great cage now stand Mercedes and BMWs, within which sit large men in dark suits and caps.

'Come. We must hurry. Konstantin will be waiting.'

'Who's Konstantin?' I called after her, but she didn't hear me. She was already under the arch and hurrying through the traffic on Voznesenskij Prospekt.

Konstantin Shelakov was waiting at the service entrance on Voskovaja Street. A short man in his early fifties, he was stamping his feet against the early-morning cold and smoking a cigarette. He nodded like a spy when he saw Katarina, then turned, dropped the cigarette, and slipped through the door.

'Who is he?' I said as we followed.

'Sssh,' hissed Katarina.

To get to the complex of archives and storerooms that lies beneath the Hermitage you must first find your way in low gloomy light through a maze of narrow corridors, all of which look the same, and the combination of any three of which would surely defeat the most dedicated of intruders. As we twisted and turned, I half expected, at every moment, to find the bones of some poor soul who, after hours of searching, had finally given up hope and just sat down to die, and when at last we came into the humming and light of what seemed to be some sort of waiting area (straight-backed wooden chairs around the room's edge, a door in the far wall with a glass and mesh window) I was glad of the air and the space.

'Wait here,' said Konstantin. He crossed the room, punched a code into a box on the door, stepped through and was gone.

Katarina and I took our places on the hard chairs in the low-humming silence. I looked around. There was a skylight overhead – also meshed – beyond which was what looked like a pale grubby sky. This seemed odd: I'd thought we were still underground – I hadn't noticed us climbing. I glanced at Katarina. She was playing with a button on her coat lapel, turning it around and around on its thread. She seemed nervous.

'What does he do?' I said after a while.

She looked up. 'Excuse me?'

'Konstantin. I was wondering what he did –'

'Did?'

'*Does*. His *job*. I was wondering what it is –'

'Why?'

'No reason. I just wondered.'

She looked nervously at the door, as if she were worried that it would open any minute and something bad emerge – or perhaps that it might never open at all.

'What is it?' I said.

She looked back, paused a moment as if deciding whether I was worthy of a secret, then put her lips to my ear. 'He buys and sells Mercedes cars,' she whispered.

'Cars?'

'Sssh –'

'But I thought –'

A buzz and the door opened. Konstantin nodded.

'Now,' said Katarina.

He led us through a series of small, brightly lit rooms, his long coat swirling behind him. Each room was empty, save for a table in the centre and a small, straight-backed chair. In the fourth room (or maybe fifth – I lost track), a man in a dark-blue uniform was waiting, a set of keys in his hand. He nodded at Konstantin (who nodded back), then turned and unlocked a door behind him. Reaching around, he flicked a switch. A ceiling light blinked on, off, then on again. He stepped back.

'OK,' he said, for the first time looking me straight in the eye. 'Five minutes.'

I hesitated, three sets of eyes on me. 'Do I go in?' I said.

'Five minutes,' said Konstantin.

I looked at Katarina. She shrugged.

'Right,' I said.

Not taking his eyes from me, Konstantin edged up the sleeve of his coat and tapped on the face of his watch. 'Five minutes.'

'OK.' I took off my coat, set it on the table. 'I'll be going then,' I said.

You'd think there'd be a system in such a place – some sort of planned layout. Well, if there was, I couldn't see it. Everything seemed to be jumbled up together on row after row of metal shelves – paintings and boxes of stuff and even whole sets of armour. The only form of labelling I could see was a cloakroom ticket attached to each article with a piece of sticky tape. It was like some enormous garage sale – tables overflowing with bric-à-brac where everything is priceless and nothing is for sale.

It was quite by chance that I found Libbie's bear's head. It was sitting entirely on its own on one end of a shelf in the far corner of the room. When I picked it up it left a ring of dust behind. It was tiny (about the size of a table-tennis ball), and dusty as if it had not been handled in years. I turned it around. The work was exquisite – every bit as delicate and beautiful as I'd imagined it to be. It was amazing (to me at least) to think how far in years and in miles it had come – that someone who was long since dead and forgotten had once, long ago, chipped a rough nugget from the tight grip of rock way out west, and then someone had sold it and someone had carved it and someone had carried it halfway around the world – only for it to end up here, with me, in my hand.

'One minute,' said Konstantin at the door.

As I set it back down and studied the palm of my hand, I remembered something Karen's father said in his speech on the day of our wedding. The best gold, he said, like the finest love, is so soft and forgiving that just by touching it it makes you richer. Love, like gold, he said, is a gift that leaves you always the better for even its most fleeting presence.

33

Time Regained

Back in those days I could scarcely go an hour without thinking of Karen; now – thanks to Sarah – whole days can pass by without the sound of her voice coming to me in a moment of silence, or her face appearing unexpectedly in an afternoon crowd. And gone now, too – thanks to her – are the nights spent turning things over in my head, and the hours lost to useless self-pity. Back then there was always *before*; now there is only *now*.

'*Sir?*'

Back then, sitting in that plane on my way home from St Petersburg, all I could think was *maybe she'll be there standing at the gate*, even though the part of me that was really alive knew it was impossible. Only in stories do people ever really come back; only in stories does death not mean *death* – does it not mean the end of (at least in retrospect) all that was good and the beginning of something quite different.

'You're in the wrong line, sir.'

'I am?'

'Sir, this line is for aliens only. Citizens of the United States need to use the first nineteen lines.'

The immigration officer pushed back my passport. My passport was blue now, not red – an eagle on the front, not a circle of stars. No longer did the queen require of others my protection. I stepped away, fed my way back against the tide. I was a citizen now, not a subject.

But all that, then, as, on the first leg of my journey home, the plane touched down in London, was still to come. Then, stepping out into the grey light of a cold rainy morning, I was still on the inside of my old self looking out, still adrift in the calm before the marvellous fiery storm.

I crossed the road, deafened by the sound of thundering planes, and caught a cab for the city. Here I wandered around for a while, no plans, no particular destination. I sat on a bench in the middle of Leicester Square and watched the other strangers pausing with their guidebooks and pointing, and the five-layer tramps begging money or just lying in their bundled-up filth like overdressed tourists on a beach. For so long now, it seemed, I'd looked forward to coming back – but now I was here it didn't feel like I'd hoped it would. I could see it, but not feel it. Certainly it was familiar (as a child I'd crossed this square twice a day for over a decade on my way to and from school) – but it was distant, too, like your old school in pictures.

At Waterloo station I bought a ticket for Guildford and sat on the concourse drinking coffee and watching the people go by. Ever since I was a little boy I have been scared of missing trains, and so, every minute or so, I studied the great clicking board. *Maybe she'll be there at the station,* I kept telling myself, then cursing myself for such foolishness. Being bereaved is like suddenly becoming two people: the one who has lost and been left behind and the one who has to carry on.

I took a seat by the window and watched the city creeping backwards, all hunched up and blank-faced. For a while I counted satellite dishes bolted to the back walls of dark narrow houses, but soon gave it up. I tried to read to bypass my nerves, but all I could think of was Karen in the car (our car), all I could see was her checking the time then gathering her keys, then the sound of the slamming door, the crunch of tyres on gravel.

'Ticket, please.'

For distraction, I tried to think again of Libbie Custer and the bear.

'Sir?'

I closed my eyes and thought of the poor defeated creature lying in the darkness of that cage in the stinking sweating heat of the SS *Liberation*'s hold, while Libbie was crossing the continent, heading for the Paris–London boat-train.

'*Sir?*'

And it seemed to me then some kind of a miracle that it had somehow managed to survive such abuse, such uprooting, and that, consequently, there were bears in New York City now where once (and quite properly) there'd been none.

'Well, *do* you?'

I opened my eyes. 'What?'

'Have a *ticket*, sir?'

The train was slowing, coming into a station. 'Where are we?' I said – though I knew. I pressed my face to the glass, searched the platform for one figure, one face. *I'll meet you at the station. I'll catch the twelve-thirty.*

'You're aware, sir,' said a voice above and behind, 'of the consequences of travelling without a ticket –'

And then there she was, her arm raised, waving.

A hand on my arm.

I turned. 'What?'

'I *said* –'

I fished around in my pocket – all thumbs – pulled out the tiny piece of flimsy card, thrust it at him, spun back to the window.

I'll meet you at the station.

But the platform was empty.

'OK,' sneered the ticket-man.

She was gone.

I walked the half-mile to the house in a trance. As I approached I was aware of the sound of voices. I paused in the shadow of a tree across the road. There was a big yellow skip in the driveway, and a pick-up truck and white van with *Brough and Barker – Builders* in blue letters on the side.

The voices were coming from inside the house, and as I crossed the road and headed up the path to the door I could hear a radio too: Lionel Ritchie, 'Tender Heart'. The door was open, the smell of sawdust in the air.

'Hello?' said a voice behind me. 'Can I help you?'

'I'm sorry,' I said.

'Sorry?' The man was in overalls, his shoulders and the top of his head covered in a fine white powder as if he had terrible dandruff.

'I used to live here,' I said.

'Oh?' said the man.

'A long time ago,' I said.

'So?'

'I was just thinking . . . I just wanted –'

'Just wanted what?'

To come home. To have things as they were. To be who I used to think I was.

'I've got work to do,' he said.

'Yes, of course.'

Something, as I was leaving, made me stop at the door. 'So what are you doing?' I said. He frowned. 'I mean, what are you building?'

'Stripping the whole place,' he said. 'Getting rid of all the old shit.'

He was watching me still as I left the house, as if he were wary, thinking me dangerous or mad. Fifty yards down the road, I turned to look back. He was gone. I stepped into the shadow of some trees and waited.

The van and the pick-up truck were gone by four o'clock. At ten past, with the light already fading, I was back in the driveway. Careful not to be seen, I eased myself between the old stone wall and the skip. One leap and I was in.

It was mostly rubbish – bits of skirting thrust through with rusty nails and lumps of old plaster, a length of twisted curtain I didn't recognise. This I dragged free, releasing a cloud of choking dust.

I don't know what I was looking for – and, anyway, I didn't find it. All I found was an old Roberts radio that used to sit on my work-bench in the garage. I pulled it out and blew off the dust. I switched it on. It didn't work, of course – but that didn't matter. I climbed out of the skip and moved off down the road, the radio gripped tight by my side. With every step I took I became more certain that the radio was what I'd been looking for and that holding on to it and never letting it go was vital. I carried it all the way to the station and sat with it clasped in both hands on my lap. In time the train came and I boarded it, taking a seat, as before, at the window. As the train moved off, I gripped the radio even tighter than before, as if it were my last real connection with the world of the past.

34

A Woman of No Importance

When Libbie arrived in London in the summer of 1891, she found a city in a great tumult of change. The railways were burrowing their way beneath the streets, causing chaos and a thick choking dust (this made worse by a heatwave – the hottest for thirty years), while, above ground, great baroque stations were rising, and ever more bridges and tunnels and, in the West End, twelve-storey, 400-room 'monster' hotels, and huge new department stores teeming with shoppers seeking goods from all over the vast sprawling empire. In the working-class East End, the tide of immigrants was at its height, providing the fast-spreading factories, docks and squalid sweat-shops with the endless natural flesh-and-blood resource they demanded, and without which nothing could be dyed, stitched or beaten into shape, and then sold on for a profit scarcely a penny of which would accrue to the Jews or Italians or Irish or Poles whose bodies were bruised and made prematurely aged by the glorious sanctified great God of commerce. It was a city of riches made richer every day by cruel and systematic abuse – a place waist-deep in a stinking moral darkness whose elegant face could be lighted now and wondered at at the casual flick of an electrical switch.

With three weeks to pass before her ship left Southampton for America, Libbie Custer embarked on a series of sight-seeing trips around the city. She took tea in Mayfair at the Royal Hotel and bought presents for home at the new stores in Kensington. She went riding in Hyde Park and attended three dinners at the American Embassy in Grosvenor Square. It was at one of these – a 'themed' evening commemorating the thirtieth anniversary of the beginning of the Civil War – that Libbie made the acquaintance of Robert Todd Lincoln, son of the late president and currently American ambassador at the Court of St James – and it was through him that she first heard the name Florence Maybrick.

Born in Alabama, Florence Elizabeth Maybrick became, at the age of twenty-five in 1881, the wife of James Maybrick, a dour and successful cotton-broker from Liverpool. A rather dim, flighty woman with, so it is said, the most penetrating blue eyes, she was (besides the blueness of her eyes) apparently so entirely unremarkable that even her own mother, the three-times-married (and three times widowed) Baroness Von Roque (herself quite a case, but for entirely different reasons), described her as 'mediocre' and 'not a woman of much penetration'. She was, indeed, a woman of no importance – and so, were it not for the events that were to follow (and continue, in a sense, to this day), would she have remained. However. In the summer of 1889, at the age of thirty-seven, Florence Maybrick was arrested and tried for the murder of her husband – accused, specifically, of boiling up fly papers, so draining them of their arsenic, which, when collected in sufficient quantities, she would slip into her husband's afternoon tea. Happily for her, her husband, besides being dull beyond belief, was a well-known hypochondriac, so little was suspected in the way of foul play when, in late spring, he took to his bed – only to be nursed there by his blue-eyed, doting wife.

Well, he died, of course, but it was only then – during the haphazard police investigation that, by law, was bound to follow – that one of the Maybrick servants remembered a strange acrid smell, and another having glimpsed, months previously, a bowl filled with fly paper and 'milky-coloured' water. And so Florence was arrested and, in due course, sent for trial – during which much was revealed about her (principally, allegations of a number of affairs, to support which there were letters) that did not help her case. What did not help her, also, was the judge, Mr Justice Stephen, who was old, sick and daft, and seemed convinced one minute she was innocent and the next that she was guilty.

On August 7th 1889, under close direction from His Lordship, the court at the Liverpool Assizes found Florence Maybrick guilty of murder, and she was sentenced to hang. In due course (this was years later), thanks to a combination of a persuasive legal challenge (the trial, it was argued, had been grossly mishandled) and a general public outcry at such a harsh sentence (she had, after all, been terribly provoked by a hard and brutal bully), the sentence was commuted to a life spent in prison. Even this, however, was not enough for the American ladies of London society (including the wives of the ambassador and his deputy), and a further campaign was mounted whose aim was her immediate release.

'*A prison?*'

It was this campaign to which, in the summer of 1891, the famous name of Libbie Custer was added.

'Yes, right here – on this site.'

Twenty miles south-east of London, the town of Woking is, these days, itself a kind of prison – a comfortable, middle-class, car-washing, lawn-mowing, going-nowhere prison.

'Really? How interesting!'

And what remains of the prison itself houses, these days, the local branch of the Citizens Advice Bureau.

'So you didn't know?'

The middle-aged woman at reception shook her head. 'Heavens!' she said. 'Not a clue!' She was smiling wildly: indeed, she had about her that slightly crazed look of volunteers everywhere – as if (in her case) she'd come perhaps for advice about how best to boil the flesh off the bones of a newly murdered husband but had somehow got taken for staff.

I leaned forward, told her she was sitting where the women's condemned cell had been. The smile fled her face; a sharp intake of breath.

'Oh my!' she said.

And it was through there, I said, pointing to the wall behind her and whatever lay beyond, that Roland Jackson, the hangman, had sat waiting on a hard chair testing his ropes and raising and lowering the hard-sprung trap-door.

'You mean,' she said, glancing at the wall then away, as if she could see there some grotesque and terrible apparition, 'in Mrs Furst's office?'

I nodded. At that moment the door opened. Mrs Furst (I assumed) stepped out all breezy. 'Mr Templeton?' she said, looking straight at me.

'Pardon?' I said.

She smiled and I smiled back: the teacher and the new boy on the first day of term.

'Ten o'clock?' she said.

'What about it?' I said.

She closed her eyes, nodding. 'Come on now, Mr Templeton,' she said, her voice persuasive, almost down to a whisper, 'don't be shy!'

I glanced at the reception woman, expecting to be sprung, but she was just staring into space and didn't look too well.

'Mr Templeton?' said Mrs Furst, a note of steel now in her voice. 'Are we ready or not?'

I stood up. 'All right then,' I said. 'If you insist.'

'Splendid!' she said. 'Now, won't you come on through and we'll see what we can do?'

The rules at the prison were severe; no talking was allowed, and only one half-hour visit a month. In August of 1891, following much discussion amongst what the *Daily Sketch* called 'the Ladies of the Embassy', it was agreed that Libbie Custer – herself a widow, and a woman who, consequently, knew much about suffering and its toll – would attend, and so offer what consolation could be given to a soul about to die.

It was a glorious summer day when, at ten o'clock prompt, a carriage pulled up outside the prison gates and out stepped the 49-year-old widow of the famous general. As ever, she was dressed in black and carried a small black Venetian fan. She crossed the baking forecourt and asked directions of the policeman standing guard at the gate. A small side-gate was opened and the visitor admitted. She was shown then to a small waiting-room, where she sat on a hard chair and thought about the interview to come. *My only hope*, she later wrote, *was that I might find and deliver some words of consolation, and that, through my own experience of death's shadow. I might cause a little light to shine where there was only darkness, and so illuminate a little hope where, truly, there was none.*

At a little after ten-thirty, Elizabeth Custer was sitting upright on a hard straight-backed chair when a door at the other end of the room opened and the prisoner was led in. The prisoner was dressed in a shapeless blue smock made of thick, coarse fabric, her hair, once so abundant, cut severely now and what remained folded up into a plain white cap.

'*Now then.*'

About her shoulders was a heavy brown cape marked with a large black arrow.

'Won't you take a seat?'

Her face was pale through lack of sunlight and poor diet; her hands shook when, sitting, she laid them, palms up, in her lap.

'Look –' I said, feeling suddenly guilty.

Between her and her visitor sat a warden, so partly obscuring one from the other. From outside in the yard came the sounds of a scaffold's construction: the striking of hammers on the heads of nails, cursing, the whistling of workmen, the creaking of wood.

'You know,' said Mrs Furst, half smiling and half frowning in a I'm-here-to-listen kind of way, 'whatever occurs within these four walls will remain confidential.'

'Right,' I said. 'It's just –'

She raised a hand. 'Please sit,' she said. 'Do.' She indicated the low, deeply bowed armchair before her desk. Seeing it made me want to sit down and rest. She nodded, encouraging.

'Look,' I said, 'I really shouldn't be here. I only dropped in on my way to the airport –'

'Please,' said Mrs Furst, 'don't you think you'd be more comfortable if you sat?'

'Well –'

'*I* think you would –'

'OK,' I said. 'But just for a minute.' I circled the chair and sat.

'Comfy?' said Mrs Furst.

'Comfy,' I said.

'Now then,' she said. 'What's the problem?'

'The problem?'

She sat forward. 'Is it your finances?'

'Finances?'

'Have you money troubles? Is there debt?'

'Well, yes,' I said. There was something in her earnestness that compelled me not to lie.

'I see.'

'But that's not why I'm here.'

'It's not?'

'*No.* It's like I've been trying to tell you. I shouldn't be here at all. I *should* be at the airport. I just came to look at the prison – or rather where the prison used to be.'

She frowned; this time there was no smile to follow. She leaned forward. 'You mean you're *not* Mr Templeton?'

'No.'

'Then who *are* you?'

I told her the first name that came into my head.

The frown deepened. 'You mean the *writer?*'

'What?' I said.

Suddenly she rose, crossed to a black leather bag hanging from a coat-stand. She fished around inside the bag, pulled out a book, held it up for me to see. 'You wrote *this?*' she said.

'Well –'

'*Really?*'

Oh Jesus. Without meaning to I nodded, aware suddenly of the armchair's embrace.

'But this is amazing!'

I looked away; my cheeks were burning.

She turned the book around, held it out at arm's length, staring at it wide-eyed.

I pushed up, and on the second attempt made it to standing. 'Look, I'd better go,' I said.

She lowered the book. 'Go?'

'I have to get to the airport.'

'Airport?'

'I'll miss my plane.'

She stepped towards me; I tried to step back, but the armchair forbade it.

'What is it?' I said. 'Are you all right?' She looked crazy: there were tears in her eyes. I closed my own, and was bracing myself for the sting of a slap or the deadly insertion of a blade between my ribs, when she said something up close, her words muffled, distorted by the pounding of my blood.

I opened my eyes to slits. 'Excuse me?' I said. She was standing before me, her face flushed, the opened-out spine-broken book in one hand, a CAB pen in the other.

'Would you?' she said, holding out the pen.

'What?'

'Please? You've no idea how much it would mean –'

'Oh look, I'm really *not* . . . I didn't *mean* –'

'*Oh please!*'

But then the pen found my hand and my fingers curled around it. She laid the book open on the desk. I looked up at her face; she had the crazed adoring smile of a nun in the presence of Jesus.

'Oh please,' she said.

I looked down, paused a moment, signed the page with a flourish.

'Oh thank you,' she said, lifting the book, though, at the same time, scarcely daring to touch it.

'It was nothing,' I said. I felt wretched. I passed back the pen; she gathered it like a relic. 'Now I should go.'

I was out in the street and heading for my car when a hand on my shoulder stopped me dead. I turned. It was Mrs Furst. She had a look on her face like thunder.

'Oh God,' I said.

She dropped her hand. 'There's something I have to ask you,' she said.

I glanced at my car: it was three steps away, maybe four.

'I have to ask you – *and I want the truth now –*' She paused; the thunder drifted off. She leaned towards me. 'Is there,' she said, her voice down to a whisper, 'ever going to be another?'

'Another?' I said.

'A sequel,' she hissed.

'A sequel?' She was up close and nodding now, and I got the strongest feeling that her question only had one acceptable answer.

'Well?' she said.

'Yes,' I said, and I patted my pocket, inside which lay parts of my father's book.

'There is? Oh Lord!' The whisper was forgotten now; in the street, passers-by were starting to look. I edged towards the car, followed every step by Mrs Furst. 'Does it,' she said breathlessly, 'have a title – this sequel?'

I reached for the car door, pulled it open, slipped in, slammed it shut. At once, she was tapping on the window. I buzzed it down about an inch and a half. 'It's called *Corelli Part Two*,' I said. '*The Revenge.*'

'Revenge?' she said. 'But who –'

I buzzed up the window, started the car, pulled away. As I turned at the corner, heading north for the airport, I glanced in the mirror. There on the pavement, where there'd once been a prison, a small crowd had gathered, their arms raised in a wave, and their faces turned towards me, pale and pious, as if I were Jesus Christ and they my abandoned disciples.

35

Gene

'What's that you're reading?'

I gripped the book, tried to shut down my ears.

'It's not that Corelli book, is it?'

Shortly after Libbie Custer's visit to Woking prison, the sentence of death imposed on Florence Maybrick was commuted by the Home Office to a term of life imprisonment, of which she served fifteen years. The reasons behind the Home Secretary's decision for mercy remain –

'Hey –'

– remain, still, unclear. However, rumours –

A nudge; I braced myself. Another. I looked up. '*What?*'

'You OK?'

'I'm fine,' I said. 'I'm just trying to read.'

'Sure thing.'

I focused again on the page. The stewardess was clinking glasses in the aisle.

Gene, from Duluth, leaned back in his seat.

However, rumours that the woman was pregnant at the time of her arrest and incarceration (and therefore could not, by English law, be –

Then started tapping on the armrest.

– by English law, be –

And whistling.

– English law, be –

A creaking of a seat, another nudge.

– BE EXECUTED –

I closed my eyes. I felt him lean towards me. 'Did you know,' he said, 'that she's read the damn thing twelve times right through? Twelve times! Right through! Jesus Christ! Swears the damn thing's changed her life.' He shook his head, sighing. 'Can't see it, though. She's still got a tumour in her head the size of a goddamn tennis ball.'

My eyes froze hard on the page. *A tumour in her head.* I sneaked a look. Gene was staring out of the window – looking down at the chequerboard fields below.

I heard him turn. 'How many times you read *that* book?' he said.

'Just once,' I said. *Size of a tennis ball.* 'Or rather, this is the first time.'

'Ain't it no good then?'

'It's fine,' I said.

'What's it about?'

I folded the book around my finger, showed him the cover. 'It's a life of Florence Maybrick.'

'You mean the *nurse?*'

'The nurse?'

'The *nurse* – you *know.*'

'That was Florence Nightingale.' I turned the book, opening it at my page.

However, rumours that the woman was pregnant at the time of her arrest and incarceration (and therefore could not, by English law, be –

'So who's Florence whatsit, then?'

This time I didn't look up.

'She was the wife of James Maybrick.'

Gene the bridge engineer from Duluth shrugged. He leaned over, peering at the words on the page. 'What'd he do then, this James Maystick?'

'Maybrick.'

'Whatever. He some kind of engineer, maybe?'

'He was a cotton trader,' I said. Gene's breath was warm on my face – the same breath, the same warmth, that he breathed, no doubt, on the face of his obsessive, dying wife.

'You mean like Jimmy Smits in that movie?'

I lifted my eyes. 'Maybe,' I said. 'I don't know. He was also Jack the Ripper.'

'Jack the who?'

'Jack the Ripper. The world's first recorded serial killer.'

'Jesus.'

'He killed prostitutes in London in the 1880s. And then he was murdered by his wife.'

'The *nurse*, you mean? He was killed by a *nurse?*'

Gene's face, though swollen-looking and fleshy, was pale. There were heavy dark circles beneath his eyes.

'That's right,' I said. 'It was a scandal.' It was the face – they were the eyes – of a man who couldn't sleep for fear of what the morning, one morning, would bring.

'Jesus,' he said. He shook his head. 'I know you hear *stories*, but for something like that to happen to somebody you *know* –' His eyes, with their circles, looked bruised, like the eyes of a boxer who's beaten and he knows it, but whose corner just won't let him quit. He shook his head again, turned to me. 'So what happened?' he said.

'What happened? You mean to the nurse?'

He nodded. 'Did they catch her?'

'Yes,' I said. 'They caught her. She was tried and sentenced to death. But then, because they thought she was pregnant, they changed it to life.'

'She had a *baby?*'

'No. No baby. Turned out she wasn't pregnant at all. Either that or she had a miscarriage. At any rate, she served fifteen years of her sentence, and then they released her.'

'Where'd she go then?'

'Alabama.'

'*Alabama?* Jesus, Lord, *I'm* from Alabama!'

'I thought you said Duluth?'

'No, sir. I *live* in Duluth. I'm *from* Alabama.'

'Small world,' I said.

'Jesus Christ, you ain't wrong there.'

I looked down at my book. *Following her release, she returned to Alabama, where she died at the age of seventy-six on December 7th 1941.* 'Apparently,' I said, 'she died on the same day the Japanese bombed

Pearl Harbor.' I looked up. Gene from Alabama was gazing out of the window, looking down with great sadness at the living, breathing, tumourless world below.

Part Three

The Afterlife

36

Furniture and Flags

She always returned to her home in Georgia,* there to sit amongst her things – all her relics of their past – and attempt to recover those energies that seemed to dwindle with every year and every speech and every mile undertaken in the service of her husband's sacred memory. She'd sit in the silence of the log cabin's walls and turn over in her mind all that had happened – replaying conversations thirty and forty years distant – or walk with the aid, now, of a stick through the woods, always dressed in widow's black, her ears tuned to the sound of barking dogs or the chatter of voices growing louder, the owners of which, it had become her experience, were invariably clasping copies of her books to be signed or the para- phernalia required for the taking of souvenir photographs. On hearing them she would stop and stand quite still – neither trying to avoid detection nor to promote it, for both were useless – and just wait, then, for the moment when her name would be called and the show and her duty would begin once again. *Excuse me*, they'd say, approaching her carefully as if they feared any minute she'd take fright and run, *are you* – and she'd nod and smile, and sometimes (if they spoke with admiration for the general) she'd let them follow her back to the cabin. Here, amongst the clutter of furniture and flags, she'd watch with satisfaction their eyes grow wide (*This table*, she'd sometimes say, tapping with an elegant gloved finger on the polished oak surface, *was where the Civil War*

---

* Due principally to the success of her books (three volumes of memoirs) and frequent speaking engagements, Mrs Custer was able to afford a large house in Bronxville, New York, a cottage in the Adirondacks, and a log-built summer home in central Georgia. It was to the latter that she usually retired on returning from a trip, as she increasingly found the noise and heat of New York tiresome and enervating.

ended, and they'd stare at the thing as if at a piece of the true cross), and she'd stand for them and for the generations to come, erect and imperious, on the porch in the last of the afternoon sun as spindly legs were extended and velvet hoods ducked under and the images created that exist now on walls and on the shelves of libraries in the pages of history books. In time, of course, she'd watch even the keenest and most curious visitors go, and she'd retire then to her canvas-walled bedroom, there to dream in the cool of her mono-grammed sheets her solitary private unrecorded dreams.

'Do you have an appointment?'

With seven bedrooms and four bathrooms, three garages and a basement playroom, the house in Bronxville, New York, was apparently a 'bargain' at $2.3 million.

'An appointment?'

'An appointment, yes. You must have an appointment.'

I smiled, said I was just passing, saw the ad in the real-estate window.

The woman (Mrs Johnson, the owner, I assumed) shook her head. 'I don't care,' she said. 'I let you in, you could be anybody.' She frowned. 'And anyway, there *isn't* a picture. This is a private sale.'

I fished around in my pocket, pulled out a folded-up piece of paper, spread it out, passed it over.

'What's that?' she said, glancing down at it then back up, as if she feared it might, in some way, if she touched it, contaminate her.

'The house,' I said. '*Your* house. I photocopied it from a library in Monroe.'

'Monroe?'

'Monroe, Michigan.'

Gingerly, she took the sheet. 'Who are you?' she said, her eyes flicking back and forth as she scanned the article.

I told her, and explained what I was doing. She looked up.

'Custer?' she said.

'His wife, yes. She lived here.'

'His wife?'

'You didn't know?'

She looked down again at the sheet. 'I had no idea,' she said. She turned it over. It was blank on the back. 'Are you sure?'

'About him having a wife?'

'About her living in this house.'

I said I was sure.

She passed the paper back, considered me, sceptical. 'And you just want to have a look?'

'Just a look,' I said.

Suddenly the frown slipped away. 'And if I do show you round,' she said, smiling, 'will you put me in your book?'

'I promise,' I said.

And now I have.

In the summer, when she felt the need of company (but couldn't stand the city heat, Libbie Custer would ride the train north fifteen miles to Lawrence Park. Here, in an enclave on the edge of Bronxville filled with writers and artists, she would work on her articles for New York magazines and entertain visitors come up for the day from the city. Of these, those who knew her would find nothing strange in the vision of an increasingly elderly lady, dressed head to toe in black, sitting in the shade of the trees at the end of her garden, turning the pages of a closely written manuscript or listening to songs on her wind-up gramophone. Nor – unlike first-timers, who, on approaching across the grass, prepared themselves for either spikiness or decrepitude (or both) – did it ever surprise *them* to hear her talk with authority of events in the world, or the people – often people she'd known – whose faces looked out from the pages of the *Washington Post* and the *New York Times*.

'Come with me.'

People like the Empress Elizabeth of Austria, stabbed to death in the absence of her husband on the shores of Lake Geneva.

'Where are we going?'

Or Henry James, newly an Englishman.

'There's something I want to show you.'

Or Tsar Alexander III, long dead, his family dead now too.

'In the trees?'

We were crossing the wide lawn as so many others had done, approaching a table surrounded by chairs, set on a circular, stone-coloured surface.

'Here.'

Standing at the far edge, in the shade of those trees, Mrs Johnson pointed down towards a shape in the stone.

'What is it?' I said.

Concrete, not stone.

'Have a look.'

I kneeled down. It was the indentation of a hand, fingers splayed, and letters beneath it. I looked up. 'Seriously?' I said. She nodded. I looked down.

'She signed it – do you see?'

I squinted: it was true – three letters, LBC, straight and steady. I reached out my hand, placed it on the shadow of hers.

'So what do you think?'

I opened my mouth, but nothing came. All that came was the feeling that Libbie, in that moment, was beside me. It was a feeling that was with me still, an hour later, as I sat gazing out from the train heading south as the backyards and playgrounds of the suburbs gave way to the city's heat and grime.

37

When This Cruel War is Over

By noon I was sitting in the bar of the Algonquin Hotel on 44th Street, half looking through my father's *Life* and half watching the people passing by. As I watched them smiling, and the casual way they greeted one another with what seemed to me then (unreasonably, I know) a complete and stupid disregard for what bad things might lie ahead for them or good things might not, I couldn't help thinking about Libbie's hand and how close I'd come – and whether that, in the end, was as close as I'd ever get. I tried not to think this, and so, for distraction, I thought of Gene from Alabama/Duluth and set myself to wondering what *he'd* find when *he* got home, and how soon the cancer that had claimed Karen and taken *her* away to God knows where would come finally for *his* wife.

A clatter of bags; I looked down again at the page. *He charged and routed the rebels at Winchester.*

Voices, raised: 'Hey, be careful with that –'

And I wondered again if he, too, would go crazy like me and break out of the comfort and safety of home – to escape the familiar – only to find himself hiding out in the loud, jarring world, bereft and bemused like a deaf man abandoned on the median of a busy highway, or a child in a shopping-mall in the hour before closing.

The voices moved off down the hall; the *ping* of the lift-bell, and they were swallowed and gone. I took a mouthful of beer; it seemed like fizzy air. I settled down in my chair. *He charged and routed the rebels at Winchester, claiming the town for the north and for Lincoln.* In my mind's idle eye, then, I tried to picture the great man – the real Lincoln – but could only find the fake. Oh, he was tall and thin, all right, and wearing the president's immensely tall hat, and though his beard was huge and as dark as it should be, it was, in his case, half hanging off and half clinging to his chin, while behind him, slumped over a table scattered with cards, a man with golden hair and a uniform of blue was snoring and dribbling, his spittle spreading dark across the table's green baize. I took another sip, cleaned my glasses, read on – *for the north and for Lincoln, and command of a division for himself, then on to Tom's Brook and Cedar Creek, where the nearly beaten Sheridan promoted him to major-general* – but in the way that one memory will always beget another, all I could think of was sitting in the bright-green McGinty's Irish Pub, then standing at a screen door at some house in the suburbs, peering in. *Caroline? She left.* Then a squealing of tyres and a car disappearing, high speed, down the road. I lowered the typescript. *She left. Didn't even take her coat.* Unbidden, her image came to me. She was smiling.

Didn't even take her coat.

I closed my father's *Life*.

According to the operator, there are thirteen bars called McGinty's in the state of Michigan – but, happily, only one in the city of Monroe. I dialled the number, no idea what I was planning to say or why I was calling. I sat on the bed and listened to the ring tone.

No answer.

I reached over to the mini-bar, fished around for a beer, flipped the top, lay back.

'Yes?'

I sat up. 'Is that McGinty's?'

'Who's this?'

'Look, you don't know me but I was hoping you could help me –'

'*What?*'

'It's about Caroline.'

'Caroline?'

'Caroline Downey.'

Silence. Breathing.

'Hello?'

'Look, buddy, what do you want?'

'I told you, I was just wondering –'

'She ain't here.'

'No. I know –'

'Well, if you *know* –'

'It's just I was hoping you might know where she went –'

'Look, who the fuck *are* you? Is that Jason?'

'Jason?'

'Jesus fucking Christ –'

The phone clicked dead. For a moment I sat with the humming in my ear, the image of Caroline and her sister still before me. *She just left. She ain't here.* Then I set down the receiver and lay back on the bed. In a while I flicked on the TV: *Come to Grenada – America's paradise!* Undoubtedly there were a million places the two girls could be, and none of them sinister – and none of them anything to do with me. I flicked channels. *The Love Boat.* I chugged back the beer and tried to turn my mind to other things.

Libbie joined her new husband whenever she could, often undertaking the most perilous journeys in order to be with him at the front. Mostly sleeping under canvas and often within the sound of the guns, she determined to endure whatever he endured – to experience his life so that it might become *hers* in all its danger and deprivation.

All of which is not to say that the life of the general – and so *hers* – was without its comforts. There was, for example, Eliza, the general's 25-year-old black cook, who, on hearing of the president's Emancipation Proclamation, had simply set down the potatoes she'd been peeling for supper, then stepped out of the kitchen and away from her master's failing plantation, heading north then towards freedom, where, at Amosville, Virginia, on the banks of the Rappahannock River, she met a soldier, newly a general and newly married too, who offered his protection in exchange for her services as maid and cook. 'Well?' he said, when she seemed undecided. 'What do you say?' What she said was, 'I reckon I would,' and so the deal was made. It was an appointment of which Libbie entirely approved, freeing her as it did to concentrate on becoming the kind of wife that the general and the times required – the kind of wife, that is, devoted to the three roles articulated in *Mrs Cadogan's Wife's Companion*, the first two of which – 'On Being Your Husband's Hostess' and 'On Being Your Husband's Confidante' – Libbie was soon performing with outstanding success. In private, always an uncritical and devoted listener, she developed, in public, an unfaltering command of army politics – a skill she deployed right up to the end when her husband's name was being advanced as perhaps that of the next president – and even beyond – perhaps *especially* beyond – when the face of the martyr needed polishing when tarnished, and when a fickle and increasingly ungrateful nation needed reminding of the heroism and selflessness of those gone before.

But all that, then, was still to come – still a future unknown. *Then* there was still the future expected – that certain future decreed by the third of Mrs Cadogan's rules for marriage.

Children.

That both husband and wife wanted children is beyond question – indeed, it wasn't even a question. It was just what people *did*, what *happened*. Why, for the Custers, it *didn't* happen no one knows. It certainly wasn't for the want of trying (Custer, in his letters to Libbie, declares himself on several occasions 'in desperate need' of the 'usual *ride* before breakfast') – nor was it for the want of wishing. 'I think of the day of peace,' said Libbie, 'when little children's voices will call to us. I long for my little boy and girl.' That there was, perhaps, some physical barrier on one or either part is unknown and will remain so (Custer, as a young man, had, after all, been far from celibate and could have contracted an undetected and, consequently, untreated disease); the consequences, however, of this childlessness are not. In Custer it produced profound feelings of personal and private failure: a failure as a man – an inability to perform – made, by the absence of children, public, and, consequently, humiliating – a humiliation made all the more acute by his own presence as one of his father's ten children. How this failure – this lack of a personal stake in the future – affected his future actions

196

one can only speculate. It seems likely, however, that the lack of an heir retarded to some degree (and with no little irony) the shedding of his own youthful recklessness.

'*Yes?*'

It is, perhaps, also no coincidence that his nickname 'The Boy General' stuck – just as, looking back, it seems inevitable that he should have died young; unthinkable, indeed, that there could ever have been an elderly, subdued George Custer.

'Who is this?'

And it is, perhaps, ironic that it was in the end this over-aged recklessness which led to his great and famous, foolish defeat on that hillside one Sunday in Montana, that relieved him of having to fight (and inevitably lose) the cruel and bitter war of attrition fought between the past and what's to come, between youth and old age.

I closed my eyes tight.

'Hello?'

'Look,' I say. I'm still shaking now from a dream.

'Ah, *Jesus* –'

'I rang before –'

'I know.'

'About Caroline?'

'I *said* I know. Now, what the fuck do you want?'

Well, I just had this dream.

'Hey, I asked you a fuckin' question –'

We were standing, me and her, on the street in warm sunshine – I was smiling with the news, I could hardly believe it –

'Look, buddy, don't think I can't hear you. You think I can't fuckin' hear you?'

'What?'

There's my hand, see, on her belly. Then I look up: she's smiling too – but it's a weird kind of smile. 'Hey, what's wrong?' I'm saying, and just then it breaks the skin of her temple, round and grey like a lamb's heart but hard like a baseball, and I'm reaching and trying to force the thing back or out or something but I can't get a hold and I'm trying to get a hold but it's slippery, everything's slippery, and I'm stumbling then and losing my footing, then I'm slipping and sliding down some slippery chute and calling out and yelling –

'What the fuck?'

Click and a dial tone.

'Hello?' I say – and just then there's a tapping on my door. I turn; the door opens, as if on my cue.

'Señor?'

An ochre-skinned girl, a trolley piled with sheets. I turn away, watch myself putting the telephone back into its cradle. It occurs to me then that there are neither jokes nor dreams. And it occurs to me *then* that, thought I'd thought the war over, it goes on.

38

The Table

The war ended as it had begun: in a place nobody had heard of – at a tiny clapboard courthouse in a clearing called Appomatox. Mr Robert E. Lee, gentleman butcher, and Ulysses Grant, the upstart, street-smart butcher's boy, sat around a table* no bigger than a card table, dealing, trading, while their armies (or what was left of them after they'd finished with them) lay seething, exhausted and bitter as much in victory as defeat, in the fields and the dirt-roads all around. Absurd and polite, they talked of the weather, and whether the thing they had done could have been done better. All agreed it could not. It had been a good fight, fought to the end, and now it was over.

Except it wasn't really over at all. All that had really been completed was the military bit – the fancy-dress entrée; still to come was what was always going to follow – the main course, so to speak – the lynchings, the poverty, the shots ringing out from a Memphis motel, the cities dividing, parting like black and white seas, as if by some prophet in pursuit of applause.

'Is that the real historic table?'

Death had come and had its carnival. Now, people thought, was the time to go home.

'Sure it's it. What did you expect?'

'I dunno. Something bigger, I guess.'

Except –

'Like what?'

Except for a soldier like Custer who knew nothing else – a man for whom the army was his real and only home.

* Now part of the Appomatox exhibit in the Smithsonion Museum, Washington.

'Like I say, I dunno –'

And for Libbie, of course, whose home, then and always, was and would be her husband.

'You mean like MacArthur's? You mean like on that ship with the Japs?'

For them – and for so many like them – there was only, now, with the arrival of peace, the prospect of some sleep-walking, sleep-marching, fort-to-fort hibernation – a kind of marching on the spot while they waited for the next war, the next call to arms.

'The Japs? What Japs?'

All of which is not to say that there wasn't celebrating – for there was – it's just that for soldiers like Custer it was the sharp and shallow celebration of one job completed when there is no other in sight. He'd be lost, in time, and he knew it – he knew that all he'd gained would soon be swept away before the glad tide of peace.

'On that ship – you know. Fuckin' what's-his-name –'

Soon – but not yet. First there was Libbie to find (she'd not been allowed, this time, so close to the final bitter fighting), and their own particular celebrating to do; first there was *now*, and who cares about tomorrow?

'No, I don't fuckin' know.'

'Jesus, Rufus –'

'What?'

'Don't you fuckin' know nothin'?'

Though it was small – the table – and built of dark pine, and stood only mid-thigh on elegantly turned legs, it was well worth the eighteen dollars in gold General Sheridan offered for its purchase. When the deal was done (it cost him twenty dollars), he set it on the courthouse verandah and sent word to Custer, into whose hand had been passed the rebels' flag of surrender. When at last he appeared, he found Sheridan in uncharacteristic good humour. The table, said the older man, was a gift for Libbie – offered by a grateful nation to her 'very gallant husband'. Then, when the two men had shaken hands and General Sheridan had withdrawn, the 26-year-old Custer bounded down the steps and out across the yard, whooping and yelling for Libbie, the small, dark-pine table balanced neatly on his head.

He rode hard and found her at last where he'd sent her – in Richmond, in bed, upstairs in the rebels' own White House, her clothes neatly folded and shoes set together before the huge, ornate dressing-table last used by Mrs President Davis before the south's war was lost. He was, according to Libbie, 'tanned, but thin and worn', and in possession, he said, of a gift from General Sheridan. It was, he said, 'a piece of true history'. She would have to get up to see it.

After Richmond, the couple, the table and the white towel used by the rebels to surrender returned to Custer's command at Petersburg. It was here, while exchanging stories of the past and speculating on an uncertain future, that news of President Lincoln's assassination filtered in. At first there was shock – a stunned disbelief – but this soon gave way to anger and a call for retribution. 'Treason,' said Andrew Johnson, the incoming president, 'is the blackest of crimes,' and he asserted then (with Custer's wholehearted approval) that 'Extermination is the only true policy we can adopt toward the leaders of the rebellion. Our nation shall be purged from every disloyal traitor.'

Extermination.

It was a word that, having once entered the lexicon of political life, would prove hard to remove. It carried with it a terrible, daring honesty – an acknowledgement of what everyone knew but all were too delicate – too spuriously gentlemanly – to say: that is, that the point of war isn't *fighting*, but *killing* – that it's not about *battles* but *bodies*; that the best path is the most brutal, and the greatest heroes are and always should be those with the bloodiest hands.

Heroes like Grant. Like Lee. Like Sheridan.

And like Custer, who, on May 23rd 1864, as he rode with his men down Pennsylvania Avenue, was so proud of his part in the democratic slaughter (although he'd no clear idea where the thing might lead), and so determined that it and he should not be forgotten, that, somehow – quite by chance, of course – his battle-hardened, quite unspookable horse Don Juan was mysteriously spooked by a garland of flowers, and so took off (its rider bare-headed, golden locks flowing) past the reviewing stand and the gentlemen of the press, who couldn't, of course, help but notice (and pass on their observations to their exhausted but star-struck readers) the graceful mastery with which the Boy General managed to rein in his horse and so save the day, before returning, to great cheers, to the head of his division.

'You've reached the Monroe city sheriff's office. My name is Sherry. How may I help you?'

It was a performance that served further to underline what the public already knew of the man – that he was bold and dashing; that it was with men like Custer that the future of America lay –

'It's about a missing person –'

That it was in hands like his that the promises made by the founding fathers would be made flesh and soil, and through the action of such men that America would surely, given time, conquer first the continent and then the whole world, so creating the greatest empire known to man.

'OK, sir. How long has this person been missing?'

'Well, I don't know –'

'You don't know, sir?'

'Not exactly, no.'

'Well –'

'You see, she just took off with her sister –'

'She's with her sister?'

'And she didn't take her coat. She just left. Hello?'

'Sir, are you a relative?'

'Well, no –'

'And you can't say for sure how long she's been missing?'

'No.'

'And you say she's with her sister?'

'Yes – she's missing too.'

'Sir –'

'What? Don't you believe me?'

'If you tell me the names I'll make some enquiries.'

'You will?'

'I just said I would, sir. Now, do you have the names?'

'Caroline and Trudi.'

'And the surname?'

'Downey, I think.'

'You're not sure of the surname?'

'Well, no, not exactly. I only know them from the bar. Well, one of them. The other one – Caroline – I don't know about her. Hello? Hello? Are you there?'

On the afternoon following the grand parade, George Custer said goodbye to his men. With his wife by his side (she wearing a black velvet riding cap with a red peacock feather, so echoing her husband's famous red scarf), he rode along the entire length of the division, receiving cheer after cheer. In a brief speech, he gave thanks to 'the Great God of battles', and then to the men themselves. The victory, he said, was their victory, and he just a part of it. It was a fine, affecting speech, and brought tears to Libbie's eyes. For her – as much as for her husband – that moment in the slow-fading sunlight was one she would never forget. It was perfect – they had everything.

And then they rode away.

39

Reading the Signs

A hundred miles south of Waco on I–35 lies the city of Austin, capital of Texas. It's a small pretty city in a big ugly state, and just about the only place in the Redneck Republic where the natives won't look at you as if they'd rather be shooting you if you ask about hiring a bicycle.

I got mine from Smiling Dave's Spoke and Saddle Shop, a small, family-run concern on Sixth Street, between the Women At Work Gallery and the Blue Grove Drug Store. 'Sure thing! No problemo!' said Dave (he runs the outfit with his brother, Dave Jnr) when I asked for directions, and he was waving in my mirror, the advertised grin stretched wide across his face, as he watched me totter off.

'Take care now!'

I turned the corner out of sight into Zilker Park, where I promptly fell off, scraping my shoulder on the leading edge of a metal seat and grazing my elbow through my shirt and making it bleed.

'Hey – you OK?'

I pushed myself up on to my hands and knees. A pair of legs appeared before me, brown polished shoes, sharp-creased trousers.

'Do I *look* OK?' I said. My arm hurt like hell.

'Did you break something, you think?'

And then at last I was mostly upright again, my head pounding where I'd hit it. I squinted down at the man's face. He was chubby, maybe a foot shorter than me, hair above his ears, shiny head. 'I don't think so,' I said.

'That's good,' said the man. He smiled. He had one silver tooth set in two rows of white. 'Except for me.'

'What do you mean?'

He shrugged. He looked at my elbow. 'That hurt?' he said.

'Yes,' I said. The cloth of my shirt was already stuck fast to my elbow with blood.

''Cause it sure *looks* like it hurts some –'

Slowly, I peeled it away.

'Anything else?' he said.

'Like what?'

'Any twists? Any sprains? You fall awkward or something?'

'Well, sort of,' I said. 'Why?'

He slipped his hands into the pockets of his jacket, fished around for something. He pulled out a small pack of business cards, sliced the cellophane with his nail, separated one card and held it out. *Johnson T. Taylor*, it said, *Attorney at Law, Auto and Cycling Accidents a Speciality*, then an address, phone, e-mail, etc. 'Go on,' he said, 'take it.' He waggled it. 'Just in case.'

'In case of what?'

He frowned – but there was something behind it. 'In *case*,' he said slyly, edging forward, indicating my elbow with a nod, 'something develops.'

'Like what?'

He shrugged, bending with me as I stooped to pick up the bike. 'Who knows?'

'I'll be fine,' I said.

'Of course you will! For *now* –'

I eased on to the seat, fed my trainers into the pedal-buckles. 'Look, thanks for your help,' I said. 'But I have to go.' I pushed off gingerly. He walked beside me, his brown shoes clicking on the path. I worked the pedals; he fell behind.

Once out of the park, I headed east as Dave at the cycle shop had told me. The combination of exercise and cool air eased the throbbing in my elbow. Though I was annoyed with myself for having ignored his advice about the park ('You don't want to go in there,' he'd said mysteriously. 'No way! No, sir!'), I was soon moving well – just one of a number of cyclists out enjoying the warm summer air. I paused at a coffee shop and ordered iced tea and doughnuts. From the window I could see the State Capitol building, its dome rising pink in the sunshine. I felt mellow and glad to be where I was – grateful to be where nobody knew me and no phones or letters could find me.

Part, now, of the army of occupation, they stayed in an asylum for the state's blind but wealthy, in second-floor quarters from whose south-facing window they could see the Capitol's dome and, across the Colorado River, the city's asylum for the deaf and dumb. They gave parties and dances, where the women would sing while their husbands tried to guess what future lay ahead. For men like Custer – volunteers, not regular army – the most likely outcome was a transfer from the former to the latter, and a consequent drop in rank and pay. This, for Custer, meant an income quartered and a return to the rank of captain. It meant also that the soldiers over whom he would soon have command would have none of the zeal for a fight of volunteers, and would require, consequently, a kind of leader-ship that was new to him. No longer would he be able to win their loyalty by stirring appeals to patriotism, or by reminders of the danger posed to wives and children and homes. All that, with Appomatox and the war's end, was gone now. All that was left now for the common soldier to fight for – and all that would remain until a new threat was found – were abstractions: the idea of 'nation', of what was 'right', the unprovable worth of undertaking God's often entirely mysterious will. It was a situation to test the most flexible of commanders, amongst whose ranks George Custer would never be found. When, for example, in Texas, he saw men exhausted through marching, he'd convince himself it was weak-ness and march them even harder; when they complained of hunger, he'd deny them food; when they were thirsty, he'd cut their ration of water. He simply couldn't understand why the men now under his command weren't the whooping, virile men he'd known before – why they wouldn't march, wouldn't drill, wouldn't be *soldiers* just for the *love* – for the *rightness* – of it. It was a blindness – part wilful, part come from simple ignorance of the many shades of man – that, though useful in a killing war, in peace can lead only to discontent and disaster. Again, in Texas, a state rich in beef, he was quite prepared to let his men eat worm-ridden hogs' heads, and when, in order to supplement such meagre rations, some stole turkeys and a cow, he had the offenders lashed, their heads shaved, then paraded before the rest of the regiment. It was an event telling both of the times and of the man. Where, before, he had sought to gain his authority through respect for his daring deeds – now, when there were no longer any such deeds to be performed, he saw no other way to command but through fear of retribution. For Libbie, observing from a distance, there were signs of a disaster to come that she would not acknowledge. She would be forced to face them soon enough.

'*Are you sure?*'

Then finally, as expected, Custer's demotion from major-general in the Army of Volunteers to that of captain in the Fifth (Regular) Cavalry came at the end of January.

'Sure. The Austin Deaf and Dumb Asylum. Apparently you could see it from here on the second floor. It was just across the river.'

In preparation for leaving Texas, Libbie gave away the dogs and sold everything that couldn't be transported. What with the drop in pay and her husband's series of speculations all of which had gone bad,* it was money they would need to pay debts and help towards living expenses.

Mike Bates, chief archivist, Longmann Life Assurance, squinted across the river in the hard light, then down at the city plan, circa 1880, in his hands. He shook his head. 'They must have tore it down,' he said. 'Sorry.'

'It doesn't matter,' I said. I watched him fold the map, slip it back into its transparent pocket.

'It's hard to believe,' he said.

'You mean about them tearing it down?'

'No. *That* happens all the time. I mean about Custer.'

'Yeah, it *is* weird, isn't it?'

---

* Including, at one stage, the purchase of horseshoes for the cavalry. When they arrived, however, it was discovered they didn't fit. No one had checked.

'I guess if people knew, they maybe wouldn't hate him so much.'

'They still hate him in Texas – even now, after so long?'

'Oh *sure*. But maybe if they knew about the asylum –'

'You think him going over there and learning to sign might change things?'

'Hell, no. Not *that*. It's the riding thing that'll do it, if anything will. Him teaching them deaf and dumb folks to ride. Now that's a *Texas* thing. It's just a shame he didn't find them some oil. Reckon they'd make him a saint then.'

I stood for a while at the window when Mike was gone and tried again to square up the two sides of Custer – the vain, brutal martinet and the shy man who'd teach disabled people to ride and say nothing about it – but could not. They seemed so far apart – his actions those of two different men. I turned away – the puzzle still unsolved – and took the lift down. Back out in the street, the air had grown thick with the promise of a storm. I unlocked my bicycle and pushed off, heading out into the afternoon traffic.

When they left the city, Custer, Libbie and the faithful Eliza headed south down to Galveston on the Texas coast, then on to New Orleans. From there, in late February, they travelled by steamboat and train north to Michigan, arriving at last in Monroe. Lack of money denied them a house of their own, so, in mid-May, they took rooms in Libbie's parent's house. It was a cramped arrangement made worse by the state of her father's health. Indeed, so fast was the old man failing that only two days later, on May 18th, while Custer was riding the train south for Washington, hoping to meet the new president and secure some advancement, Daniel Stanton Bacon, at the age of sixty-eight, died.

For Libbie, the death of her father meant the last tie that bound her to the past had been cut. No longer a daughter, she was suddenly now only, exclusively, a wife. From then on there was nothing but her husband, right or wrong.

40

Destiny Manifest

'What are you thinking?'

We were sitting in the sunshine on the grass outside the office of the history department at Texas State University on the outskirts of Austin.

'Well, if you *really* want to know, I was thinking that if it's true that we're made in God's image, then it surely follows that *he* must be made in *ours* – and must, therefore, have all the same doubts and inconsistencies and downright bloody-mindedness that *we* have –'

Charlie Birdsall, assistant professor of American history, lay back and howled.

'What's the matter?'

'Oh, nothing,' he said. 'Go on.'

'OK. If you insist.'

'I do, I do.'

'Well, I was thinking, *then* – this being the case – that the *real* great mystery isn't how we came to be here or even why, but why, if we think of him at all, we think of him – of God – as a *good* God – as a kind and gentle God, as all-seeing and wise, when clearly he isn't. I mean he can't be – can he? – not if we're like him and he's like us – because we're not, are we?'

'Oh fuck.'

'What now?'

He sat up. 'I just remembered something.'

'What?'

But then he shrugged. 'Too late.'

'Too late for what?'

He lay back down. 'Doesn't matter. It was a stupid idea anyway.'

'What was a stupid idea?'

'It doesn't matter. It's nothing.'

'If it's nothing, you can tell me.'

He turned his head on the grass. 'Promise you won't be mad?'

'I don't know. Tell me and I'll decide.'

'Well, like I say, it's nothing really.'

'I know. You said.'

'OK. It's just I said I'd call Sarah. When you got here.'

'Who's Sarah?'

'One of my students. At least she *was* one of my students. Now she helps out here – at the library.'

'So?'

'Well, anyway, I told her about you, and she wanted to meet you.'

'What did you tell her?'

'Well, not the truth, obviously. I *did* tell her about your book, though.'

'And she still wanted to meet me?'

'Oh yes.'

'Why?'

'You'll see. Or rather, you won't now. Sorry.'

'Me too.'

'I said I'd call her before three.'

I looked at my watch: three-thirty. 'Where was she going?'

'Well, that's the thing. The whole reason I told her about you in the first place.'

'What do you mean?'

'Sorry. It's just that it maybe sounds a little, well, creepy.'

'*What* sounds creepy?'

'Well, you know the Little Big Horn and all that?'

'Yes. What about it?'

'And you know Fort Lincoln?'

'For Christ's sake get on with it, will you?'

'And so you know they have this thing every year – a sort of pageant – dressing up, running about, pretending to be people they're not?'

'You mean a re-enactment.'

'A re-enactment, yes. Well, anyway, that's where she's going.'

'And that's the mystery — that Sarah somebody is going up to Montana to watch some bunch of blokes making fools of themselves in the sunshine?'

'Not exactly.'

'Then what exactly?'

'Well, she's not going to *watch*. She's going to take part. She's going to be at Fort Lincoln, waving them off. She's going to be Libbie.'

'Jesus.'

'Precisely, and on the subject of which —'

'*What?*'

'Jesus — the Great Question. If he *was* the son of God, then doesn't that mean he must have been a total fuck-up too — just like us and just like his daddy?'

Later that afternoon, I was sitting in Charlie's back yard with a beer and a copy of his doctoral thesis, *Manifest Destiny — God and the Selling of Westward Expansion*. It's a mighty book — nearly six hundred pages long — that begins (thank God) with a brief overview. It was this overview I was staring at (what with the beer and the sun and general creeping exhaustion, I was fighting sleep and, gradually, losing) when the telephone rang. I pushed myself out of the chair and slipped into the cool of the house. The phone stopped ringing just as I found it (it was hidden behind a pile of papers and books and a stack of CDs, *Blood on the Tracks* on top), the machine clicking on. *Hi*, said a voice — a woman's — then something about jeans and a car needing tyres. *All four*, she said, then some stuff about his step-sister and the hospital. Then she paused as if weighing something up, then she said, *Hey, by the way, it's me, Sarah*. Another pause, then a click and a buzz.

Sarah.

I padded into the kitchen, cracked another beer, had a look at the pictures on his pinboard. Of course they were mostly faces I didn't know – groups hugging and laughing, Charlie dressed as a deer with antlers, Charlie and his brother on a sled in the snow, then the sled upturned, Charlie and his brother sprawling, laughing. I scanned them close, pausing at the white-bordered faded one of me and Charlie and Oskar at school. It seemed so long ago – like something out of another life. I thought of Oskar in the back of that police van and tried to find his face in the photo, but could not, and so I moved on (I knew if I stared too hard and too long I'd find Charlie's fading too, and even, in time, my own), looking, for distraction, for one face in particular. I figured that, if this Sarah was going to play Libbie Custer, then the chances were she had to look at least something like her – and the chances were she'd be here somewhere. Up close, my eyes slipped from one face to the next, until I'd covered them all. Nothing. I took a chug of beer, tried again. Still nothing – plenty of women and girls, but none like Libbie. I gave it up, went back out to the yard. Charlie's book's plastic cover was curling in the heat; I moved my chair into the shade of the fence and started reading.

The reader must remember that, initially at least, the Indian tribes of North America welcomed the pale-skinned men, and were in no sense the savages bent on blood that popular journals and dime novels would have their readers believe. Above all, they were peaceful (there were of course individual 'incidents', but no more and no harsher in tone than could reasonably be expected); above all they were keen to trade to trade. The whites, however, wanted more than wanted however the whites wanted more than trade – or, at least, they wanted more than trade at least they wanted equal trade more than equal trade –

I jumped at a sound; my eyes opened. I twisted round. 'Charlie?' Nothing. I sat up straight in the chair, held the book firm before me, squinted hard and with purpose at the words. *The whites, however, wanted more than trade – or, at least, they wanted more than equal trade. What they wanted was land, the ownership of which was (and still is) the most enduring symbol of one man's worth in relation to another. The problem, of course, was how to justify the taking of this land. It became both a question of authority, and how to avoid the censure of individual and collective conscience / feelings of guilt. The solution, as it turned out, was both simple and brilliant — indeed, literally divine. The authority would come from no less a source than God Himself, who, it shortly became 'obvious', had, in His wisdom, made the white man superior (after all, He had given him — not the red man — the guns and the horses — surely evidence enough), and had therefore made plain and explicit the white man's hegemony over the land. Of course, that that land contained (amongst many other things) large quantities of gold was simply a happy accident — further proof, indeed (what with the Indians placing little value on such useless material), of His great and increasingly less mysterious ways.*

I closed the book on my finger and shut my eyes. From nowhere a breeze came up, soothing. I reached down, slipped the book into the shade beneath my chair. I drained the last of my beer and pulled down the peak of my Sun-Devils cap.

The yard was deep in shade when I woke. There were voices inside the house. Retrieving the book, I pushed up out of the chair and made my way indoors.

Charlie was at the kitchen sink, washing lettuce. 'Hungry?' he said.

'What time is it?'

'Seven-thirty. You looked so uncharacteristically cheerful I didn't want to wake you.'

'Did you get the message?' I said.

'Yup. Got it.'

'Sounded like she's having trouble.'

Charlie looked over his shoulder, smiling, sly. 'You didn't find her then,' he said.

'What do you mean?'

He nodded at the pinboard.

I felt my face warming.

'She's not there.'

'Why not?'

'In fact, she's not anywhere. In photos, I mean.'

'Why?'

Charlie shrugged. 'I suppose it's the Indian in her.'

'The *Indian*?'

213

'One-eighth – or one-sixteenth, or something – Cherokee. Whatever. No pictures – that's the rule. Spanish omelette all right?'

'Jesus.'

'You don't like omelettes?'

'Is she really?'

'Really what?'

'An eighth – or whatever – Cherokee.'

'Sixteenth. And yes, she is. Her grandfather's side, I think.'

'That's weird.'

'Why?'

'She's part Cherokee and playing Libbie Custer. You don't think that's weird?'

'Not really. In fact, I think it's rather neat. After all, the delightful Mrs Custer *did* come to see the error of her ways – that is, of her husband's ways – didn't she? In fact she got quite evangelical about the damage done.' He turned from the stove, two plates in his hands. 'Which was sweet.'

'I still think it's weird.'

'And you'll tell her that?'

'Well, I would if you hadn't screwed up.'

'All of which is now un-screwed up.'

'You spoke to her?'

'I did.'

'And?'

'And she says she'll see you there. If you want to.' Another look, another half-smile. '*Do* you want to?'

'I don't know. Should I want to?'

'It's up to you.'

'When?'

'Well, I strongly suggest sometime before June 25th. After that you'll have to go a whole lot further than Dakota to find her.'

'So where's she going?'

'Home.'

'Which is?'

'Canada. Toronto, I think.'

'For good?'

'Maybe. Don't know. Anyway, should I call her – tell her to look out for you?'

'I don't know.'

'Well let me know, OK?'

'OK.'

'And in the meantime lighten up, will you?'

'Right.'

'And stop looking so fucking guilty.'

'I don't – I'm not.'

'You could have fooled me.'

'And you're saying that's difficult.'

'Oh, just eat, for Christ's sake. *Eat.*'

That night we went for drinks at the house on campus of one of Charlie's friends. On the way there, as we were heading past the library, shirt-sleeved in the warm evening air, quite out of the blue Charlie said, 'When did you find out?'

'What?'

'That she was pregnant.'

Absurdly, I found myself shrugging, though I knew the answer precisely. 'Three months, five days,' I said.

'You mean before the headaches?'

'We thought it *was* the headaches.'

'Jesus.' We walked on. Charlie paused at a driveway.

'What's wrong?' I said.

He shook his head. Behind him, beyond the pick-up with its bright-polished chrome, the house was full of light and laughter. 'Did you know she called me?' he said.

'I was holding the phone. She didn't have the strength.'

'Do you know what she said?'

'Yes.'

He sighed, seemed suddenly old. 'I can't believe it,' he said.

'Neither can I,' I said. 'But I'm learning to.'

He looked up. 'Really?'

'Really,' I said. And I realised, in that moment, that for the first time it was true.

'That's great,' said Charlie. He turned at the sound of voices –
'Hey, Charlie!' – then turned back. 'Look, you want to do this?' he
said.

'Sure,' I said. 'Why not?'

Charlie smiled. 'Fucking ace,' he said, 'fucking ace,' and then he
took my hand and led me down the path and into the brightness
and the laughter.

41

Darkness Incomplete

In the summer of 1866, encouraged by the need to protect western settlers against the godless, red-skinned, blood-thirsty savages who were squatting on American land, the United States Congress authorised the creation of four new cavalry regiments. It was to the first of these – the Seventh – that the newly commissioned Lieutenant Colonel George Armstrong Custer was appointed. Whilst, at the time, unremarkable (Custer's star – once so bright – had dimmed considerably of late, and, besides, Lieutenant Colonelcies were low currency indeed), it was an appointment the consequences of which would come to define all that was (and is) best and worst about American expansion, and one that would provide, through prints and books, movies and websites, the definitive image of glorious and heroic defeat.

But this, then, was the future, and as yet unknown. For now there was Kansas. For now, at the very western end of the Kansas Pacific Railroad, there was Fort Riley.

The Custers arrived on the morning of October 16th, moving into one half of a double house for officers. The accommodation was spacious, with a wide verandah that looked on to the central parade ground. So much better than she had feared, it was, to Libbie 'like living almost in luxury' – although, in time, its appeal would begin to pall; in time, due in no small part to the endless, unceasing Kansas winds, it would come to seem to her what precisely it was – an isolated post in a hard cheerless land known to many as 'America's Siberia'. For the time being, however, there were shopping trips to Junction City to be enjoyed, and many dinners, much dancing. There was even a buffalo hunt attended by a real Russian prince. And, of course, above all, there was Armstrong. He was with her every morning and returned to her every night. He was, she said, despite his troubles, 'growing so much dearer and dearer every day', and she professed herself at a loss to know how he could get any better. In short, to Libbie, the move, despite all its disappointments and hardships, meant, at last, the start of what was to come – the beginning, for real, of what she told herself would be a great and glorious future.

But that, again, was the future. For now there was a regiment to organise, and work to be done. There were settlers to protect and land to be annexed, and revenge to be exacted for the massacre by the Sioux of Crazy Horse of that bellicose fool Captain William Fetterman and every one of his 81-man force near Fort Phil Kearney in Montana.

'*Charlie says you're writing a book about Custer.*'

It was a massacre that, in time – when the war that was coming had finally come and gone – would be revenged a thousandfold – when, in time, the great plains were free at last of the murdering red man, but stained for ever with the red man's blood.

'Well, actually it's about Mrs Custer.'

'He had a wife?'

'He did.'

'Well, I'll be damned. You hear that, Rosemary? Fella here says he's writing a book about Custer's *wife* –'

'Her name was Elizabeth,' I said. 'She wrote three bestselling books about her husband and lived to be ninety-one years old.'

'You don't say! You hear that, Rosemary?'

Rosemary smiled. Rosemary, quite clearly, was drunk.

'Hey, Rosemary – you OK, honey?'

Then Rosemary was swaying – all skirts and surprise – collapsing straight down like a detonated building.

The party wrapped up with Rosemary's departure in an ambulance (initial reports had her suffering a small stroke, though this later turned out not to be true), the guests drifting away this way and that into the still evening air. Charlie and I headed for the football field and sat in the home-team dugout. He'd smuggled a bottle of wine out for me under his jacket; he popped the cork with a penknife, and opened a can of Coke for himself.

'Drink?'

I put the bottle to my lips, took a mouthful, swallowed. The wine was heavy and warm. I set it down before me on the raised turf. We sat for a while, then, in silence, just watching the bugs flitting madly in the moonlight. I closed my eyes.

I heard Charlie stirring beside me, as – through an incomplete darkness – Karen's face slid before me, half-smiling, then was gone.

'You know one thing that really pisses me off?' he said. He sounded agitated – as if there was something inside him getting ready to burst out.

I opened my eyes. Her face, once so delicate and fine – had been bloated, disfigured, her beauty quite gone.

'What?' I said. She'd been, in the end, quite unrecognisable: I could have passed her in the street and felt nothing but pity.

'War memorials.'

'Yeah, they get me too,' I said. 'Every time.'

He reached for the bottle, took a drink, passed it over. 'What?'

'I thought you'd quit,' I said.

He shrugged, looked away, looked back. 'I'm serious,' he said.

'Serious?'

'About fucking war memorials. I mean how they always say "In memory of the sacrifice, blahblahblah . . . Second World War, 1941–1945". Don't they know the bloody thing started in 1939? Haven't they ever heard of the invasion of Poland or Czechoslovakia –'

I took a drink, set the bottle back down. I couldn't believe he was drinking again – or how casual he was about it.

He was staring at me hard; his gaze turned mine away.

'They probably mean *their* war,' I said. 'Or at least their part in it. I don't suppose you can expect them to feel sorry about things they weren't a part of.'

Charlie grabbed the bottle. 'Yeah, but what pisses me off is the *attitude*. It's like, "If we weren't there, then it's not important." It's like they're saying if an American didn't die, then nobody died – like nobody else counts. Jesus, it's like the fucking Nazis: it didn't matter if a Jew died, because a Jew was vermin – just nothing – and who gives a shit about nothing? Or the Indians and your precious fucking Custer. He and his buddies could blow them away till kingdom come and it wouldn't matter, what with the Indians being no more than the shit on your shoes –' He trailed off, raised the bottle to his lips, drank long and hard.

We sat in silence.

'What's happening?' I said, after a while.

He said nothing; he drank until the bottle was empty, then tossed it out on to the field. The bottle skidded on the smooth turf, twirling, truth or dare. We both sat and stared at it, watching it slow, waiting for its verdict.

'It's you,' I said, as it settled, stopped.

'What?' said Charlie.

'Truth or dare.'

'Fuck off.'

'But you've got to.'

'I said fuck off.'

'Do you want me to go first?'

'I want you to fuck off.'

'OK. Truth.'

'What?'

'You ask me something and I have to tell the truth.'

'I know how it works.'

'Well go on then.'

Charlie glanced at me: he was sweating, his eyes red-ringed and tired. He looked away, out across the field, to the bottle and beyond. 'OK. Question. When she was sick – really sick – did you ever wish she'd just hurry up and fucking die? Did you ever just get so sick of caring – so tired of trying to say the right thing when there is no right thing to say?'

I thought a moment, though I knew the answer. 'Yes.'

I felt Charlie's head turn.

'You did?'

I nodded.

He looked away. 'Me too. Sometimes I fucking prayed she'd die.'

'I know. So did I.'

'For Christ's sake, it was like sitting forever in the dusk just waiting for night to come on, even though you know you're going to have nightmares when it comes – you just want it to come so you can get through it somehow and make it to morning, and not have to wait any more.'

I looked at Charlie. He had his head hung down, his hands clasped above it in a casual attitude of prayer. After a while, he looked up and over. 'You know this book of yours,' he said. 'Do you know how it's going to end?'

'Yes. Sort of.'

'Well, do you or don't you?'

'I do.'

'How?'

'She dies. That's how it ends.'

He shook his head. 'That's not how it ends.'

'You've got a better idea?'

He shrugged.

'That's how everything ends,' I said.

'Maybe.'

'Are you saying you believe in some kind of afterlife? Some kind of other dimension?'

'I don't know. Maybe.'

'Jesus. You two really would have got on.'

'What?'

'You and Libbie. She believed in all that stuff – at least she wanted to. She used to talk to him. To Custer. Used to swear he was there, standing beside her, protecting her.'

'Jesus. Talk about a fucking nightmare.'

'And she used to talk sometimes to his statue in Monroe. She wasn't crazy, though.'

'Sounds crazy to me.'

'Hey, *you're* the one who *believes*.'

'I said I don't know. I said maybe.'

'Anyway —'

'What now?'

'Now it's your turn.'

'My turn for what?'

'And I choose dare.'

'You can choose what you like. I'm not doing it.'

'You don't know what it is yet.'

'Well, whatever it is I'm not doing it. I'm thirty-nine years old, for Christ's sake —'

'So?'

'And I'm a fucking assistant professor. How's it going to look, me running around with my pants on my head?'

'You won't have to. All you have to do is come with me.'

'Where to?'

'Back to Monroe.'

'Monroe, *Michigan*?'

'Will you do it?'

'I can't.'

'Chicken.'

'I have classes.'

'It's recess.'

'To prepare. Classes to prepare.'

'Bollocks.'

'I can't just *go*.'

'You can't spare a few days?'

'Why do you want to go back there anyway?'

'Because she went back there – with him. After the court martial. Because that's where they were when the war really started. And, besides, it'll be fun.'

'It'll be a fucking long drive is what it'll be.'

'Then you'll come?'

'I'll think about it.'

'Good. Because the plane leaves in an hour.'

42

Nadir

Bright-spurred and newly booted, the Seventh United States
Cavalry left Fort Riley in March, part of General Hancock's spring
campaign. The mood was optimistic: all were assured that the
campaign would be a glorious and a short one. The Indians, all
knew, would be so intimidated by the expedition's sheer size and
obvious martial intent that either they'd be overrun or they'd turn
at the first chance and flee.

Which – the latter – they did. Again and again, Custer would
arrive unannounced at an Indian village, only to find it just
recently abandoned. Time and again he'd find fires still burning
and blankets still warm; it was as if their purpose was to mock him
and make obvious to all the fruitlessness of his pursuit. An
ungallant foe, they simply would not stand their ground and
fight like soldiers; at the first chance they'd scatter, only then to
disappear into the vast empty hinterland like summer rain in the
heat of midday. At the newly burned ruins of Lookout Station,
only fifteen miles from Fort Hays, there were bodies to mock him
too. Three traders, badly tortured, their corpses 'so mangled and
burned as to be scarcely recognisable as human beings', were left
in his path where he'd be certain to find them, their eyeless
sockets blind now and useless. It was an image of savagery that
would stay with Custer and often return to him, and one that
served further to undermine the fitness of the men under his
command for the terrible, dangerous work ahead. Already under-
paid and undernourished, some chose desertion, while, amongst
the officers, there was general agreement that suicide would be
preferable to capture. Such, indeed, was the universal horror at the

red man's apparently gratuitous thirst for torture and blood-letting, that there was bred in this and all regiments on the frontier a profound and deep-seated *personal* fear of capture, which led, in some, to a fatal debilitating paralysis, while in others it provoked a wild and reckless abandon which would often prove, in the end, just as deadly.

And then, uniquely, as befits a commanding officer, there was Custer himself. While it is undeniably true to say of him (and it is no small thing to say, and accounts, in large part, for his ever-enduring iconic appeal) that he never once – however bad the odds – exhibited any sign of fear in the face of any enemy, white or Indian, it is important, also, to assert that the circumstances on the frontier in which he found himself – the long stretches of tedium broken now and then by the hardest, most savage fighting, the generally poor and diminishing quality of his men – were not without consequences of their own, for, as discipline flagged, and his attempts to arrest the decline became more and more extreme, he became ever more isolated – his actions producing greater and greater ill-feeling amongst the men – until he came to believe (and with good reason) that there were very few people he could trust. In this way, then, the command of the regiment was soon polarised into pro- and anti-factions – a critical division that would never be overcome and would lead, in time, to disaster.

'*So you're saying he was right to go?*'

All of which, though, at least in the short term, George Custer could have tolerated. The role of command, after all, is by its very nature an isolated one. However, what he *couldn't* stand was being separated for months seemingly without end from Libbie – for she it was whose faith in him was endless.

'I'm saying it was just about the only decent thing he did after the civil war. Not that you can blame him, I suppose. Not *really*.'

She it was who shared his belief that God had marked him out from the others – that He had planned, for George Custer, some special, vital role.

'Well, it doesn't sound like it.'

Perhaps general of the army, perhaps senator, perhaps (whisper it low) even *president*.*

We were sitting, an hour later, in the fierce cool of the Long Horn Bar and Grill, one end of the departures concourse at Austin International airport.

'What I mean is,' said Charlie, 'is that after the war the game changed. Just keeping the whole show together was no longer enough. All that could ever be enough now was *more* – more land, more living space, more gold.'

'But there was the little matter of the land's original inhabitants?'

'Well, yes and no. They were certainly there first – before the white men, that is. But that doesn't mean they were *first*. Take the Sioux, for example. They didn't just happen to be there, minding their own business. No – on the contrary. Just as the land was taken from *them*, *they* took the land from others. They slaughtered others just as they themselves in time would be slaughtered. In a sense, you could say they got paid back.'

'They also wanted their own living space.'

'Precisely.'

'So there's no difference. Just one of degree.'

'No. If there *is* a difference, then I suppose it has to do with honour. Generally speaking, when the Sioux made a treaty – whether with the Cheyenne or with the government or any other tribe – they'd tend to stick to it. On the other hand, when the US made a treaty, nobody – not even President Grant – felt any compunction to stick to it, what with the treaty being a treaty with vermin, and so worthless, except as a tactic. Of course some people managed to persuade themselves and others that *this time* the treaty was for real – that *this time* they'd stick to it – but then – surprise, surprise! – something would always happen – a body conveniently found, some completely unreasonable date for incarceration on some fly-blown reservation missed – after which, amid much

* Custer's aspirations towards the presidency have long been a matter of dispute between historians. Whilst it is true that at the height of his fame Custer would certainly have been seen as a possible winner (by either party), there is little evidence to suggest that the general himself – or those in his intimate circle – really considered a move into politics desirable.

tut-tutting about the obviously unreliable natives, the treaty would be torn up and the army sent in to 'save' the poor settlers from the red man's wicked wrath. Which is where your man Custer comes in.'

'And goes out.'

'You mean the court martial?' Charlie shook his head. 'You know that's fucking unbelievable. What the hell was he thinking of?'

'I suppose Libbie. Someone told him there was cholera or typhoid or something at Riley. So he just left his command with a detachment of men – some of whom died on the way – and got on his horse and rode until he reached her.'

'And *was* there cholera?'

'Nope. What there was was what Libbie described as "one perfect night", then a telegram in the morning from Hancock demanding his arrest.'

'And then?'

'Then, stripped of his sabre, he was taken to Fort Leavenworth, where, at the end of October 1868, the court martial found him guilty on all three counts, the members ruling that he should be "suspended from rank and command for one year, and forfeit his pay for the same time".'

'So what did he do?'

'Nothing. There was nothing he *could* do. He was finished: no career, no money, not even a place to live.'

'The end of Custer then.' Charlie was fishing around for something in the pockets of his jacket.

'What are you looking for?'

He pulled out a hip flask. 'I'll drink to that,' he said, unscrewing the top and taking a swig.

'Where'd you get that?'

It was a grand thing – silver, engraved.

He lowered the flask, passed it over. 'Would you believe I found it?'

'Where?'

He shrugged. 'In a store.'

'You mean you stole it?'

He grinned. 'It's not stealing if they don't know it's gone,' he said.

'Christ.'

The smile bled away. '*What?*'

'You're a fucking professor. You can't go around stealing things. What if you get caught?'

Then crept back. 'What do you mean "if"?'

'You mean you did?'

'Yup.'

'When?'

He cocked his head, put his finger to his temple in a parody of thinking. 'Well,' he said, 'the first time was June 17th 1997 –'

'The *first* time?'

'The second, now, let me think. Oh yes, that would be August of the following year. A Tuesday, I think.' He scowled suddenly, glaring at the flask. 'Look, are you drinking that or what?'

'Jesus, what happened?'

He reached over, took it from me. 'Don't fucking hog,' he said. 'I hate fucking hoggers.'

'Charlie –'

Another shrug, another slug.

'I was drunk – seriously fucking drunk. In fact –' that grin again '– I was so fucking drunk I was sick all over the sidewalk. Which is how they caught me. I was too sick to run. I *tried* to run, but I kept slipping and sliding. That's what you get with Nike trainers and vomit – no fucking purchase.'

'What about your job? What about the university?'

'Quit,' he said.

'You *quit*? *When?*' I thought of his empty office, the boxes in his house. 'Jesus, Charlie –'

'Sssh.'

He was squinting, as if he was trying to listen hard.

'What is it?'

'Isn't that us?'

'What?' I turned, trying to see what he could see.

'Sssh.'

And then there was the announcement: *Would all passengers on American Airlines flight twenty-three to Minneapolis . . .*

I turned back. Charlie was gazing, blank-faced, into space. 'Are you OK?' I said, but he didn't respond. 'We'd better go,' I said; I touched his arm, and in that moment – just *for* a moment – as he made his way back from where he'd been, I saw the boy I'd known in school – he was standing in the sun against a dark red-brick wall – the carefree boy who'd existed before the afternoon sun had crept its way behind a cloud and the coolness of evening came on.

43

A Necessary Martyr

We arrived in Monroe late evening. Charlie was asleep (sleeping it off) for most of the drive from Detroit, the low talk on the radio interrupted now and then by strange muffled exclamations come from what I guessed were uneasy, fitful dreams. Once, maybe thirty or forty miles from the city, he woke up with a start – or seemed to – his hair all wild and eyes fierce. 'Is it over?' he said, but when I twisted in my seat and asked what he meant, he just sighed and lay back down, the moment having passed.

The Knights Inn was full (a convention of upholstery cleaners was in town), as were the next three motels I tried. Each time, heads were shaking before I'd hardly finished my sentence. 'And there's no sleeping in the lot,' said one particularly sour-faced clerk helpfully, adding that the fine for such an offence was now forty dollars. 'Would that be in advance?' I said, but he just scowled.

We ended up eventually at the Lazy-I Motel at the end of motel row. Though it had the chipped and faded look of an old piece of furniture left out in the rain, it *did* have rooms (the appearance of the former presumably explaining the availability of the latter), into one of which I staggered with Charlie, laid him on the bed and left him to it. I was tired from the driving and sick of the whole damn enterprise, and, lying back on the bed in my own room, I really couldn't have cared if the Custers themselves had suddenly turned up and tapped on my door. I just closed my eyes and was gone.

It was light when I woke, my limbs stiff, my shirt cool with sweat from a dream. I tried to remember it, but the act of remembrance, as ever, made it flee. I pushed myself up, inched my way to the shower.

Charlie didn't respond when I knocked on his door. I cupped my hands to the window and peered in. He was just as I'd left him, his arms outstretched like a man crucified. He clearly needed to sleep. I crossed the forecourt and climbed up a bank on to the road. The highway was already busy with trucks, the morning alive with the blasting of their horns.

It was a long walk into town, and I was already tired by the time I reached the memorial. I crossed the grass and sat on a bench. The Monroe memorial is a Bell 'Huey' helicopter perched high on a pole, the sort of gunship that, thirty years ago now, had carried young Americans to their deaths in the jungles of Vietnam. This one, these days, is home to several squadrons of swallows (or swifts – whichever have the long tails), their nests built in what were once rocket launchers. From these they flit in and out on their simple frantic errands, now and then gathering on the top edge of a plaque beside a rosebush upon which are engraved the names of the dead. Here they'll sit for a while, twittering like children in the play-ground, until something unheard makes them fly and they're off again, swooping and darting around the helicopter's flightless bulk, their simple joyous song neither tribute nor reproach – their singing just singing for the sake of it, their flying just flying because they can.

'Mornin' to you.'

I smiled.

'It's a fine one, ain't it?'

I'd seen the old man coming from way off, watched the morning light glinting off something in his hand he held down by his side, tried to figure out as he approached what it was.

'It is,' I said. 'You working?'

Turned out it was a small wood-handled scythe.

'Yup,' he said. 'You just sittin'?'

'Just sitting,' I said.

'OK then.'

Closer up he was younger than I'd thought – late forties, fifty tops. He smiled and turned away. He was wearing gloves, and was dressed in baggy jeans and a faded but neatly pressed camouflage jacket, Nike trainers on his feet – the kind that have bulbs in the heels that flicker when you walk. I watched him circle the helicopter, sticking to the centre of the path, then he suddenly veered off into the grass beyond. Here he paused for a moment, looking around him, then, having first removed his jacket and set it carefully over a railing, he set to work, scything the long grass with elegant sweeping motions, only stopping now and then to check on where he'd been and how much he had still to do. After maybe half an hour, he set the scythe down in the grass and wiped his forehead with the back of his hand. I waved when I thought he was looking in my direction; he hesitated for a moment, then waved back. Then he picked up the scythe and resumed his work. The distant blade made a tiny whooshing sound as it cut the air, a *chink* sometimes when it struck a stone. With the sun warm now on my face, I closed my eyes, listening to the rhythm.

'You OK?'

I opened my eyes. He was standing before me, the scythe hanging down by his side. His tanned face was shiny with sweat, his shirt dark-patched beneath his arms.

'What time is it?' I said, aware as I did so of my dream's last carriage disappearing again round a bend.

'Nine-thirty,' said the man. He sounded certain, though he wore no watch.

The dream was the same dream I'd had the night before – though this time only a fragment.

'It's Sunday,' he said, as if that settled something.

In the dream, I'd been standing – for some reason unknown or at least unexplained – on the shores of some vast inland sea, watching for something, waiting.

'All day,' he said, and he smiled.

I pushed up, sat straight. I asked him if he had finished working.

He turned to look back at what he had done. I followed his gaze. The grass was level now around the memorial. He turned back. 'I guess so,' he said, then: 'You need a ride someplace?'

We talked about Custer on our way into town (it was Reno and Benteen, he said, that were really to blame – how they'd not come to Custer's aid when there'd still been time), and then I asked him about Vietnam. Yes, he said, he was there,* but there was something in the silence that followed, then, that didn't encourage any further enquiry – so I left it, changed the subject. Instead we talked about Monroe. Did I know, for example, he said, that when the Custer statue was moved for the last time, both the Masons and the Knights of Columbus tried to outbid each other for the rights to transportation – each one aiming, if chosen, to point the horse's ass in the other's direction? He also told me, as the statue came and went and we headed downtown, that it wasn't despite his faults (and there were, he said, many) but because of them that George Custer was so quickly rehabilitated.

'How so?' I said, as he drew the car to a stop at the kerb.

'Well, he was just what they needed,' he said. 'A necessary martyr. A high-profile death – a sacrifice – to rekindle the public's will for slaughter.'

'You mean an excuse?'

'If you like. And who better to offer than Custer – the Boy General – a man so desperate to regain his lost glory that he was pretty much guaranteed to go and get himself killed.' He ducked forward, peering out through the windscreen as if seeing the city for the first time. 'This OK for you?' he said.

'Sure,' I said. I reached for the handle, paused. 'So it was a conspiracy?' I said.

He shrugged. 'It was politics. Grant was looking for an epitaph: "Here lies the presidency that gave us the west."'

'And he got it – thanks to Custer?'

'Well, it didn't do him any good – it didn't stick. If anybody remembers him as a president at all (which they don't), it's as the Man Who Did Nothing. Oh sure, some people will tell you this

* According to Dean Priebe, editor of the *Monroe Evening Sentinel*, Lieutenant-Colonel Lloyd C. Alexander (US Army, Retd) served two terms in Vietnam, during the second of which he was awarded the Congressional Medal of Honor for 'conspicuous and selfless bravery' at the Battle of Da Trang in the autumn of 1967. Though wounded in both hands and under near-constant attack, he saved the lives of two of his severely wounded men by carrying first one then the other to safety across several exposed paddyfields. Though one man later died from his injuries, the other survived and is currently a United States Congressman representing the state of West Virginia.

manifest destiny crap – but that was just bullshit. All anyone remembers about him was the Grant of the civil war. Shiloh. Vicksburg. Trenches full of blood.'

'And bringing back Custer.'

'Maybe. But then who cares about Custer any more?'

'People here seem to. At least some people.'

'You mean Ian Evans?' He smiled. 'Did you know he's done time?'

'What for?'

'Got caught passin' bad cheques.'

'And they sent him to *prison*?'

'Up in Spareville. Six months.'

'*Six months?*'

'Well, it seems the chances are he would ordinarily have got some kind of *suspended* sentence – maybe a time collectin' garbage or plantin' trees or some such thing – but poor old Ian just had to get himself caught when the governor was up for re-election and lookin' for some see-how-tough-I-am examples to parade before an ungrateful public.'

'And Ian was one of them.'

'Uh-huh. Not that it was all bad news for him, seeing as how it was through his time in Spareville that he met the future Mrs Evans – or should I say Custer – when she started writin' to him, sayin' how sorry she was for him and how the Lord had forgiven him already and how he had to start forgivin' himself.'

'Which he did?'

'Which he did. But not until she promised to visit him, and only *then* – when he saw, to his utter amazement (this was God's work, for sure), that she looked not unlike a certain other person – when she agreed to be his bride.'

'Which she did?'

'Which she did. But only after he'd agreed to go straight and pass no more bad cheques.'

'Which he did?'

'He did.'

'And they were married?'

'On 25th June 1990. A happy day for all.'

'Are you saying you went?'

'Sure I went. *Everybody* went. Now, you OK from here?'

'I'm OK,' I said. I got out of the car, stepped back and watched it go. Then, crossing the street, I tried the door of McGinty's. It was closed. I walked on, strolling this way and that through the Sunday-morning streets, my eyes out for Custer and his sweet, forgiving, God-fearing bride.

44

Sighting the Enemy

He returned to the army on October 5th, arriving at the Seventh Cavalry campsite on Cavalry Creek at noon. For Custer, it was like coming home. Already there to greet him were his brother, two-time Medal of Honor winner First Lieutenant Tom Custer, and others of the small but loyal Custer clique. With his hair cut short and surrounded by a dozen foxhounds, he at once set about re-establishing his authority, buoyed up by General Sheridan's publicly stated faith in his abilities.* Having welcomed hundreds of new recruits from Fort Dodge on the Arkansas River in Kansas (many of whom were immigrants and could speak very little – if any – English, and had joined up only for the free passage west and would soon desert), he embarked on a new regime of even sterner discipline and drilling, selected some as sharpshooters, and, in an effort to enhance morale, ordered that each company should have horses of a similar colour. Since this involved, in many cases, *existing* officers and men having to swap trained mounts, its general effect – instead of enhancing corps morale – was to create disaffection amongst those upon whom he would come in time to rely. This was, in a sense, typical Custer: a bold idea rashly implemented, whose long-term consequences (principally, the encouragement it gave those merely considering desertion to act) had not really been thought through. It was an example of why, for every ally he made, he seemed to make two enemies – chief amongst whom was (and

* Sheridan to Custer: 'Custer, I rely on you in everything, and shall send you on this expedition [against a large band of Indians camped along the Canadian and Washita Rivers] without orders, leaving you to act entirely on your own judgement.' These instructions would be echoed later – and with much consequence – before the Little Big Horn campaign.

would remain, right up to the end and beyond) Captain Frederick Benteen.

A southerner who fought for the north during the civil war (thus so displeasing his father, who said, 'I hope the first bullet gets you!'), Frederick William Benteen took an immediate dislike to Custer who, though younger in age, was senior in rank. He disparaged the younger man's charisma and 'show', thinking him shallow, his success borne of politics and unseemly preening. It was an opinion shared by many outside the Custer 'family', and one that nothing in the coming campaign would change. Indeed, what happened on the Washita River served only to further the older man's antipathy to the younger. It was a hatred that would in the end cost many lives and turn its host into an old man wracked with drink and disgrace.

But that was all to come. For now, there were six thousand Indians camped at various points along the Washita River in Oklahoma Territory who needed subjugation. The job fell to Custer and the Seventh.

On November 23rd, with the band playing Custer's favourite song, 'The Girl I Left Behind Me', the regiment totalling seven hundred and twenty cavalrymen left camp and headed south. The winter that year was particularly bitter, with snow falling in heavy drifts. Soon the men were freezing and the band silent (their instruments having frozen), but they pressed on, arriving late in the evening four days later at the first – Black Kettle's* – village. While the Indians slept, Custer held officers' call, detailing his plan of attack. As he would with such consequence at the Little Big Horn, he divided his forces, in order to strike from all sides at once. At dawn the next day a bugle sounded the charge and the Battle of the Washita commenced. In total, it took ten minutes, and resulted in the deaths of approximately one hundred and twenty-five

* Chief of the Southern Cheyenne, Black Kettle was a well-known advocate of peace with the white man. Indeed, on the morning of Custer's attack, he was sleeping in his tent having been trying – and failing – for many days to locate General Sheridan, to whom he had been told by Colonel William B. Hazen to report, in order that his peaceful attitude be officially recognised. During the first minutes of the attack, he gathered his wife and children and tried to flee, but all were cut down and killed in the river's icy water.

Americans – twenty-five cavalrymen,* one hundred Indians. It was deemed a great victory – a success little tempered by the knowledge that a great number of the Indians killed were women and children.

Of the women who survived, some managed to escape across the river and into the trees, while some were taken prisoner. Amongst the latter – specially selected by Custer as a possible interpreter – was a pregnant seventeen-year-old Cheyenne girl named Monahsetah, only daughter of Chief Little Rock who was killed during the battle. She first came to Custer's attention when another captive Cheyenne woman performed for the two of them what Custer thought was some sort of elaborate tribal introduction, but which was in fact a ceremony of marriage. To what extent his ignorance of the ceremony's significance was genuine (or, indeed, the extent to which Benteen's later claims to have seen the two of them 'many times in the very act of copulating' was more than just the act of a bitter and spiteful, passed-over officer) is uncertain; what *is* certain, however, is that when the regiment returned to Fort Hays in April the following year, Monahsetah was with them.

For Libbie, the presence in the camp of the young Indian woman (and, particularly, her knowledge of the rumours so eagerly broadcast by Benteen) forced her to consider again the nature of her husband's (and therefore her own) enemies – and never more so than when the young woman's baby was born, and there followed at once prolonged and quite absurd speculation that Custer himself was the father. The fact that Monahsetah was already seven months pregnant at the time of the Washita fight did nothing to stop the talk (nor did her offering the child to Libbie – an offer immediately refused on her behalf by her husband); it was talk which, for Libbie, simply served to illustrate further that his was a position of siege from both inside and outside the army – one that, consequently, demanded from her nothing but total and

* Including Major Joel H. Elliott, Frederick Benteen's best friend, who, unknown to Custer, left the battle to pursue some fleeing Indians and disappeared. Fearing the arrival of several hundred more braves from camps further downriver, Custer decided not to look for him, thinking he was most likely lost and would in his own time return. His mutilated body and those of his men were later discovered a few miles downstream. Benteen accused Custer of having abandoned him, and never forgave his commanding officer. He would later have his revenge.

publicly declared support. That, of course, it was Custer himself, as much as – indeed more than – any other, who was, and would be, through a combination of arrogance and insensitivity, responsible for his own position she never, in public at least, conceded.

'*You wanna hear a story?*'

This was an enemy she chose not to see – one from which even Custer couldn't escape.

'What kind of a story?'

'A funny story. Concerning a man who tried to kill himself by jumping off a bridge.'

It was the one in the end that would kill him.

'It doesn't sound very funny.'

The boy beside me at the counter of the Custer Grill and Deli dipped his head, sipped his coffee, and came up smiling. He was nineteen or so, maybe twenty, his thin face pale in the shadow of his cap. 'Oh, it's funny, all right,' he said. 'You wanna hear it?'

'Sure.'

He leaned forward, stretching his arms across the counter and lowering his head until his chin was touching his coffee-cup. He squinted hard, concentrating, as if there was much to remember and much to get right. 'Well, let me see now,' he said. 'The way I heard it was there was this man one time who was lookin' to kill himself and so he got in his car and he drove out of town to a bridge across a river. Well, when he got to the river he parked up his car in the middle of the bridge and climbed up on to the ledge.' The boy twisted his head, still squinting. 'You with me so far?'

'So far,' I said.

'OK.' He turned back, fixed his eyes again on the wall behind the counter. 'Well. Like I say, he climbs up on to the ledge and he jumps. Thing is, though, him not botherin' to look before he jumped, he didn't see that the river was real low and there was nothin' but mud. So, instead of killin' himself, he just sinks into the mud and gets himself stuck.' He turned again. 'Ain't that a funny story?' he said.

I nodded and stood up. The morning was slipping already and there were things I had to do. 'Well, I'll see you,' I said.

'Where you goin'?' said the boy.

'I have things to do.'

'But I ain't finished the story. Don't you wanna hear what happened?'

'OK. Tell me. What happened?'

The squinting fled the boy's face and was replaced by the broadest of crooked-teeth smiles.

'Well?' I said.

'Can't you guess?'

I shook my head.

'Ain't you gonna try?'

'I don't know,' I said. 'Maybe he got rescued and later ran for president.'

'Nah,' said the boy, suddenly solemn. He sat up straight. 'The tide came in, is what happened.'

'It did?'

'Yes, sir,' he said, shaking his head, as if disbelieving his own words. 'And that man – he *drowned*. Hey, where're you goin'?'

'I gotta go,' I said. 'But thanks for the story.'

The boy frowned. 'What you gotta do?'

'I have to go to church.'

'You *do*?'

'I do.'

'*Wow* –'

'So I'll see you,' I said, and I thanked him again.

'Any time,' he called as I let the screen door bang and made my way out into the sunshine.

The service at the Custer church was just breaking up when I got there, so I waited on the grass in the shade of an oak tree. I watched the worshippers filing out, each one pausing at the door and blinking in the sunlight. When the last of them was gone and their voices had drifted back and away, I made my way inside.

'May I help you, sir?'

The man was standing beside a table just inside the door, the collection plate held tight in his hands. He seemed a little nervous.

'Can I just sit?' I said.

'Of course.' He glanced down at the plate. 'Would you care to make a donation? For a dollar you can sit just as long as you like.'

I took out my wallet. 'What about ten?' I said. 'What do I get for that?'

He smiled. 'Ten dollars? How does the best seat in the house sound?'

'How about a tour instead?'

'A tour? Sure. Now, we have the regular tour, which is where I tell you all about some dead people neither one of us ever met. Or there's the other one.'

'Which is?'

'The George Custer tour. Which is where I show you where they walked on the day they got married. In fact, you get to walk it too. You even get to kneel where they kneeled and stand on the exact steps they stood on when the soldiers raised their sabres in an arch.'

'And this tour starts when?'

He turned and set the plate on the table. 'Well,' he said, turning back, 'as luck would have it, the next tour starts right away.' He paused. 'First, though, we have to choose sides.'

'Sides?'

'Bride or groom. You want to walk where *he* walked or walk where *she* walked?'

'I think I'll take him. If that's OK.'

'No problem. You about ready?'

'Ready,' I said.

And so we set off, shoulder to shoulder, beginning outside and then coming back inside and moving at a slow pace down the aisle. We paused before the altar. Crossing himself, he knelt; I followed. 'Blahblahblah,' he whispered low, turning then to me.

'What?' I said.

'Blahblahblah,' he whispered again.

'OK,' I said. 'Blahblahblah.'

He pushed himself up, turned. I followed. 'Hope you're not already married,' he said as we moved back down the aisle and out into the sunshine.

'No,' I said.

'Well, you are now,' he said. 'Where've you got planned for the honeymoon?'

'No honeymoon,' I said, moving away. 'Don't you know there's a war on?'

'But I was a-hopin' for Charleston!'

'Sorry,' I said. 'No can do.' I walked down the path. 'See you,' I said.

'I'll wait!' said the man from behind me. Something in his voice made me pause. I looked back. He was standing there on the steps, tears in his eyes and a small cotton handkerchief raised high in one hand.

When I got back to the motel Charlie was sitting by the coffee machine in reception, his hair this way and that, clothes ruffled. He looked like shit.

'You look like shit,' I said.

He raised his cup. 'Thanks. Coffee?'

I sat. 'How are you feeling?'

'Like shit. Where'd you get to?'

I told him about the boy and his story and the man in the church. 'Jesus,' he said.

The phone behind the desk rang; a clattering in the back room, then the man from last night appeared. He picked up the phone. '*Yes?*'

'So what now?' said Charlie.

'I don't know,' I said. 'I'm not sure why I'm here.'

'Oh fuck.'

'What?'

'Then why did you bring *me* here?'

I shrugged.

The desk clerk set down his phone.

'Hey, you guys OK?'

'Well,' said Charlie, 'as a matter of fact —'

'We're fine,' I said.

'You in town for long?'

Charlie shook his head.

'I don't know,' I said. 'Maybe.'

The desk clerk made a half-smile. 'OK. Well, if there's anything you need –' He turned away. In a moment came the sound of a TV from the back room.

'Well?' said Charlie.

'That guy,' I said. 'In the church.'

'What about him?'

'He asked me if I was married.'

'So?'

'I said no.'

'Well, you're not.'

'I know.'

'Well then.'

'It just felt strange. Like I was lying. Like I was being unfaithful.'

Charlie said nothing.

'Charlie?'

'What?'

'There's something I want to tell you.'

'Don't.'

'But you don't know what it is.'

He stood up.

'Where are you going?'

'I don't know.'

'Charlie –'

'Just out maybe. You coming?' He was staring out across the parking lot, out towards the highway and beyond.

'I didn't mean to hurt her.'

'Just don't,' he said. Then he stood a while in silence, just watching the cars – me too. Then he said, 'What do you say we go see Custer?'

'Now?'

'You think he'll be in?'

'I don't know.'

'Let's try.'

'OK.'

'And then you can tell me.'

'Tell you what?'

'How none of us failed her. How we all did our best. How she lived nothing but a happy life until she died.' He turned. 'OK?' he said. He was smiling, but there were tears in his eyes.

'OK,' I said.

'OK,' said Charlie. Then he crossed the lobby to the door and I followed him, while, behind us, from the back room, came the sound of canned laughter, then a man's muffled voice, then the distant clattering of applause.

45

Reconstruction

On August 13th 1876, two months after the disaster in Montana, hundreds of grieving citizens crowded into the Methodist church on Loranger Square for a service dedicated to the memory of the six Monroe men who had fallen. The ceremony commenced with a roll-call of the dead – the three Custer brothers, George, Tom and Boston, George's nephew, 'Autie' Reed, his brother-in-law, James Calhoun, and their friend, George Yates – and continued with the required fulsome (and, of course, entirely partial) history of the tragedy. The Reverend Mattoon absolved the general of all blame, dismissing charges of rashness as the work of 'mean and shallow men'. Custer, he said, was a hero worthy of all men's admiration – a man whose abilities were deep as they were broad. He was, he said, 'never idle. When he laid down the sword he took up his pen,'* and he claimed, then, that, had time allowed, he would surely have gained distinction as a writer. He spoke of the hardships of campaigning – the heat in summer, the freezing winters – singling out Libbie for particular praise. She had willingly shared with him, he said, 'the soldier's tent', and had 'buckled on his armour', sending him forth then to do the Lord's work. For, he went on – his voice growing low, pious and sincere – it was clear to all who had eyes to see that the Lord had made the land for which Custer and his men had fought and died for 'civilisation and for Christianity', and he

---

* Custer wrote a series of articles for *Galaxy Magazine* about his life in Kansas. These proved immensely popular, and were eventually gathered together in a book. Published in 1874 as *My Life on the Plains* (referred to by Captain Benteen as *His Lie on the Plains*), the book is a detailed, somewhat turgid account of the period, unsurprisingly devoid of any self-criticism. It was an immediate bestseller and made the author a considerable sum. This he soon lost.

concluded then with a statement of 'manifest truth' to which all present (and far beyond) could subscribe – namely, that the Indians were mere barbarous heathen and simply had no right to claim any authority over the land, and, by so doing, stay the inevitable God-given tide of progress. It was a speech of outstanding sentimental power, making, as it did, of an entirely avoidable military disaster a selfless and saintly God-annointed crusade, and so, to Libbie's ears (and to the ears of many), confirming what she knew to be true – that her husband was a hero brought down in the service of God and that his actions had been entirely dedicated to the betterment of America and her sprawling grateful people.

Not that they were *that* grateful.

On the contrary. Attempts to raise her pension from thirty dollars to fifty met opposition in the Senate and were permanently stalled. And if that wasn't enough, in the weeks following Reverend Mattoon's stirring address, she discovered she was broke. She discovered that, though he may have been brave and charismatic – that he may have done the nation the greatest service by giving his life – he was, in business, a perfect fool. She also found that, at the time of his death, those insurance policies which he'd told her would amply provide for her in the event of anything 'happening' to him had been allowed to lapse and were, consequently, worthless, and that, as a result, all things combined (there were monies owed on fruitless land speculations and personal notes now due for payment), she owed a total of four thousand dollars – a huge debt in 1876, and one that she had no means of paying. All she had, after all, was an immensely famous – and immensely dead – husband.

She thought of teaching, but dismissed the idea as she'd already tried it, briefly, at Sunday school and had hated it. Besides, it was too poorly paid (particularly for women, who received approximately a third of their male counterparts' salary) to make any kind of dent in her debt. She thought of clerical work, perhaps at one of the many government offices in Washington, and applied to the United States Pension Office. Her letter eventually found its way to President Grant, who offered to make her postmistress of Monroe.

This offer, however, she turned down flat. She would not take anything from Grant, whose view of her husband – publicly expressed – had been far from complimentary, more than implying as it did that his death (and the deaths of those under his command) had been entirely unnecessary and exclusively his fault – the massacre a result of the rashness so eloquently dismissed as false by Reverend Mattoon.

'*So this is it?*'

So, unemployed and in debt, what should she do? As a woman – indeed as a *lady* – she had few choices – fewer still if she stayed in Monroe.

Charlie leaned forward, peering out at the house through the windscreen.

So, one morning in the spring of 1877, she packed her bags and boarded a train.

'This is it,' I said.

And headed, like so many before her, for the glitter and hope of New York.

'So what do we do now?'

'What do you mean?'

'Well, do we just go and knock on the door?'

'Of course.'

He sat back. 'Jesus,' he said. 'This is weird.'

'Come on,' I said, pulling on the handle and stepping out. 'You ain't seen nothin' yet.'

She rented a room in Newark, New Jersey, and began the search for employment. She tried the New York hospitals, hoping for some kind of charitable work. When no such work was forth-coming, she considered enrolling in the nursing programme at Bellvue hospital, but was politely and firmly persuaded that, what with her age and obvious emotional state, this would not be appropriate. While she was there, however, she learned that the newly formed New York Society of Decorative Arts was looking for a part-time secretary. She applied at once, and, after some initial doubts ('She came, a pathetic figure in widow's weeds,' said the society's director, 'which seemed to hold the shadow of heart-rending tragedy'), was given the job, three days a week. Although not enough to even begin to pay back her many debts, it was a start. It was enough, at least, to pay her room and board. She would, for the time being at least, neither freeze nor starve.

Founded by Candace Thurber Wheeler, widow of the famous engineer and surveyor, the society was a source of employment for 'decayed gentlewomen' brought low by circumstance (this often widowhood, thanks to the recent war), a place in which they would be taught to use whatever natural talents they possessed in embroidery or needlework (this was later, after Libbie's arrival, expanded to include classes in decorating china and pottery), the results of which (assuming they were up to standard – and much, at least to start with, was not) would then be sold on and a portion of the profits returned to the women. It was, in effect, a benevolent workhouse, and always hugely oversubscribed. Initially, it was Libbie's job just to order and organise correspondence; in time, though, as her relationship with Candace Wheeler bloomed into friendship, she took on more responsibility, until she became more a partner than a mere employee. Thanks to an increase in her salary, she was able to move from her basement room in New Jersey, and in late May, with the first anniversary of the Little Big Horn approaching, she moved to New York, taking a room at the Glenham Hotel on Fifth Avenue.

Perhaps the most difficult aspect of the new and impoverished state in which Libbie found herself (aside, of course, from the sudden loneliness and emptiness of widowhood) was having to bear what was her effective exclusion from society. Once the sweetheart – and later wife – of society's darling, now she was nothing but a once-famous, fast-fading widow. Where once – and only recently – she'd travelled everywhere in the city in carriages, often on her way to the most glittering parties and balls, now she travelled mostly on foot, and spent most nights alone, just thinking of the past and scarcely daring to consider the future. Whatever future there had been was gone now – taken from her – leaving her now just this low-voltage, low-volume half-life – a life of work and remembering, of meals taken silent and alone. The idea that this would all change – and soon – would have seemed to her then quite impossible.

'Nobody's in.'

'So what do we do now?'

Back then, as she sat at her desk at the society or at home in her one gloomy room, she knew that all she'd ever have and all she'd ever be was what she had and what she was now.

'I don't know. Go back to the motel, I suppose. Hey, where're you going?'

Back then, she knew for certain that the better part of her life was over.

'Round the back,' Charlie called, already on his way. 'You coming?'

'Jesus, Charlie –'

A clattering and a curse.

'Charlie?'

He was lying on his back in the gloom of the empty lean-to car port. He lifted his head. 'What the fuck –' All around him, scattered like strange metal seeds, were hundreds of bullets – round, roughly made things, circa civil war.

'You OK?' I said.

He pushed himself up. 'No, I'm not fuckin' OK.' He picked up one of the bullets, turned it around in his fingers. 'These people,' he said. He paused.

'What about them?'

He looked up. 'You reckon they've got guns to go with these?'

I looked around. There were none in sight – though there were plenty of cupboards. 'Look, maybe we should go,' I said.

'Go?'

'Come back some other time. Maybe I'll ring first.'

Charlie stood up, started patting himself down. 'You can go if you like. Me, I've got to meet these fuckers –'

'But they're not here –'

'Somebody's here.'

'How do you know?'

'Listen.'

I listened. 'What?'

'Don't you hear that?'

'Hear what?' There was nothing – at least at first. Then something. Singing.

'Where's it coming from?' I said.

'Sssh.' Charlie held up his hand. 'This way,' he whispered, creeping his way like a thief or a spy through the gloom towards the back of the house.

She was sitting, half-lying, on a pink and white lounger in the middle of a roughly cut lawn, earphones clamped to her ears and her eyes closed tight, her voice raised melodious in song.

Charlie stopped, maybe twenty feet away. 'Who's that?' he whispered.

'Eliza,' I said.

'Who's Eliza?'

'The maid.'

'Whose maid?'

'The Custers'.'

He turned. He was frowning. 'You mean the Custers or the people who *think* they're the Custers?'

I shrugged. 'I don't know.'

'OK. Let's ask.'

'Charlie –'

But he was off across the grass and I had no choice but to follow. He stood beside the chair. I hung back.

'What's that?' he whispered.

'What?' I looked around, expecting discovery any second. I kept thinking of the bullets – and the gun that was bound to be around somewhere.

'What's she singing?'

I turned back. 'Marvin Gaye,' I said.

'What?'

'Marvin Gaye. Now, can we go?'

But then before I could stop him, Charlie was leaning forward, his first finger tapping on the black woman's shoulder.

'Charlie!'

She sat up with a start. Charlie and I gave a sort of jump backwards.

'Who the hell are you?' She pushed up, struggling, pulling off the earphones. 'What the hell you doin' in my garden?'

Charlie cleared his throat. 'We've come to see the general,' he said.

She rolled off the lounger, setting herself on her feet. She was huge, her skin glistening, her eyes blinking hard. 'The general?' she said, her face creasing with disdain.

'Custer?' said Charlie.

I eased out from behind him. 'I was here before,' I said. 'The surgeon?'

She considered me, scowling. 'You ain't no surgeon,' she said.

'I know,' I said. 'There was a mix-up. I'm really just a lieutenant –'

Charlie turned. 'What?'

'You see, when I got here, Libbie was sick, and they thought I was the surgeon –'

Eliza shook her head. She seemed to look at me now with a mixture of pity and disgust. 'Listen, boy,' she said, a weariness creeping into the mix, 'you ain't no surgeon, and you ain't no lieutenant –'

'Well, no,' I said. 'Not really, *obviously* –'

'What you is,' she said, 'is a white boy with too much time on his hands. What you is is a waste of my tannin' time –'

'Tanning?' said Charlie. 'But –'

She turned her gaze upon him. It was withering. She stepped towards him; Charlie stepped back. 'You think,' she said, 'I was always this black?' She drew herself up, until the two of them were nearly nose to nose. 'Well, do you?'

Charlie sort of shrugged. He was sweating now too.

'Well, no sir is the answer.' She raised a hand, finger out, started jabbing his chest. 'When I STARTED this MORNIN' I was JUST about as WHITE as YOU – OK?'

'OK,' said Charlie.

She stepped back. 'Now then,' she said, looking at us both. 'Suppose you boys just turn yourselves around and go back to wherever you came from.' She raised an eyebrow. 'Would that be a good idea?'

I looked at Charlie. Yes, we agreed. Good idea.

'Well, that's jus' fine,' said Eliza. 'And when the general gets back from court – *if* he gets back from court – I'll surely tell him you called.'

'Is it, like, a court martial?' I said.

Eliza shook her head. 'Shoplifting,' she said, her weariness complete.

46

Monuments

We were having dinner that night at Roscoe's Real Steakhouse on Johnson Street when, quite out of the blue, Charlie announced he was leaving.

'Leaving?' I looked at his steak. He'd barely touched it.

'Going home,' he said.

I looked up. 'You mean Texas? But I thought –'.

He shook his head. 'Not Texas.'

'Then where?'

'Home.'

'You mean England?'

'Where else?'

'But why?'

He sighed, turned to the window, looking out to the parking lot and beyond. 'You see that?' he said.

'What?' I followed his gaze.

He nodded towards something. 'All that.'

'All *what*?'

There was nothing to see: just the empty parking lot, a patch of scrub, then the highway, more scrub. Then nothing. Flat land. 'I can't see anything,' I said.

'I know,' said Charlie. 'Me neither any more.'

A truck drew into the parking lot, paused a while, hissing. The driver got out, moved around the front and started checking something inside the wheel-arch.

'What's the matter?' I said.

He turned to look at me. He seemed pale despite his tan – and for the first time every year of his age. He shrugged. 'I guess I'm just tired.'

'Then take a holiday.'

'Tired *of.*'

'Of *what?*'

'Everything. Nothing. I don't know. The scale of things here, maybe. Maybe I'm tired of looking out and seeing nothing going on for ever. And when I *do* see something, I'm tired of it being so fucking big. I'm tired of feeling out of scale.'

'And you think going to England will fix that?'

'Maybe.' Another shrug. He smiled. 'Doesn't home always seem smaller when you get there?'

'But it isn't your home. You haven't lived there for ages. You don't know what it's like.'

'I know it's small. People-sized.'

'Yes, and cramped. And wet. And everyone's got shitty teeth.'

'*You* haven't.'

'You think these are real?'

He smiled, looked away. We sat a while in silence. Then he said, 'I was thinking of buying a seat – you know, with a plaque?'

'For Karen?'

He nodded. 'Somewhere to sit, you know?'

'There's already a plaque.'

'Can't you have two?'

'You can never have too many plaques.'

'I'm being serious.'

'I know.'

'Well?'

'I think it's a good idea. She always did like sitting.'

Charlie laughed.

'I mean for pictures. Having her hair cut. That sort of thing.'

'And the cinema. Don't forget the cinema. I remember when we were kids –' He paused.

'What is it?'

'Nothing.' He looked up. 'I really *am* going, you know,' he said.

'OK. You said.'

'And I'm going to quit drinking.'

'And smoking?'

'Smoking? Fuck *that*. Smoking may kill you, but at least it doesn't ruin your life.'

'Is yours ruined?'

'Nearly.'

'Nearly isn't ruined.'

The waitress came with our drinks.

'Cheers,' said Charlie. We clinked glasses.

'So when are you going?' I said.

'Soon. Tomorrow. Early. You won't see me before I go.'

And I didn't. Tapping on his door next morning, I got no answer. I asked the desk clerk, but he hadn't seen him go. 'Must have been real early,' he said.

I've not seen Charlie since that evening in Monroe, when he told me about the seat with its plaque that is yet to appear. Whether he ever made it to England I don't know. He certainly never contacted me if he did. There was – and would be – too much to see in each other. I'm sad, but glad also. I suspect he is too.

With her husband returned at last to his home at West Point, Libbie returned to hers in New York, resuming, then, her work at the society. In addition to this, she took up the role of paid companion to a wealthy Rochester widow now resident in the city, to whom she would travel every evening, and with whom she would talk of the west and of her life long gone. It was a life of routine – and she was grateful for that, after all that had happened – but one untroubled by happiness. Every day was a journey of harmless monotony, every evening, on returning from her duty of smiling concern, a time spent in melancholic introspection. Her life, it seemed, was set in a pattern that only old age and, in time, death would alter.

But it was not so.

For that would be to reckon without Henry James, and, indeed, without George Armstrong Custer.

Libbie met the great writer at one of Candace Wheeler's soirées on his return to America following the publication of *Portrait of a Lady* in 1881. They talked, of course, of her husband (the two men were near contemporaries) and of Vienna, which she longed to see, and of the great man's work.* Her husband's life, he suggested, was one worthy of literature, containing as it did 'the great sweep of tragedy'. It was a story, he said, that the world would care to know.

It would be, he said, if she chose, a monument to the times and to the greatness of the times.

And Libbie did.

For, ever since her husband's death, she'd been in search of some fitting, enduring memorial – something that would show him 'as he should be known' (and continue to show him to future generations) – somewhere where the truth could be told and all lies expunged. This she'd found, for a while at least, in the hastily written *The Complete Life of General Custer* by British ex-pat dime novelist Frederick Whittaker, to whom she'd confided much personal information, but, though initially successful, sales of the book had soon dropped, thanks in large part to its wildly over-blown style and many inaccuracies. Such failure, she came to believe, would be the fate awaiting any such history compiled by someone 'who does not truly understand'.

Which meant anyone, of course, but her. It was she alone, after all, who knew the truth. If anyone were to speak, it must be her.

So, a week later, sitting at her desk beneath the gaze of a bust of her husband made by the artist Vinnie Ream (it was a plaster model, the intended reproduction in bronze of which proved too costly and was therefore abandoned), Libbie embarked, cautiously at first, on her own, true version of her husband's remarkable life. It was to be an exercise in memory more painful than she had imagined, as, for so long, she had avoided the cruel luxury of remembrance by trying to keep busy. Now, though, with the work begun, all that changed; now she had no choice but to give herself up to it – to find herself 'always looking back in the waking hours and dreaming the saddest dreams of my beloved'. The effort exhausted her – particularly the fear of not doing the story the

* Some years after their meeting, the writer published a story, 'The Altar of the Dead', about a man who lives his life entirely in remembrance of his friends. Eventually, of course, he meets a woman who does likewise, although her life-long dedication is to the memory of one man, her great love.

justice it deserved – and made her, at times, quite ill. But, uncaring, she pressed on, though her hand would cramp up and her eyes start to falter. So exhausted, indeed, did she become, that when at last she was done and the book was completed, she took to her bed, quite drained by the cost of such intimate recollection, and there she stayed for three days and three nights.

Harper and Brothers Publishers were the first and last people she tried. They took the manuscript at once, for a modest fee, and published the book, *Boots and Saddles, or, Life in Dakota with General Custer*, in March of 1885. It was an instant success, followed, in due course, by two further volumes. The first of these, *Tenting on the Plains* (1887), covered the period immediately following the civil war; the second, *Following the Guidon* (1890), the winter campaign of 1868. Combined, the three books present a picture of the general as a dashing, vital, heroic man – a portrait, indeed, no less laudatory than Whittaker's, and, as with Whittaker's, Libbie's Custer is a man whose faults are only those of over-abundance – in generosity and sensitivity and love for his wife and for his men. However – hagiography though they may essentially be – this is not to say that the books are without interest, for, while short on intimate revelation, they are long on the details of frontier life, and though this at times makes reading them heavy work, there is, generally speaking, a naive kind of charm about them – a self-deprecation that sat well with readers. The public was also gratified to have their view of the Indians as savages confirmed by one who knew: it was clearly her belief – and theirs – that the Indian, though 'noble', was a distinctly, self-evidently second-class creature – that his role, as ordained by God, was, once tamed, as simple beast of burden. It was a view guaranteed to salve the nation's increasingly troubled conscience – and they loved it (and her for it), the *New York Independent*, for example, claiming the book to be 'so genial and sympathetic that the reader becomes attached to the author, her gallant husband, the servants, the soldiers, and indeed, to nearly every character in the volume'. So positive, indeed, was the reaction that one reviewer even suggested that copies be supplied 'to every school, college etc. in the land', in order that such a glorious example of, on the one hand, manliness and, on the other, shy, devoted womanliness be available as instruction to all. But more than this – more than the simple, thankful plaudits she received – the book's success (and that, increasingly so, of its sequels) meant, for Libbie, a return to the public's attention she'd once enjoyed. After years in the wilderness, she was back, centre stage. It was a position she would never again entirely relinquish – a platform from which, for the rest of her life, she would battle all the doubters and proclaim her husband's greatness.

47

The Bridge and the River

At around twelve o'clock on June 23rd 1888, the mayor of New York climbed the three steps that led up on to a podium situated for the occasion on the walkway in the middle of Brooklyn Bridge. He shuffled his papers, raised his eyes to the crowd and began. 'Ladies and gentlemen,' he said, 'we are gathered here today to celebrate a birthday. A fifth birthday. For today, ladies and gentlemen, the East River Bridge – known to all, now, as the Brooklyn Bridge – is five years old.' Another pause. Beside him then, drawn together as if cued in tentative applause, the hands of the deputy commissioner of public works were joined (much to his evident relief) by other hands, and then others, until all, that lunchtime, on that fine summer's day, were clapping. Then, reasserting his authority by lifting up his arms (it was, to one spectator, as if he wished to embrace not only all those present but also all those for whom work or indifference had proved such a hindrance to their attendance), the mayor silenced his audience and continued. 'Thank you,' he said, 'thank you, thank you.' Clearing his throat, he glanced down at his notes. 'Now, as I was saying, today we celebrate our beloved bridge's birthday –'

A shriek, then, from the crowd, heads turning, fingers pointing.

'What is it?' said the mayor.

'Look!' said a voice. 'Up there!', and all did so (including, reluctantly, His Honour), their necks craning, eyes squinting into the sun.

A figure – a man* – high up, dark against the light, his

---

* Benjamin Bushnell, a former day-labourer employed during the bridge's construction at ten cents an hour, who contracted caisson disease ('the Bends') through working for long periods underground in compressed air. Having, consequently, been unable to work for five years, his wife and four children were starving. His suicide was an effort to persuade the city of New York to pay compensation to others similarly injured.

arms outstretched, hands hanging on to the heavy wire cables.

'What shall we do? said the deputy commissioner of public works.

'Do?' said the mayor – but, before he could think up any kind of a plan, another woman (or perhaps the same one – they all looked the same to him) was shrieking again – a long cry this time, like, ironically perhaps, the cry of a woman giving birth – and it was all far too late. The crowd moved as one to the edge of the bridge, those at the front (amongst whom, all shoulders, was, of course, the mayor) craning over and looking down, in general, at the grey distant water, and, in particular, at the dark thrashing figure who, though a minute ago had seemed intent on death, now, it was clear, was fighting for life.

It was a fight that soon ended, a stillness overtaking the body like a shroud drawn slow across a corpse, which then, water-weighted, sank down beneath the surface. A few bubbles, a few ripples on the surface – then nothing. A silence in the crowd, then a murmuring, a shuffling of feet. Eyes slid away from eyes. Nobody knew quite what to say.

Amongst the crowd, two women – one dressed dark in mourning black, the other outfitted as if for some western-themed fancy-dress ball – contributed their silence to the whole – until, that is, a young man – a reporter with the *New York Herald* – stepped away from the edge (he'd been scribbling in his note book, scarcely able to believe his luck) and approached, excusing his presumption by removing his hat.

'Ladies,' he said (he was smiling – but not too hard, given the circumstances), 'may I have your thoughts?'

'Thoughts?' said the lady in mourning. She seemed genuinely shocked.

But the other was less so. 'My name,' *she* said, 'is *Miss* Annie Oakley,* appearing tonight and every night in Mr Buffalo Bill's

---

* 'Little Miss Sure Shot', Phoebe Anne Oakley Moses Butler (1860–1926), was a child prodigy, performing unequalled feats of marksmanship. She joined Buffalo Bill's *Wild West Show* in 1885 and stayed for seventeen years, during which time she travelled the world, delighting audiences with her act. This included shooting a cigarette from between the lips of a volunteer at thirty paces. These volunteers included, memorably, a startled Emperor of Prussia.

Wild West Show, and *I* think it's all an entire tragedy is what *I* think it is.' She turned to her companion. 'Don't you agree, Miss Elizabeth?' she said.

Her companion, still pale, said nothing.

The reporter was frowning, his doubting pen suspended. 'Are you *really* Annie Oakley?' he said.

'Really,' said the woman, lifting her rhinestone-studded Stetson and nodding. 'And *this,*' she added, turning to her friend, 'is *really* Mrs General George Custer. Now what do you think about that?'

What he thought about that appeared next day in the *New York Herald. Tragedy on the Bridge,* ran the headline; then, beneath it, a little smaller, *Death Still Stalks the Custer Name.*

'So you've everything you need?'

In an echo of an earlier time and another American tragedy –

I looked up from the clippings file. 'Yes,' I said. 'I think so.'

'Well, don't hesitate to ask –'

I said I wouldn't; smiling, Cheryl Stapper moved off, was lost in a moment in the library's aisles. I went back to the file, scanned the clipping.

– of an earlier time and another American tragedy, there was amongst the guests who witnessed the deceased's fatal jump one Mrs George A. Custer, wife of the late general, accompanied by members of Buffalo Bill's Wild West Circus,* *the hit show currently playing to packed houses on Broadway. When asked to comment on the terrible scene, the pale and drawn widow said, 'Oh, when will the bloodshed end?'*

'You've a problem?'

I'd been staring at the thing for an hour, unable to screw down my mind.

'Well, not a problem exactly. More a question.'

This anguished question, echoed by the tears of her immediate companion Miss Annie Oakley, the famous lady shot, is one surely all Americans must ask themselves today –

---

* Although she never visited the scene of the *actual* Battle of the Little Big Horn, Libbie did visit the *Wild West Circus* many times, and is said to have particularly enjoyed Buffalo Bill's entirely partial and patriotic rendering of 'Custer's Last Stand'.

Cheryl Stapper closed the cabinet into which she'd been peering. She turned, smiling. 'I'm all yours,' she said. 'Fire away!'

Today, as the ship that is Our Nation gathers steam and advances into the unknown waters of her second century, and the legends of her past drift slowly into history –

'Well, it's about some people I knew. When I was over here before.'

She frowned, her mind already working. 'You mean in America? Whereabouts?'

'Here.'

'In Monroe?'

'Two girls, yes. Two sisters.'

'You mean the Downey girls?'

'You know them?'

She shook her head. '*Of* them. I never met them.'

'So what happened? Are they OK?'

She opened her mouth to speak, but something changed her mind. 'Will you wait here?' she said.

'Why?' I said. 'What is it?'

She stepped away. 'I won't be a minute,' she said, and then, for the second time that morning, she turned and was gone. I sat awhile, just waiting, wondering. I replaced the clipping in the file and closed it. *I won't be a minute.* I looked at my watch. Three minutes and counting.

The first time – so many years ago – she'd come to New York, the city had been gripped by a harsh winter chill. The streets had been thick with ice (she'd watched, quite transfixed, a horse lose its footing and slide on its belly what seemed like the whole length of Broadway), the East River itself completely frozen. She'd stood, then, a young girl, on the Brooklyn side, the arms of her beloved around her, the two of them looking out, silent except for their breathing, at the buildings of Manhattan, with all their promise of wealth and arrival. They had seemed such an age away – such a bridgeless expanse – though one she'd felt certain she and he would be crossing. How long, she'd wondered, was it going to take?, and she'd gripped her husband's hand. He'd drawn her to him then, as if he'd heard the question; then, stepping away, he'd led her across the promenade and down the wooden steps to the frozen water's edge where a carriage and four was waiting, horses steaming in the chill air. The carriage was surrounded by people – sixty, maybe seventy – each one of them wrapped up in long coats and mufflers. A man at their centre shouted out, calling for volunteers. Heads were turned, boots inspected. A hand, at the back, was raised. 'You, sir?' said the man at the centre. 'Me, sir,' said the man at the back. 'Very well, sir. Step this way.' The man at the back stepped forward, his hand in the hand of a pretty, dark woman. He led her through the throng and up into the carriage. The crack of a whip then, the call of the driver, and the carriage moved off, uncertain on the ice, every turn of the wheel drawing gasps from the crowd. Some felt certain the ice would crack and the carriage plunge deep into the dark and freezing waters, and they looked away, just as others – equally certain – couldn't help their staring. They winced at every yard, until soon, fully halfway between here and there, it paused. Voices far apart on both banks were stilled. It was a moment of time and motion suspended – a daredevil feat unsurpassed. 'What's happening?' people whispered (to speak any louder they feared would crack the ice). 'Why have they stopped?' They peered (some with the aid of brass or silver telescopes), but could not see. Soon, though, the carriage moved on and they sighed, relieved, unaware of the cheers that rose on the river's other side as the carriage and four, the two passengers and the driver, circled slow in an arc and then came to rest in the city of New York, where the river meets the good solid earth.

48

Heading West

'I'm sorry. We've just had a new system installed, and it took a while to locate anything. Anyway, here it is –'

Cheryl Stapper laid a copy of the *Monroe Enquirer* before me on the desk. Though it was only a month old, the paper was already yellowing, the picture that dominated the front page almost sepia in tone. It was a photograph of what looked like the end of a fence and the corner of a field. At its centre was some kind of ditch, within which lay two mounds the size and shape of bodies, each one covered over with a length of tarpaulin.

'Are you all right?' said Cheryl Stapper.

Corpses.

'Jesus,' I said. I felt cold. 'What happened?'

She leaned forward, took a look at the picture as if for the first time. 'I don't know,' she said, shrugging. 'I guess they just died there and somehow got buried. Anyhow –'

I looked up. 'What do you mean somehow got buried?'

Another shrug. 'Of course, nobody knows for sure. At least it seems we won't for a while – not until the report gets released. *Then* I suppose we'll know.'

'I can't believe it.'

'I know. They *do* seem to take their time, that's for sure. But then I suppose they figure they've got plenty of time to play with. I mean if those poor souls have been in the ground maybe a hundred, hundred and fifty years, then to an archaeologist that's just about what five minutes is to you and me, and I suppose they think another few weeks won't make much difference.'

'*What?*'

'Well, one thing's for certain – they're not going anywhere, are they?'

I looked down again at the paper. *Uncovered*, read the caption. *The bodies of two men presumed to be soldiers of the Indian or civil wars rest in peace while awaiting their removal to the archaeological department of the University of North Michigan.* My heart skipped a beat, then started to settle. I blew out a breath.

'Are you *sure* you're all right?' said Cheryl. 'You look a little pale –'

'Well, I thought –'

'Yes?' said Cheryl.

'Nothing,' I said. 'I'm fine.'

A beeping: the pager on her hip. She peered down at the message. 'Oh darn it,' she said. She looked up. 'I'm afraid I have to go. Mr Webb's had another of his turns in French History. He will keep on reaching for the *Life of Napoleon!*' She turned away, took a step, turned back. She nodded at the paper. 'Page four, I think,' she said, suddenly beaming. 'Isn't it marvellous!'

When she was gone, I turned the pages, lifting the first three and easing them over. I scanned the fourth page, my eyes alerted for a name. Nothing. I checked again.

Again nothing.

Then something. I leaned forward. *Heroes Return*, I read. Then underneath: *Following their miraculous recovery from the freak accident that took the life of their father, sisters Trudi and Caroline, daughters both of Monroe, spent their first day as orphans at the family home. (Picture, page 6.)* I turned the page.

And there they were. Trudi and Caroline, linked arm in arm.

Again I leaned forward, peering close. They were staring straight at the camera, and, although they were both frowning slightly, it seemed as if there was something else going on – something deeper.

I picked up the paper.

Freak accident –

I held it to the light.

– that took the life of their father.

And then I got it.

'Did you find what you were after?' said Cheryl Stapper.

I looked up.

'So what's so funny?' she said. She was holding a pile of books and smiling.

'Oh, nothing,' I said.

I looked back at the picture. Somewhere deep behind the frowns the two girls were smiling – I was sure of it. 'I was just thinking,' I said.

'Thinking?'

'About what people have to do sometimes to survive.'

Cheryl frowned.

'Anyway,' I said.

She glanced at the paper. She looked halfway to saying something, but nothing came. Instead she just smiled.

I closed the paper.

'Are you done now?' she said.

'Sure,' I said.

'Do you think you'll be back?'

I shook my head, thinking then of the picture of the girls on that front porch – how they'd stood, arm in arm, smiling like innocents finally released.

'Well, take care,' said Cheryl, 'and take care of Libbie.'

'I will,' I said. 'You too.' Then, gathering up my papers, I crossed the library, passing out through the doors into the mid-morning sun that dappled the pavement. Here I stood for a moment, glad of its warmth on my face. Again I thought of the girls, pictured their smiles. Then I moved on, heading for my car, smiling too and ready to go.

In the summer of 1872, parties of engineers and surveyors of the Northern Pacific Railroad appeared in the valley of the Yellowstone River – and, by so doing, violated the Laramie Treaty of 1868.* It was an action whose consequences – though limited at

---

* Under the terms of the treaty, the government agreed to end construction of the road leading to the Montana gold fields and close all forts on this route. In return, the majority of the Sioux and Cheyenne agreed to live on territory 'north of the North Platte River and east of the summits of the Big Horn Mountains'. Significantly, those Indians who refused to sign the treaty, declaring it their right to roam freely, included the Sioux's most respected leader Sitting Bull, and Custer's contemporary and ultimate nemesis, Crazy Horse.

first to a few skirmishes between Indians and whites and a sub-sequent (and always temporary) halting of railroad construction – would, in time, entirely change the face of America. Indeed, from that first day on – from the very first moment when, observed from afar, geologists, down on their haunches, considered the qualities of the rich Dakota earth, and surveyors looked for ways through the thickly wooded hills – the peace that had existed for thousands of years was destined to end, for it was in that moment – that first digging of the dirt – that the Indian wars began.

For Custer, the call to the Dakota Territories could not have been more welcome. Bored and restless in Kentucky, he wanted action, and here at last it was – even if his role was to be, in this case, rather less than the glorious one for which God, he was certain, had made him. Indeed, his task was to be a defensive one – to protect the Northern Pacific Railroad's workers against small marauding bands of Sioux. Anyway, if hardly ideal, it was at least something; and, at noon on April 10th, the Custers arrived at the Seventh's camp at Yankton, accompanied by the usual menagerie of dogs and birds, the latter including a pelican. While other officers' wives took rooms in the town at the St Charles Hotel, Libbie chose to stay with her husband in camp. The accommodation was strictly rudimentary (and made worse when the weather closed in and the men on sentry duty lost fingers and toes to the freezing temperatures) – but she'd rather endure this than 'be left behind, prey to the horrors of imagining'. From now on, she swore, she would always be beside him, and so she was, when, on May 10th, to the cheers of a crowd led by the territorial governor, the 'Glorious Seventh', with its Golden-Haired Boy at its head, set out on the journey that would take them further west still – as far west, indeed, as a white man could travel and still be in America. It was a journey to the frontier from which many would never return. For one man in particular, it was a journey that would take him from life into history and thence into legend, and change for all time the course of a nation.

49

What Will Happen Starts Here

'*So you in town for Saturday?*'

Fort Abraham Lincoln, five miles south of Bismarck, deep in the Dakota Territories, was still under construction when at last the Seventh Cavalry arrived.

'Saturday?'

Built of local pine, and set on a plain beside the slow-winding Yellowstone River, it was to be, when completed, the largest and most important fort in the west – the source from which all operations against the hostile Sioux and Cheyenne would spring.

'Saturday. The re-enactment.' A shake of the head, disbelieving. 'You saying you came all the way out here and you don't even know about the re-enactment?'

It was – the command – for Custer, all that he knew he deserved. He was back where he belonged – leading from the front, furthest man from safety.

'I thought it would be on Sunday.'

'Sunday?'

All there was before him now was danger and glory. From such a place as this, life, to him, seemed rich with endless possibilities.

'Well, Sunday *is* the anniversary – *isn't* it?'

Another shake of the head. Sunday, apparently, was the Lord's day, and not, consequently, for fighting.

'Shame somebody didn't tell *him*,' I said.

The desk clerk at the Last Stand Motel frowned. 'Tell who?'

I nodded to the picture of Custer behind him on the wall. He half-turned, then turned back. 'Tell him *what*?' he said.

'About Sun–' I started, but something as vast and vacant as the land in the man's eyes made me stop. 'Never mind,' I said. I fished around for my wallet. 'So will you be there then?'

'Where?'

Jesus.

'On Saturday.'

He was studying my hands as I opened my wallet, as if he was half expecting something weird to fly out. 'You want a bath?' he said suddenly, still staring.

'Now?' I said.

He cocked his head, unsure. 'That a joke?'

'Obviously not,' I said. I pulled out the cash, set it down on the counter.

'So you don't want a bath then,' he said.

I sighed inside. 'How much,' I said, 'is a bath?' It sounded like the start of some music-hall routine.

He shook his head, taking the money and counting it. 'No baths,' he said, 'at the Last Stand Motel.' Then he looked up – I was sure in some way triumphant. 'You want a bath, you want Bismarck.' He pushed the money into the front pocket of his jeans and he smiled. 'OK,' he said. 'Is there anything else?'

'Yes,' I said. 'As a matter of fact there is.' I was tired and he was seriously pissing me off.

'Oh?'

'Ice,' I said.

'Ice?' he said.

I leaned forward. 'You know – frozen water?'

'What about it?' he said. His lip (I was sure) made a tiny, mean curl.

'Well,' I said, 'do you have some? Or do I want Bismarck for that too?'

'Machine across the yard,' he said.

'Right,' I said. 'Thank you.' I huffed, turned to go.

'Don't work, though,' he said, as my hand found the door. 'If you want a ice machine that works –'

'Don't tell me,' I said, 'Bismarck.'

'Nope,' he said. 'I got one sitting right there in my kitchen.'

Jesus Christ.

He smiled. 'So you want some?'

'Yes,' I said, my teeth clenching. 'If it's not too much trouble.'

'No trouble,' he said. 'No trouble at all.'

The Custer quarters, when completed, comprised an elegant two-storey house with a verandah and rooms out back for Eliza and the other servants. Set on one side of a large square (the other three sides of which were made up of – and still are today – barracks for the men, other officers' quarters, stables and the armoury and quartermaster's stores), it had a commanding view across the parade ground and the flat lands beyond. From her second-floor sewing-room off the small master bedroom, Libbie could see the river in the distance and the blue hills beyond. For her, after the weather and the perils of Yankton, Fort Lincoln and the house were a huge relief, bringing with them as they did the opportunity of creating their first real home – which, in short time, she did, sewing curtains and arranging with great care the furniture and keepsakes brought out from the east.

Despite its precarious isolation from the rest of America, life on the post was punctuated, thanks to Libbie, with regular social events. Indeed, within a month of their arrival, within walls freshly painted and upon floors newly polished, she arranged a dance for the officers and their wives, which the former attended in full dress uniform, the latter in their carefully folded and stowed grandest dresses. There were evenings, too, devoted to cards, and theatricals produced by the enlisted men at which the general commanding and his wife were guests of honour. At one such event, a soldier named Mckean, taking the role of an Indian chief intent (for no apparent reason, other than, of course, his blood-thirsty nature) on the torture and murder of a miner and his son, emitted from the makeshift stage a series of bellowing cries so loud and chilling that two of the wives in the audience fainted. Upon reviving them with smelling salts, the post surgeon assured them most persuasively that such events as depicted were no more than fantasy and should be disregarded. At this, it is recorded that the ladies smiled but 'seemed unconvinced' – which, of course, they were right to be, as, within six weeks of the play's production, the mutilated body of a miner named Loggins from Oxford, Mississippi was discovered by a patrol on the banks of the Yellowstone, along with that of his fourteen-year-old son. Found naked, not only had their tongues been cut out and penises removed, the thighs of both corpses had been slashed to the bone and their eyes gouged out. It was the first of many such incidents – none of which was discussed, of course, around the Custer table. Here, with monumental foolishness or perhaps just self-delusion, all the talk was of glory and the coming campaign. For Custer and his brothers – for Tom and Boston and their cousin, little Autie Reed – defeat and death were conse-quences suffered only by others. Never having been beaten, they thought such a thing (if they thought of it at all, which they did not) impossible – and it was thanks to this attitude, of course – this complacency and arrogance – that, long before the coming cam-paign began, the campaign was lost. Even then, on those calm distant evenings, as the meat was being carved and the wine poured with care into fine crystal glasses, the bodies around the table, though warm to the touch, were already shadowed by onrushing mortality. Already, each one of them – the men – were unknow-ingly sick with the disease of uninterrupted former victory. It was a sickness for which there would be no cure but death.

That night, lying in my bed at the Last Stand Motel, for the first time in weeks and for what (although I didn't know it then) would turn out to be the last time, I dreamed of Karen. She, too, was lying on a bed, but still and straight like the wife of some knight on a tomb. Her hands were crossed in peace on her chest. I reached out in my dream, covered them with mine. They were cold, stone. Appalled, I stepped back, stumbled, and then I was falling, down and down into some endless depth of space.

'*Hey, what the fuck –*'

I opened my eyes. The room was dark. I lay still a moment, listening to my hard-thumping heart.

'Hey, man –'

It was banging so hard I felt sure any minute it would bang itself out. *Be calm, be calm,* I told myself, *there's no need to panic,* and I tried to sit up, but my head was still thick with the remnants of sleep and dreams, my shirt and shorts cold with sweat, and I gave up, lay back, stared in the gloom at the ceiling. I closed my eyes, knowing suddenly and for certain I had to retrieve the dream – to somehow make whatever had been wrong in it right – but of course the dream had fled in the moment of first waking.

The revving of an engine then, and voices – from outside somewhere, beyond the black and blue flimsy-curtained window.

'You gotta problem?'

Again I tried to push up. This time I made it halfway, locking up on my elbows.

'Yeah, man, you're the problem.'

I let my eyes close, the better to concentrate, to isolate.

'Well, fuck you –'

'No, fuck you –'

They sounded so far away, the voices. And drifting. Everything was drifting.

You don't live here any more.

Then, in the eye of my mind, Karen was smiling, her words not bitter now but just truthful. I opened my mouth to speak, but nothing came and then suddenly I was sitting at the wheel of a stationary car, the engine rumbling beneath me, the window down. I turned my head. Karen was standing maybe twenty feet away, her face a mask of sadness. I tried to ask her what was wrong – I felt the breath in my lungs, but still no words came. I reached for the handle – but there was no handle. I looked up. Karen was gone – and so was something else. Something, in those moments, had come to an end. Again, I lay back, listening for my heart. I closed my eyes. My heart, for the first time in months, was calm, its beat regular.

50

Water and Gold

The western summer of 1874 was a season of drought and disappointed hope. Water, that summer – always scarce – seemed, then, due to the searing, unbroken weeks of heat, as rare a thing as gold; while gold itself – long promised in large quantities as a cure for the nation's depression – had yet to be found. As the land grew brittle and streams ceased to run and then ceased to *be*, even the small but steady trickle of miners, with their wagons filled with tools bought with hard-borrowed dollars, began to falter and dry up as banks in the east open on Friday stayed closed Monday, never to re-open, and the man in the White House looked on, saying nothing, his hands useless as if tied. All around him the country seemed to be failing – drying up, in the west, for want of water, and, in the East, for the desperate need of gold.

Gold.

Gold would solve everything.

But, so far, all there were were rumours.

Rumours that Dakota's Black Hills – so sacred to the Sioux – weren't really black at all, but gold.* Rumours that her rivers ran yellow in the sun, and that only a man with no hands could fail to gather the stuff in such quantities as to make that man rich. Rumours, in short, of nothing less than salvation.

And it was all right there.

All a man had to do – all a nation had to do – was reach out a

---

* The Sioux arrived in the Black Hills around 1770. They displaced the Kiowa who had displaced the Comanche who displaced the Crow. The Sioux were, of course, displaced in due course by the white man. In 1980, descendants of the original Sioux (but not the Kiowa, Comanche or Crow) were offered $105 million in compensation. This offer was rejected. The rejection stands to this day.

hand and take it. No matter that that salvation lay buried – lay inert, lay uselessly squandered – in your neighbour's back yard. Times were desperate. It was all ends and means.

And the means?

Well, Custer, of course. Fearless, foolish, vain Custer. Let him be the point of America's great sword. If there's gold, let him find it, and if there's not, let him take the blame. Let the nation be reminded of how he'd once been court martialled, then generously, humanely reinstated.

But above all let him go.

And this he did. At ten o'clock on the morning of July 2nd 1874, with the regimental band playing 'The Girl I Left Behind Me', the Black Hills expedition, with Custer and his brothers Tom and Boston at the head of ten companies of the Seventh Cavalry, moved out of Fort Lincoln, glad of the freedom of the country that lay before them and high on the prospect of fame. Behind them, adrift, the women watched them until they were gone, and then turned away, back to another summer of heat and dust and fearful lonely dreams.

At first, Libbie and the other wives filled their days with distractions. They sewed and sang and planted vegetables in whatever shade could be found in the hard scorching earth. Sometimes, Libbie travelled to the shops in St Paul or to Bismarck to meet friends from the east.* Here, unfashionably tanned, she'd sit drinking tea, and describe, when asked (and she was always asked), the delights of the frontier. Always, too, of course, they asked about the general – and always – of course – she told them what they (and she) wanted to hear. The frontier, she told them, was a beautiful place, and the general as gallant and attentive as ever. Here, amongst the tea cups and the cake stands, she found herself retailing for the first time the half-truths that would turn in time into lies. Here, in the cool of the parlour in a Bismarck hotel, she first sketched the image to the dissemination of which, in due

---

* This source of entertainment, however, was soon closed to her, as such trips involved crossing the Missouri River, which, at the best of times, was a precarious business, the river being prone to sudden flooding, and the captain of the vessel being most often drunk and, consequently, incompetent.

course, she would dedicate her life. No mention was made of the armies of grasshoppers who, just as soon as they'd risen from the earth into sunlight, had destroyed every one of her carefully nurtured plants – nor of the swarms of mosquitoes that arrived every evening and against which there was scarcely any protection. And neither, of course, did she tell them how the general, in recent months, had begun to withdraw, or how, lately, alongside the brave and confident, dashing soldier that everyone knew – the man who believed *to his soul* in eventual and permanent victory – there had come to exist someone else – another man, this one secretive and solitary, whose gaze seemed perpetually focused elsewhere, somewhere much closer at hand – at a place, a future perhaps, that only he could see.

'*You mean the general? No, sir. The general's still in his quarters.*'

'And Mrs Custer? Is she here?'

She didn't say that this vision – whatever it was – was one that tensed up his body as if in expectation of some terrible blow, and made him stare out at the night from her sewing-room window as if he were listening to something that, though she tried and tried, she never could hear.

Captain Myles W. Keogh (aka Richie Stevens, a welder employed by the New York Transit Authority)* was leaning back against his pick-up, his eyes closed and face turned up to meet the mid-morning sun. He shook his head. On the far side of the motel's parking lot, the other members of his troop – maybe twelve, maybe fifteen, of them – were chattering like children on the first day of the holidays, chugging back beers and smoking cigarettes, the blue of their uniforms already growing pale with the fine Dakota dust.

'No?' I said.

---

* Myles Walter Keogh, thought by many to be the last white man left alive on the Little Big Horn battlefield, left his native Ireland at sixteen, following which he fought with the French Foreign Legion in Algeria, then for the Papal States against Napoleon II (for which action he was decorated by the Pope), after whose defeat he sailed for America just in time to fight for the Union in the civil war, then for the Seventh Cavalry against the Sioux and Cheyenne. Though he died at the Little Big Horn, his horse, Comanche, survived, and can now be seen in a glass case, stuffed, at the University of Kansas. The body of Captain Keogh himself was removed from the battlefield in 1877, and his remains reinterred in the family plot at Auburn, New York.

Again he shook his head. He sighed, smiling with obvious pleasure at the warmth of the sun. Mrs Custer, he said, was already at Fort Lincoln, preparing the house for her husband's return.

'His return?' I said. 'Where's he been?'

At this he opened his eyes. 'Where're *you* from?' he said.

I told him.

'In England?' he said.

'In England,' I said.

He frowned, let out a whistle of breath. Then he closed his eyes and leaned back again into the sun.

The arrival of I Company, United States Seventh Cavalry, had woken me that morning at eight, their wheels and then their voices drawing me from a still and dreamless sleep, and sitting me upright, disconnected, blinking hard.

'Sergeant?' I said.

He opened one eye. 'Yes?'

'You didn't say where he'd been – where he was coming back from.'

'I didn't?'

'No, sir,' I said.

He opened the other eye. '*Paha Sapa*,' he said. 'The Black Hills.'

'You mean looking for gold?'

'No, sir,' he said.

'No?'

He pushed himself up, started dusting off his jacket. 'I mean *finding* it, sir. I mean saving this country from depression.' Then he stopped patting his shoulders and pockets and cast a glance at his colleagues, then back. 'Hey,' he said, 'you want a beer?' Then he frowned. 'You *do* drink beer in England, *don't* you?'

Like a burglar setting lookouts to watch for police, General Custer, on first entering the sacred Black Hills, laid a network of pickets before and all around him whose job was to alert him to the expected presence of the hostile, war-like natives. Despite this protection, he moved slowly, deliberately, expecting to find, at every turn and upon every hilltop, evidence of the enemy with whom, he had come to believe, he must, in the end, do battle.

But they never came.

He never saw them.

But they saw him – and were watching him still when, on July 30th, at a little after three, two prospectors in the column's vanguard, on sieving a stream, found, in the fine mesh, the first signs of gold.

51

Under the Eyes of Abe Lincoln

They were camped in the short grass, a mile off the highway, their tents and trailer-homes scattered at random around a flagpole, from which flew (or rather hung, there being – despite the plains' exposure – not the slightest breath of wind) a newly pressed, brightly coloured star-spangled banner.

Richie Stevens spun the wheel of his pick-up and sent us jumping, springs creaking, up the deep-pitted dirt-track that led to the camp. He turned. He was smiling. 'So you ready?' he said.

'Ready for what?'

Up ahead in the distance, way beyond the camp, rose the huge, heavy bulk of Mount Rushmore, the stern faces of Washington, Jefferson, Lincoln and Roosevelt looking down, vast and sandy-coloured in the mid-morning heat.

He turned back to the track, still smiling.

'Who's here?' I said.

'Wait and see,' he said.

'Why won't you tell me?'

He shrugged, as the ground beneath our wheels levelled out, and we headed, rolling smooth now, towards a small knot of cars, finally parking between a Lexus and a beaten-up old Chevy.

He switched off the engine, then turned to consider me. 'Look,' he said, the smile gone, replaced by a frown, 'there's something you should know.' He screwed up his face. 'These people –' He paused.

'Who are they?' I said.

'They may seem a little, well, *strange* –'

'Strange?'

'Like they're maybe a little *obsessed*. Which I suppose they are –'

'OK. So they're strange. But who *are* they?'

'I didn't tell you?'

'No. All you said was I'd be wanting to meet them. Which I am. Except I don't know who they are.'

He glanced in the mirror.

'What is it?'

'Nothing,' he said. He started undoing the silver buttons on his US army tunic.

'What are you doing now?'

Then he was twisting in the seat, pulling out his arms. This done, the tunic removed, he bunched it up roughly and stuffed it under his seat. Then, glancing again in the mirror, he gave me a look. 'Can't be too careful,' he said. 'Like I say, these people, they're a little obsessed.'

I sighed. 'Look –'

'Indians,' he cut in.

'Indians?'

'That's who they are. And not just any Indians neither. These boys are *real* Indians.'

'You mean Sioux?'

'And Cheyenne.' He was serious now. 'I mean *relatives*.'

'And they're here for the battle – the re-enactment?'

He nodded. 'Every year.'

'Well, at least they get to win.'

'Kind of.'

'What do you mean?'

'Well, they *win* OK, but it don't do 'em much good. They still get to go home to their shitty little houses.'

I thought of the Lexus. 'They can't all be poor,' I said.

He shrugged. 'Ninety-nine per cent.'

'And the one per cent?'

He was rolling up his sleeve, then removing his sergeant's stripes. 'You want to meet him?' he said.

'Who?'

'The one per cent.'

'Who is it?'

'Come with me.' He reached for the handle, stepped out of the car. 'You OK?' he said.

I was looking at the Lexus – at a sticker in the window.

'What is it?'

Fuck You Custer. A crude cartoon of a man on his back, his body riddled with arrows.

'Nothing,' I said. 'It's just –'

But Richie Stevens was already on his way, heading through the short grass towards the flagpole at the centre and the circle of trailers around it.

By the time George Custer, at the head of the seventh, arrived back at Fort Lincoln (having driven the men hard – over twenty miles a day), news of his discovery had raced like a brush fire right across the nation, igniting a gold mania that no word of caution could dampen. At once, in the east, men – emboldened by reports of vast deposits in the Black Hills – sold or abandoned what little they had and began heading west.

'*Wait here.*'

That the west was a dangerous land and the hills not theirs meant nothing to them; they would go, regardless – they *had* to – and hope that God or providence or Custer would protect them.

'So where are *you* going?'

Sergeant Stevens (he was looking like a sergeant now, walking with studied military-looking purpose) crossed to the trailer and knocked on the door. He glanced back; I half waved, but he didn't seem to see me. A voice then, muffled, then he climbed the two orange-box steps, twisted the handle and disappeared inside.

'Hey!'

Maybe a half-hour later and I was looking away, watching the people moving to and fro, doing errands or just talking, when Richie called from the trailer. 'You comin' or what?' he said. He was red-faced as if he'd been drinking. I crossed the grass and climbed the steps.

It was gloomy inside, a smooth-running aircon box turning the heavy air cool. It took a moment for my eyes to adjust, but when they did I saw there were four of us in there – me and Richie and two others – one of whom was large and oldish-looking, the other young and slender. The older man was dressed up in an outfit of decorated skins; the younger man wore nothing but a loincloth. Both had Nike trainers on their feet.

'Hello,' I said. Richie was beside me and a little behind. The two men nodded, grave like judges.

Silence. Just the humming of the aircon.

'Well, it's nice to meet you,' I said.

I stepped forward, held out my hand towards the older man. He raised his hand lazily, took mine, shook it.

'What do you want?' said the younger man. When he turned his head, I saw he'd something attached behind his ear. He was lean, his chest hairless, his shoulders dappled with spots of paint, a lightning bolt across one cheek.

I turned to Richie.

'He's writing a book,' he said. He sounded hesitant. 'Like I said – remember?'

'A book?'

'About Mrs Custer,' I said.

The two men glanced at each other.

'Why?' said the older one. His voice was so deep it seemed to vibrate something inside me.

It was a good question; one I had asked myself many times over the past months and years – always without coming up with a good answer.

'It's what I do,' I said lamely.

Silence.

I thought again of the Lexus.

'Nice car,' I said. 'The Lexus. Is it yours?' I smiled at the older man.

'It's mine,' said the younger man. Suddenly, from out of nowhere, he smiled. 'You wanna drive it?'

'Drive it?'

He sat up – and in that moment of movement, it came to me who it was.

'You're Crazy Horse, aren't you,' I said.

The smile dipped. 'No pictures,' he said.

'What?' I didn't have a camera.

Then at once the smile returned, lighting the place up with a line of white teeth. He pushed himself up. He was shorter than me – maybe five-seven, five-eight. He padded to the door. I stepped back. He was barefoot. He opened the door, twisted back. 'You comin'?' he said.

'Where?' I said.

'You ever *driven* a Lexus?' he said.

'No,' I said.

'Well?' he said.

'OK,' I said.

I looked back at Richie. Richie gave a shrug, an I-didn't-know-this-was-going-to-happen kind of look on his face. 'I'll see you later,' I said.

'OK,' said Richie. He sounded a little nervous.

'You OK?' I said.

He hitched up a smile. 'I'm fine,' he said. 'I'll just hang out, have a talk with our friend here.' He looked sharply at the older man. 'If that's OK with you –'

The old man shrugged. He was fishing around in his pockets for something. He pulled out a TV remote, squinted at it a moment as if he'd never seen it before, then pressed a button, slow and deliberate. A TV high up on a bracket in the far corner sprang into life. *Over fifty?* said a voice. The old man huffed, pressed another button. In an instant, the face of Jack Klugman appeared.

'Ah, *Ironside*,' said Richie.

'*Quincy*,' said the old man, his eyes narrowed and scowling hard at the screen.

The Lexus belonged to his father. His father, Jimmy Longfoot (who was one-quarter Sioux, making his son, I figured, one-eighth), was a jeweller who owned a chain of cut-price stores across the Midwest – a man who, according to Jimmy Junior, his son, was loved and loathed by his fellow (partial) Sioux in about equal measure.*

'Why hated?' I said, as I tried to move the gear-stick to drive. I rattled it. 'And why can't I shift this?'

'There's a button,' said Jimmy Junior. 'Underneath.'

My fingers found the button; pressing it released the stick. We hummed forward. Soon we were rolling across the short grass with all the slow, steady grace of a liner.

'Where are we going?' I said. According to Jimmy Junior, the car cost over one hundred thousand dollars. This fact made me nervous. I touched the brake gingerly as the grass met the track.

He slid down in his seat, set his feet in his Nikes up on the dash. He was naked, still, but for the loincloth. He pointed to the highway. 'Down there, turn left,' he said.

'OK,' I said. 'Whatever you say.'

'I say left,' said Jimmy Junior.

'I know,' I said. I turned to look at him. He was poking at his navel, removing little bits of fluff.

His father, he said, was hated because he'd made a success of things, and not just sat on his ass and whined. And, besides that, he was a friend of Muhammed Ali (they'd sparred together in upstate New York before the first Joe Frazier fight), which also didn't help, what with there always being bad blood between blacks and Indians. I said I didn't know that – about the bad blood. Oh yeah, Jimmy said, leaning forward to crank up the aircon, *everyone* knew *that*. Not me, I said. We drove on.

'See it?' he said suddenly, after we'd been driving maybe eight, ten miles. He dropped his feet from the dash and pointed up ahead. I leaned forward.

'See what?'

'Me!'

'What?'

I couldn't see anything – just the road and scrubland and mountains all around.

* According to *Money Magazine*, Jimmy Longfoot Snr is currently worth $145 million.

'There!'

'Where?' I squinted harder, trying to see what he was looking at. And then I saw it.

A figure on horseback carved in three dimensions in the side of a mountain.

'See now?'

'Jesus,' I said. Even at a distance it was huge – despite being only so far half-formed – man and beast half-emerging from the rock as if struggling to break free.

'What do you think?'

I couldn't speak. The car slowed.

'Hey, what are you doing?'

'Who the hell did that?'

'KZ.* And it ain't finished yet. You like it?'

The car stopped on the shoulder. 'It's amazing.'

Jimmy turned to me, frowning. 'It's *me* is what it *is*.' He nodded at the mountain. 'Don't you *see*?'

I looked at him. Amazingly, there was a likeness. 'When's it going to be finished?' I said.

'Dunno,' said Jimmy. 'Hey, you see what he's doing?' he said. He straightened his right arm, first finger extended.

'He's pointing,' I said.

'And do you know what he's pointing at?'

I said no, I didn't.

'Custer,' said Jimmy, lowering his arm.

'Custer?'

'Uh-huh. He's just seen Custer break into the sacred lands and steal the Indians' gold, and he says he's gonna get him.'

'And did he?' I said.

* The late Boston-born sculptor Korczak Ziolkowski worked on the presidents' sculpture at Mount Rushmore, before accepting the commission from Chief Henry Standing Bear to create a monument to Crazy Horse 12 miles away. He began the project in 1948 and was still working on it at his death in 1982. His work has subsequently been continued by his widow Ruth and six of their ten children. The sculpture, on completion, will stand nine storeys high from the horse's hooves to the tip of the forty-foot feather. Crazy Horse is pointing, some say, not at Custer, but at Lincoln, as if mocking the former president's desire for a peaceful and unified America. The facial features of the great warrior are a matter of great contention, as no authenticated photograph of Crazy Horse exists.

'You bet,' said Jimmy. 'Got him good. Bust him up bad.'

'Then I suppose he learned his lesson, eh?'

He nodded. 'Reckon he did,' he said. 'Hey, you wanna go get a piece?'

'A piece of what?'

'The rock. Pieces they're chipping away. It's only five dollars.'

'Sure.'

'You got money?'

'I've got money,' I said, suddenly remembering the loincloth. 'You?'

He shook his head. 'No, sir.' He turned to me, serious-faced. 'I don't need money. This is my land.'

'Of course,' I said.

'That's me up there,' he said.

'I know,' I said.

'I'm Crazy Horse. I'm here for my people. Come Saturday, I'm gonna bust up that Custer real good.'

I said nothing.

'Real good,' he said. 'Hey, you gonna put that in your book – what I said?'

I twisted the key; the dashboard blinked awake. 'I guess I will,' I said, pressing the button on the gear-shift and slipping the thing into drive.

52

Blind Man Sighted

By the spring, while nearly two thousand miners were panning the rivers and blasting the rock of the Sioux's sacred lands, the Custers – George and Libbie, along with Tom and Boston – headed east to New York for a vacation before preparations began for the expected decisive summer campaign. Here, while, for the general's younger brothers, the trip meant the opportunity to visit friends and spend much accumulated back-pay, for their older sibling it was a chance to do business – to position himself financially, socially and politically, so that, come the autumn, he'd be able to take full advantage of the fame and gratitude that would naturally accrue to him in the wake of what all felt certain to be the coming, inevitable, spectacular victory. For him and for Libbie, their lives, in that spring, seemed at last to be falling into place – all the stars aligning, so to speak, guaranteeing success. This time next year (next year, of course, was election year)* not only would the landscape of their lives be entirely changed, but also the place from which that landscape could be viewed. From the Black Hills to the White House was just one short and certain stride.

From the start, however, that stride was a stumble – his ambitions, quite clearly now, at a century and a half's distance, just the consequence of foolishness and vanity.

Now – but not then.

* In the election set for November 1877, President Grant was intending to seek a third term. Unpopular and surrounded by rumours of scandal, in this he was thwarted. The Democratic nomination was, at this time, undecided. In the event, the election was a close-run thing, and though votes were bought, sold and stolen on both sides, the winner was declared to be Republican Rutherford B. Hayes. The only notable thing about his administration was the refusal of his wife, 'Lemonade Lucy', to serve alcohol at the White House.

Then, each obstacle, each failure, was merely something to be ridden out and beaten – each failed investment an indication not of idiocy but of courage thwarted, each harsh unfettered word uttered against the president and the president's grasping brother evidence not of childlike naivety but of the upstanding honesty of the people's noble champion. For George Custer, there was nothing in sight, then, that could stop his advance.

'*So?*'

He was victory-blind in the land of those covering their eyes.

'So what?'

And all around, peeking out from between their fingers, they were watching and waiting for the drama that was Custer to play itself out.

'So was I right or what?'

'You mean about them being strange?'

We were back on the highway – me and Richie – headed south for Fort Lincoln.

Richie flicked his eyes to me. 'You don't think so?'

Yes, I said, I thought they were strange.

'But?'

'But nothing. You're right. They're strange.'

We drove a while then in silence. I looked out of the window – at the scrubland passing by and distant mountains. I thought again of Crazy Horse carved in that rock, his arm outstretched, hair flowing backwards behind him – of how much he'd had in common with Custer –*

'Hey, you know the old guy?'

– and whether he also knew that the final confrontation was coming and all that was left for him and his people was barely one more summer of the life of freedom they had known for generations.

---

* The two men did indeed have much in common. They were born and died within a year of each other. Both had happy childhoods and rose to lead fighting men at the age of twenty-three. Both were humiliated at the height of their fame (both attempting to be with the women they loved), and both recovered to gain even greater fame. They both loved horses and were happiest when riding alone across the plains. Neither man drank. Both were called 'Curly' as children.

I turned away from the window. 'You mean Sitting Bull?'

'You knew it was him?'

'I knew it was him,' I said.

'How?'

'I don't know. Lucky guess, I suppose. Anyway, what about him?'

Richie shrugged. He sounded disappointed, like I'd spoiled his great revelation.

'Ah, nothing,' he said. 'Nothing really.'

'Come on. What?'

Another shrug. 'Like I said, it was nothing. Just that one minute we were sitting there watching TV, then the next he's down on his knees, howling and chanting.'

'You mean like in some kind of trance.'

'I don't know. Maybe.'

'Maybe he was having a premonition.'

'Premonition?'

'About Custer.'

Richie flicked his eyes from the road then back. '*What?*'

'Well, you *said* they were strange. Obsessive. I think you were right.'

'You mean you think that they really think that they really are who they're pretending to be?'

'Maybe. I don't know. Do *you* really think you're Captain Keogh?'

'Me?' He shook his head. 'Can't say as I do. Except maybe when I'm running up that hill and there's some guy that drives a Lexus on my ass.'

'So you've never had a vision.'

'White boys don't have visions.'

'You mean it's an Indian thing – seeing into the future?'

'I don't know. Maybe it is.'

We turned off the highway at a sign: *Fort Abraham Lincoln One Mile*.

'You know Libbie Custer had a vision,' I said.

He turned again. 'No kidding,' he said. I couldn't tell if he knew or not – if he was just humouring me.

'Shapes in the sky,' I said. 'When you guys rode away. She said she felt it was a premonition. Of course she never saw him again after that. Nobody did.'

'*They* fucking did,' said Richie.

'I mean apart from them.'

I looked at Richie. He was staring straight ahead. He seemed tense now, his smiling all gone. Without saying another word (he hardly looked like he was breathing), he drew the car off the road and headed for the makeshift car park in a field.

I was glad to leave Richie behind and all talk of reconstruction and re-enactment. I felt the need to return (at least for a while) to the real, present world, and so I picked my way through the throng of blue uniforms and, after a deal of searching, found my car. It was dusty already, the inside like a cauldron. I opened all the doors and sat a while in the shade, leaning back against the boot. All around there were voices – commands and responses – and the distant crunching of marching feet. I felt suddenly weary. I let my eyes close.

Sometimes, looking back, the route from there to here seems a mystery – a tangle of twisting paths through a dense and impenetrable jungle; sometimes it's as clear as a straight sunlit road. And sometimes, if you're lucky, it doesn't matter – or will come to not matter – as you turn your gaze ahead and just start walking.

The sound of a bugle woke me. *There to here.* The sun was lower in the sky now, the shadows on the parade ground longer and leaner. *Here.* I pushed myself up, and was dusting off my trousers when the bugle called again and I twisted, squinting in the sun, searching for its source.

The parade ground was busy now – soldiers in blue ranks, a tall man with yellow hair dressed in a buckskin suit standing on a low-railed dais. A shouted command. The crunch of boots. A distant *hurrah!* The man on the dais raised an arm, then turned and seemed to beckon towards a small knot of people behind him. One of them – a woman, slight, dressed in white, dark hair – detached herself and approached the dais. The man in the buckskin suit held out his hand; she took it, then gracefully ascended the steps to stand beside him. All turned then, individually and as one, towards the flagpole in the centre. Another call from the bugle – a slow, romantic, melancholy sound. Slowly then the flag was lowered, as, like a fluttering falling thing, the day became dusk.

That night I drank beer and watched TV, lying on my bed, the curtains drawn. As the shows came and went (but not the fake laughter which seemed ever-present), I thought about the day – about the boy in the Lexus, about Sitting Bull, about Richie – about how seriously they all took such a fake endeavour.

I turned out the light at midnight; the moon rose at once beyond the curtains. I lay in the dark, re-enacting in my head the movements of the soldiers on the parade ground. They twisted and turned, dust rising, sweat falling, then froze before the man on the platform. He raised an arm; he turned and motioned to the woman in white. 'My darling,' he said in my half-dream, and, in my half-dream, then, she smiled and I knew her – her face, I recognised it – knew her like a man knows the house he will one day call home.

53

Custer Cut

At three o'clock in the morning on May 17th 1876, at the camp several miles to the south of Fort Lincoln, those men of the glorious Seventh United States Cavalry who'd managed to sleep at all were woken in their tents by the call of a distant-sounding bugle. Those who had not – those to whom, through excitement or fear, sleep had been denied – were mostly already dressed and waiting, some checking their Model 1873 Springfield .45-calibre breech-loading or trapdoor single-shot carbines or their Model 1873 Colt .45-calibre six-shot 'Peacemaker' revolvers, while some (those who could write) had spent the hours before dawn writing letters to sweethearts, to wives, to mothers and fathers – the letters that would, in too many cases, so long outlive their writers and find homes, in time, yellowed, the ink fading, in glass cabinets in museums, propped up, their private contents laid bare for all who cared to see. Others were already loading their horses: standing in the mist, spreading the blankets on their animals' glistening backs and tightening their twenty-pound stiff-leather McClellan saddles. They counted their ammunition (one hundred rounds for the carbine, twenty-four for the pistol), and stowed as best they could their overcoats, blankets, mess-kits and rations. Pots and pans rattled in the close, moist air; leather creaked, men cursed. Some liked to talk; others preferred silence. Around all, besides the mist, hung the weight of expectation. They were going to march, and they were going to fight. Some, they knew, were going to die.

At five, with the mist slowly rising, the bugler sounded the general call, so signalling that the time to break camp had come. Two hours later, the regiment, marching in column, platoon by platoon, approached Fort Lincoln, there to take its final leave before riding west. At its head was General Terry, expedition commander,* accompanied by his staff, then the forty Arikara scouts. After them came the band of the Seventh, then the cavalry itself, in whose lead rode, of course, General Custer. He was dressed in his favoured buckskin (as were, in imitation, others of his officers) and wearing a low-crowned, wide-brimmed hat; his boots were polished, his horse and his spurs gleaming in the sun. He looked to all the model of confidence, the very image of victory made flesh.

'*Are you sure?*'

Only the wives of the Arikara scouts seemed to see something else, for, while the wives of the soldiers wept at the knowledge of imminent separation, the Arikara women sat crouching on the ground, silent as if in the presence of death.

'I'm sure.'

'It's short.'

'I know.'

'OK then. One Custer cut coming up.'

Balancing on a stump in the sunshine, I braced myself. I closed my eyes, awaiting the scissors' first cut.

It wasn't that she cut his hair for vanity (it had long been thinning – a lack that required disguise), nor even for the good sense of it (it was cooler on the hot trail that way), that made Libbie remember the clicking of her heavy sewing scissors that day and the tumbling at her feet of Autie's long golden locks. It was because she knew (and he knew that she knew) that the real reason for their cutting was neither vanity nor sense – but that it lay, unspoken, elsewhere. It lay in the knowledge that a man cannot lose to a savage's knife what he does not have. It was, of course, something not only she knew; other wives knew it too, and they, too, that morning, stood

---

* When Custer fell out of favour with President Grant, he was denied command of the Dakota column during the 1876 expedition. As commander of the Department of Dakota, Brigadier General Alfred H. Terry assumed theoretical charge. Custer, however, retained the leadership of the Seventh Cavalry (following intercession on his behalf by Terry), and was, therefore, consequently, the expedition's *de facto* commander.

clipping and trimming, some silent, unable to counter stark fear with bluff, some talking – *over*talking – of the future. Silent or not, this future was a future that, for many of them, would never come; all that *would* come for them would be empty chairs and silence – and their husbands' curls swept up and preserved, some artfully under glass, some trapped in lockets and taken out on the anniversary of a hard and brutal death.

'That'll be twenty-five cents.'

I opened my eyes. 'How much?' For a moment I scarcely recognised myself: having my scalp shorn close seemed to bring out my features, accentuating them and giving my face an anxious, almost haunted look. I wondered if such a look had greeted Custer when Libbie handed him the mirror.

The barber was wiping his scissors on a rag. 'Twenty-five cents,' he said again. He looked up. His head was shaved even closer than mine. He smiled. 'Custer cut, Custer prices. Twenty-five cents.'

I pulled out a dollar. The barber made change. 'Did he know, do you think?' I said.

'Who, *Custer*?'

'That he was going to die. Do you think that's why he had his hair cut?'

He shrugged. 'Fuck knows. Maybe he just got sick of the lice.'

'He had *lice*?'

'*Everybody* had lice.'

'So you don't think it was down to some premonition.'

Another shrug. 'Could have been. I don't know. Maybe it was just Libbie. *She's* the one with the premonitions. Maybe she just didn't want anyone to recognise him.'

'And did they?'

'No, sir. I don't believe they did. They weren't looking for *him*. They didn't *care* about *him*. He was just one more. So they cut him up bad just like the rest.'

I stood up, brushed the hair from my clothes.

'So you going?' said the barber.

'Going where?'

'Where'd you think?'

292

'No,' I said. 'You?'

He shook his head. 'No, sir.'

'Barbers don't fight?'

'You got it.'

I looked at his close-shaved head. 'So why the Custer cut?'

He raised a hand, drew it over his scalp, as if confirming its continued presence. 'Lice,' he said.

'What?'

'Uh-huh. Got it from my little girl.' He frowned. 'Hey, you got any kids?'

I shook my head. I thought of the comb, the scissors, felt a sudden, definite itching on the back of my head. 'No kids,' I said.

'Shame,' he said. He was packing up his stuff.

'Is that it?' I said.

'Nope.' He drew the string taut at the top of his US army-issue canvas bag. 'I got one more customer.' He slung the thing over his shoulder, turning, looking beyond the soldiers and the horses and the women in their dresses, squinting at the two-storey Custer house, glowing cream in the early-morning light.

'Not *Custer*,' I said.

He turned back. 'Sure. You wanna come watch?'

'Won't he mind?'

'Mind?' The barber shrugged. 'I imagine he has other things to think about.' He stamped his boots, shifting two small clouds of dust. 'Besides,' he said. 'Who cares if he does? He's only an accountant.* What's he gonna do? *Audit* you to death?'

He was standing in the parlour, his back to the piano. She was playing a Viennese waltz. She seemed tiny, dressed all in a blue so dark it seemed black, her hair piled high on her head and secured with a half-dozen silver clips. I couldn't stop watching her. It was her, but not her. She paused in her playing when, while we stood in the doorway, the barber gave a cough.

* This particular Custer (and there are many) is not, in fact, an accountant. In the real world, William J. Martin is an IT consultant currently attached to a large sportswear manufacturer's.

'Yes?' she said, not turning her head.

She was here, but not here.

'Haircut,' he said.

The general flicked his eyes first to the barber, then to me. His buckskin tunic and breeches were pale, his boots black and shiny at the calves, dusty at the feet. He was bare-headed, his face thin and tanned, his locks – truly golden – twisting like a girl's to his shoulders.

'Outside,' he said, still looking at me, drawing my gaze from his wife.

'OK,' said the barber. 'You're the boss.'

Reluctant, I settled my eyes on his. They were a pale, sharp blue. They looked like a boy's eyes. I imagined them open, rolled back in his head, unblinking in the heat of the hard Montana sun, uncaring, thanks to death, as the women on that hillside set about him with their knives.

54

The Girl He Left Behind

I stepped back into the hall as first the barber then the general passed by me, their heavy boots clumping on the polished wooden floor. At the door, the barber stepped aside. The general pushed on the screen door, stepped out into the light. The barber followed, glancing over his shoulder as he went. '*Fucking Custer,*' he hissed, raising his eyebrows and grinning. I smiled. He turned away. The screen door banged behind him.

I stood for a while in silence then, half holding my breath, half-expecting the piano to start up again. It didn't. I moved back into the doorway and eased my head around the door.

She was standing at the window, looking out through the dusty pares at the activity on the parade ground.

I knocked on the door. Without turning, she said, 'You shouldn't be in here.'

I said I was a friend of Charlie's.

Now she turned. 'Charlie?'

'From Austin,' I said.

'I know.'

I stepped into the room, glanced around. 'He said I should call in.'

'He did?'

'He did.'

'And now you have.'

'Yes.'

Silence. A clock ticking.

'Look,' I said. 'If this is a bad time −'

For a moment I thought she'd say yes and I was ready to turn

295

around and go. But then she sighed, shrugged. 'It's OK,' she said. 'It's nearly over anyhow.'

'Over?'

She nodded towards the window. 'Five minutes and they're gone. Me too.'

'You're going home?'

'Didn't Charlie say?'

'Say what?'

'Oh, it doesn't matter.' Outside, from the parade ground, a bugle called, then again.

'I have to go,' she said. 'Will you wait?'

'Of course.'

She crossed the room, pausing at a mirror by the door. She stared at herself staring back.

'Wish him luck,' I said.

She smiled in the mirror. 'It's a bit late for that.'

'Not if he takes the Gatling guns.'

She frowned, quizzical.

'Never mind,' I said. 'Break a leg.'

'Thanks,' she said.

One last glance in the mirror, then she turned and was gone. I moved to the window and watched her make her way down the steps. Either side of her, two rows of blue-coated soldiers stood stiff to attention and saluted. Head high, imperious, she passed between them and made her way to her husband, who was mounted already on Dandy, his favourite horse.* Removing his hat, he leaned down; she rose on her toes. They kissed; he whispered something, then sat himself up, clicked his spurs and turned away. For three, four, five paces, Libbie followed him, the tips of her fingers trailing his saddle, his boot, his blanket. Then, the connection cut, she dropped her arm and stood quite still as, before her, the band playing, her husband rode to the head of the column and the column moved off across the parade ground and on to the

---

* Custer alternated between two horses: Vic (Victory) was a light sorrel virtual pure-bred with three white stockings and a bald face; Dandy – his favourite – was a dark-brown army horse with a little white blaze on the forehead.

scrubland beyond and soon was lost to the distance and to history amid the fine rising dust.*

He killed his first buffalo at the age of fourteen; by the age of twenty-three – a chief now – he'd led raids against the Crow, Blackfeet, Shoshoni and Arapaho. By 1862, his targets were the white men who, having trampled and defiled the sacred Black Hills, proposed then to move him and his people elsewhere. When he refused (though others did not – Red Cloud amongst them), they said, 'Sitting Bull, Chief of the Lakota, unless you do as we say we will kill you and keep on killing until all your people are gone.' They said he could not resist them. But he did. He gathered those of his people who wished to fight around him, and those of their cousins, the Cheyenne, and prepared to fight and, if necessary, to die. Together they made camp, the largest ever seen, in the valley of the Rosebud River, and held a sun dance. Here, Sitting Bull sliced strips of flesh from his arms, then he danced until he passed out.

'*So how did it go?*'

Once revived, he told of a vision – a vision of soldiers falling into the camp from the sky.

She was pulling off her gloves, finger by finger. 'OK. It *went*.'

It was a vision that meant that a great, final battle was coming.

She paused, looked up. 'Can I ask you something?'

It was a vision that meant victory.

'Sure,' I said.

She hesitated.

'What is it?'

* In actual fact, Libbie and her sister-in-law Maggie (wife of First Lieutenant James Calhoun) spent the first day with the cavalry, camping that night on the banks of a small river a few miles from Fort Lincoln. The following morning, they said goodbye (Libbie clinging on to her husband's side in an uncharacteristic show of anxiety) then rode back to the fort with the paymaster and a small guard. Libbie turned for a last look at the column. She later wrote of this, 'It was a splendid picture. The flags and pennons were flying, the men were waving, and even the horses seemed to be arching themselves to show how fine and fit they were. My husband rode to the top of a promontory and turned around, stood up in his stirrups and waved his hat. Then they all started forward again and in a few seconds they had disappeared, horses, flags, men, and ammunition. And we never saw them again.'

'Well, did he seem *OK* to you?'

'You mean Charlie?'

'He didn't seem at all, well, *strange*?'

'What do you mean?'

She shrugged.

Silence. The ticking clock. Outside, the parade ground was near-deserted, the spectators moving off to their cars and the beer tents. Only the women who'd played the Arikara wives weren't moving. They were sitting in the far shade talking, their voices raised sharp, now and then, in laughter.

After a while I said, 'You know I think it's a real shame it didn't work out.'

She looked up. 'What do you mean?'

'At the university. I really think that giving him tenure might just have made it stick.'

'What?'

'Well, if they'd have just shown a little faith that he really *had* quit by giving him that tenure – I mean, if they'd really got behind him –'

Sarah frowned. 'What are you saying? He *got* tenure.'

He got tenure.

'We're moving off-campus. A bigger house. Didn't he tell you?'

Oh shit. I looked away, stared at the picture of Custer on the wall. I felt suddenly warm. Guilty.

'Didn't he?'

I thought of the boxes lining the hall, the empty shelves. 'No,' I said.

'Why wouldn't he tell you? I thought you two were friends.'

I thought of him shaking his head.

'We are.'

I'm going home.

'So I suppose he told you then that we're getting married.' She cocked her head, smiling, cynical. 'He didn't, did he?'

'He never said married, no.'

'Well, we *are*. As soon as I get home. It's all ready. Charlie's got it all ready.'

I said nothing.

'*What?*' she said.

'Charlie's not there,' I said.

'Not where?'

'Texas. Austin. He left when I left. I thought you knew.'

She shook her head. 'You're lying.'

'Why would I lie?'

She snapped her head away, then back. 'Why are you doing this?' she said. Her voice was trembling.

'I'm not doing anything,' I said.

She scowled. 'Who *are* you anyway?'

I told her.

'Never heard of you,' she said. 'Charlie never mentioned you.'

'Charlie didn't mention a lot of things.'

'What's that supposed to mean?'

'I mean like getting married. Like not getting tenure.'

'But we *are*. He *did*.'

'He's gone,' I said.

She shook her head. 'You're *lying*,' she said again, though conviction was ebbing now.

'I'm sorry,' I said, and it was then, out of nowhere, that it came to me – the whole set-up. Why he'd been so keen to tell me about Sarah, and to have me come here. I was here to tell her what he'd not had the guts to: that he was going – that he was *gone* – and that he was never coming back.

For a moment she rallied. 'Sorry? You mean –'

I shook my head. She crumpled, stepping back and sitting hard on a seat in the window.

'You had no idea,' I said.

She looked up. Her eyes were filled with tears. She opened her mouth to speak – but no words came. All that came was the sound, far off, of the Arikara women as they wailed for an audience of tourists and ghouls.

55

Voices from the River

Returning to Fort Lincoln was, for Libbie, like going back, fully grown, to a place she'd known in childhood. Everything, suddenly, seemed distant, smaller than she remembered, quieter. The rooms of the house that had so recently been filled with the laughter and talk of the Custer boys and their childish pranks were deserted now, the sound of her piano in the parlour no longer the delicate and cheering thing it had been, but mournful, now, and hollow – and though she tried (she had, after all, in the strict shadow hierarchy of officers' wives, a position to maintain, and others looked to her for a lead), she couldn't settle to the old ways: everything, with Autie's departure, had changed. Her last happy days, she knew, in the garrison were gone.

At night, she couldn't sleep for worrying; she replayed in the dark hours those visions in the sky that had so alarmed her on that last far-off morning – while, on the rare days when the infantry wasn't summoned at the sight on the hills of silent, watching figures who'd disappear as quickly as they'd come, she'd busy herself tending to her chickens or wasting precious water on the ragged, scrawny vegetables that seemed so reluctant to rise, always trying to ignore the rumours that everywhere were passed from one mouth to another, each time growing wilder in the absence of news. She didn't listen when they said that the reservations were emptying of all but the young, old and sick, nor when they said that the camp of Sitting Bull was their destination. Instead, for distraction, she'd spend afternoons in her sewing-room and evenings on the porch with the other wives, singing along to Katie Gibson's guitar, though all the time trying, despite herself, to hear beyond their songs and the trumpeter's calls for the sound of the steamship *Far West*,* hoping for news that would settle her fears.

But it never came.

All that came was news of General Cook's 'skirmish' way south of the Little Big Horn River, and sometimes, now and then, Autie's letters from the field – letters that told of the march – of how expectations were high, morale good, and how beautiful was the country and how clear the rivers. 'Do not,' he wrote in one, this after three weeks away, 'be anxious about me,' for he hoped, he told her, 'to have a good report' to send by the next mail. She replied at once, her tone confident and bright, with stories of camp life, and a reminder (lest he'd forgotten) of his vows to avoid drink and cards, closing then with a word about their certain life to come. 'With your bright future,' she wrote, 'and the knowledge that you are positive use to your day and generation, do you not see that your life is precious on that account, and not only because an idolising wife could not live without you. As ever tonight, I shall go to bed and dream of my darling Autie.'

'*What will you do now?*'

He never got the letter.

'I don't know. Maybe I'll go to England with you.'

Nor would it have done him any good if he had, for, by the time it arrived in the Little Big Horn Valley, General George Armstrong Custer was dead.

'What about school?'

And beside him lay the bodies of his brothers Tom and Boston, his cousin little Autie, his brother-in-law James Calhoun, and nearly two hundred others of his men.

'I'm quitting school.'

All had been slain in hot blood and lay now, deathly still,

---

* The *Far West* provided river transportation for the Little Big Horn campaign. Skippered by Captain Grant Marsh, she carried a cargo of rations down the Powder River to the Yellowstone River. She was moored at the mouth of the Bighorn River when news came of the Custer massacre. Forty cavalrymen, along with Captain Keogh's horse Comanche, were transported east towards Bismarck, stopping at Fort Lincoln, from where the news was relayed to the widows and to the world.

scattered on the low-rising hills above the river. Below them, the once-great camp was deserted.*

'You can't just quit.'

'Why not?'

'I don't know. What if he calls?'

'Who?'

'Charlie.'

'He won't call.'

'How do you know?'

Sarah shrugged. 'I just know.'

The first to find them, later that day – Captain Benteen amongst them – were struck by how white they appeared. From a distance, scattered in groups and singly from the low brown summit of Custer Hill down to the banks of the slow-flowing river, they seemed, to some, to be certainly the bodies of slain horses, while, to others, they looked more like the corpses of sacrificial lambs. Up close, however, to those who could stand it, they were clearly the bodies of men. Stripped naked, and already rotting in the heat of the fierce Montana sun, each man – what was left of him – was a shifting mask of flies, which, when disturbed, moved sullenly away, so revealing that man's ghastly fate. Barely a man was complete. Limbs had been hacked off, skulls crushed with rocks; genitalia had been severed and thrust into mouths. Fingers were gone, and noses, eyes; the hill, in parts, was nothing short of a slaughterhouse, the ground black with blood and the grey of intestines.

And Custer?

He lay, it is said, stripped like the others (save for a sock and the sole of one boot), propped up like a mannequin against the bodies of two others, one arm stretched out, resting as if for balance, the other by his side, fingers wrapped tight around the handle of a pistol. His head was back, in the attitude of a man who is searching the sky in vain for water, his eyes wide, reflecting the perfect blue of the sky. Some say that, beyond the indignity of brutal death itself,

* Custer's 'last stand' was said by one Indian brave to have lasted 'as long as it takes a hungry man to eat his dinner' – approximately, it is thought, twelve to fifteen minutes.

his body alone had remained untouched. But they are wrong. He, like the others, had been horribly treated; unlike the others, however, he had had performed upon him one particular rite.

'*How do you know?*'

Sewing yawls had been thrust, one into each ear, to help him in the next life hear better the cries of the swindled and abused.

'I can feel it.'

Not that Libbie knew of this – any of it – except in the way that, *feeling* it to be so, she knew it.

'What do you mean?'

We were sitting, Sarah and I, side by side now on the steps outside the Custer house. 'I mean, don't you sometimes feel things you don't know?'

'You mean like second sight?'

'Maybe.'

I half-turned away. The parade ground was quiet now, the soldiers long gone. 'What else can you see?' I said. From out of nowhere, my heart had started pounding

'Like what?'

The rustle of skirts. She was looking at me – I could feel it, feel her eyes. 'I don't know,' I said. '*I'm* not psychic.'

'I didn't say I was psychic.'

'Well, you're certainly *something*.'

A pause.

'Like what?'

Well, you're certainly something. Jesus.

I shrugged.

Silence. Just breathing. The heat and the shade.

'Look –' I said.

She said nothing. I turned. She was looking away. 'She knew, you know,' she said after a while.

'What?'

'Libbie. She felt it. The moment he died.' She turned. 'She was sitting in her sewing-room when something passed over her. Something cold. And from then on, she was just waiting.'

'For what?'

'Confirmation.' She pushed herself up. 'Anyway, what were you going to say?'

'When?'

'Just now.'

'It doesn't matter.'

'Probably not. But what was it anyway?'

'It was just something I was thinking. It doesn't matter.'

'About Charlie?'

I looked up. 'How did you know?'

She shrugged, tapped the side of her head. 'Psychic, remember?'

'Yes, of course.'

She smiled. 'So?'

'Well, what if he *doesn't* call?'

'He won't. I told you.'

'Well, how do you feel about that?'

'Are you a psychiatrist now?'

I looked away again. The sun, though high still and hot, was inching down, imperceptible, inexorable. 'Sorry. Like I said, it doesn't matter.'

'No. It doesn't. Because he won't.'

And she was right. He didn't. Not even on the days before our wedding, when, every time the phone rang I'd catch something in her eye – a certain look – and I'd convince myself she was thinking it might be him. But it never was. Always it was just someone wanting to say how happy they were, or asking for directions to the church, or most often it was a call that had nothing to do with weddings at all, but just something ordinary, mundane. At any rate, whoever it was, it was never Charlie. Wherever he was, he was keeping quiet – wounded like the rest of us and hiding, anonymous, in the carnival world.

Epilogue

This morning, along with the contract for my book, a letter arrived from a firm of New York lawyers, informing me of the death from cancer of Lena Blue, my late mother's friend. She was sixty-seven years old and had died, apparently peacefully, in her sleep, having finally abandoned all forms of treatment. Included with the letter (in which the author, a Mr Bresler, is pleased to confirm that Ms Blue has bequeathed to me various articles of china which will, in due course, find their way to me) was a photograph of two women in their late forties or early fifties, one of whom is my mother. In the picture, they are standing in front of the bear enclosure at Central Park Zoo. My mother is smiling, her friend looking away to the side, her image slightly blurred as if something, in the moment of exposure, has caught her attention.

Anyway, that was this morning. Now it is late afternoon. Now, with the dusk already falling, I realise I have spent the best part of the day prevaricating. With Sarah away, ending up doing nothing all day is easy. But I must begin. (Think of the contract.) So, with *Blood on the Tracks* on the stereo, I pull on my white gloves and turn on my typewriter, ready at last to begin. The thing sits there humming before me, expectant, challenging.

I stuck the picture of my mother and her friend along with all the others on the wall above my desk. By any standards it is a strange community – as, with a few exceptions, they have only me in common. There is Charlie, smiling, and Oskar in his uniform at school. There are the two sisters, Trudi and Caroline, their picture clipped from the pages of the *Monroe Enquirer*, and a blurry shot of a tram and a tram-stop, and two people, a man and a woman, standing shoulder to shoulder, looking awkward, or maybe just cold. Leaning forward (this is another excuse not to begin, I know – but still I do it), I peer again at what can be made out of the man's features, and am surprised again to find that the man is me. He seems like a man come from another, other life – a life certainly not my own.

And finally, of course, there is Libbie. Both of her. What I have to say about them is – it comes to me again – why I'm here today, sitting here at this desk. They are both smiling, one dead, one merely absent. *Come on*, they seem to be saying (only I can hear them), *begin, begin.*

And so I do.

Looking down at the keys, I place my fingers above them like a pianist awaiting his cue. There is much to be said, a long journey to be taken, and for a moment a weariness overtakes me. But this passes, and I roll in some paper, close my ears to the sounds of the day. A deep breath, another. *Fort Abraham Lincoln*, I write, *June 5th 1876.* I pause, look up, take one last look around, look down, then: *At a little after three a rider appears*